KEEPING FAITH *with the* PARTY

KEEPING FAITH
with the
PARTY

Communist Believers Return from the Gulag

NANCI ADLER

INDIANA UNIVERSITY PRESS
Bloomington and Indianapolis

This book is a publication of

Indiana University Press
601 North Morton Street
Bloomington, Indiana
47404-3797 USA

iupress.indiana.edu

Telephone orders   800-842-6796
Fax orders   812-855-7931

Manufactured in the United States
of America

Library of Congress Cataloging-
in-Publication Data

Adler, Nanci.
  Keeping faith with the Party : Communist
believers return from the Gulag / Nanci
Adler.
    p. cm.
  Includes bibliographical references and
index.
  ISBN 978-0-253-35722-9 (cloth : alkaline paper) — ISBN 978-0-253-22379-1
(paperback : alkaline paper) — ISBN
978-0-253-00571-7 (electronic book)
  1. Ex-convicts—Soviet Union. 2. Ex-
convicts—Soviet Union—Attitudes.
3. Kommunisticheskaia partiia Sovetskogo
Soiuza. 4. Allegiance—Soviet Union.
5. Political persecution—Soviet Union.
6. Labor camps—Soviet Union. 7. Communism—Soviet Union—Psychological
aspects. I. Title.
  DK268.A1A35 2012
  364.80947—dc23

                        2011037563

  1 2 3 4 5 17 16 15 14 13 12

For Zoë and Noah

Party official turned inmate: "When they chop down the forest, the chips fly, but the Party truth remains the truth and it is superior to my misfortune. . . . I myself was one of those chips that flew when the forest was cut down."
Fellow prisoner Ivan Grigoryevich's response: "That's where the whole misfortune lies—in the fact that they're cutting down the forest. Why cut it down?"

Vasily Grossman, *Forever Flowing* (1972)

CONTENTS

PREFACE

Early on in this research, an interview I conducted with a Gulag survivor somewhat inadvertently proved to be an excellent illustration of precisely the kinds of issues I was aiming to address. It was a follow-up to a previous interview almost ten years earlier. Right after I got to Moscow in the spring of 2006, I called Zoria Serebriakova to talk to her about my new project. As it happened, she had just finished reading the Russian edition of my book on Gulag survivors, published by Memorial,[1] and she was eager to share her thoughts about it.

She picked me up outside a subway station on the outskirts of Moscow and we talked for the hour it took to drive to her dacha, which had been home to Old Bolshevik Leonid Serebriakov, then Andrei Vyshinskii, and then to Zoria and her mother again when they returned from exile. Zoria was so anxious to express her opinions that we skipped the small talk and started our discussion even as I was climbing into her car.

Zoria passionately expressed her outrage at the interaction between the ex-prisoners and the government when the survivors were released from the Gulag. Her outrage, however, was not directed at the *unapologetic behavior of the government's representatives,* but rather at the *ingratitude of the returnees.* Zoria was so affronted by their ingratitude that she incredulously asked, "How could it be that they were not grateful to the government when they were released from camp?" Underscoring her argument, she declared, "Those times were full of opportunity."[2]

Yes, she acknowledged that I had accurately reported the bitterness expressed by many Gulag survivors, but she herself had been a prisoner, and she claimed that her embittered fellow prisoners were misguided. So the people whom I had described as victims and survivors were considered by one of their own as ingrates who had failed to appreciate the opportunities afforded them in the post-Stalin era. Zoria rightly claimed the authority of personal experience, but over-claimed the right to invalidate the experience of others who did not share her ideology. It was the self-evident quality of her convictions that I found so enlightening, because I realized that Zoria's justification for adherence to Communism was as self-evident to her as the justification for individual freedoms was self-evident to me. Although we seemed to be talking about the same Gulag and post-Gulag events, we were not, because our incompatible interpretive frames changed their meaning. Until I recognized this, Zoria's judgments seemed counterintuitive.

I knew that Zoria had been a privileged returnee under Khrushchev, and that she subscribed to the "returnee as hero" stance. I also knew that her mother, Galina, had spent twenty-one years in Siberia, and then went on to become a Party propagandist after release. So I was not too surprised by Zoria's unwavering loyalty to the Soviet regime. But I was unprepared for her inability to recognize the validity of the bitterness of so many of her fellow returnees. This group—and they were in the majority—described themselves as having been victimized by the state both during camp and after their release.

Although Zoria's allegiance to the Party, both during and after camp, was a minority view, she was not alone. There were others, like Lev Gavrilov, who entitled his memoirs "z/k," which he defined as meaning *zapasnoi kommunist* (reserve Communist). In the camps, he had demonstrated his allegiance by extracting his own gold teeth and offering them to his interrogators in support of the war effort. Some prisoners sang patriotic songs while in camp, wrote poetry about the day they would be reinstated in the Party, and glorified the "humanist principles" of socialism and the heroic struggle to attain them. Although such responses did not represent the views held by the majority, they do represent something about the interaction of repressive regimes and their captive populations. The incorporation of such an interpretive frame would enable subjects of a total or totalitarian system to effortlessly avoid internal and external conflicts.

While I felt comfortable about disagreeing with Zoria's perspective, I felt uncomfortable because of my difficulty in making sense of her authentic feelings. A goal of this study is to explain how and why this minority point of view makes sense to people like Zoria. To accomplish this goal, I realized that it would be necessary to view such perspectives from within the experience of the loyalist Gulag prisoner or survivor.

I would like to gratefully acknowledge that this interview, along with my understanding of Zoria Leonidovna's opinions, benefited from a third encounter in 2009. At the first International Conference on Approaches to Stalinism (Moscow,

December 2008), in a paper I presented to the Biography Section, I had recounted the conversation with Zoria described above. Zoria was not in the audience, but her friend was, and told Zoria that I had portrayed her as a Stalinist. Zoria contacted me a few weeks later to complain about this presumed portrayal of her as a Stalinist, and to assert that she reviled Stalin and held him personally responsible for mass murder. Zoria argued that if one does not emphasize how different things were after Stalin, then it is a justification of Stalin. I explained that the entire discussion centered on the post-Stalin, post-camp period. I had not portrayed her as a Stalinist, but in the course of reviewing the context of the reported conversation from which her friend drew this inference, I could see how some might mistakenly so label her. This mistake could occur if people failed to make the same sharp separation between the Stalin regime, which she disowned, and the post-Stalin Communist Party, which she supported. This separation was apparently more ideologically relevant for Zoria than for most of her fellow returnees, as illustrated by her response to their ingratitude to the post-Stalin Communist Party at the time of their release.

When Zoria and I revisited our previous conversation, she concurred that she had declared then, and affirms now, that the returnees' bitterness was misguided. Rather than being angry with the Communist Party for imprisoning them, they should have been grateful to Khrushchev and the Party for releasing them. Most of Zoria's fellow returnees did not share Zoria's loyalty to the Party, did not absolve it of its behavior under or after Stalin, and, by and large, were not accorded the same favorable treatment as Zoria by the post-Stalin Party. (For Zoria's life story, see chapter 3.)

In the pages ahead, as I examine various attitudes toward the Party through the narratives of victims and survivors, the focus of this study is on those stances that might be considered by some to be counterintuitive. This points to the larger question of how a repressive regime becomes incorporated into the attitudes and behavior of the people it controls, with the consequence that its citizens behave in ways that place the polity above their own individual interests.

From the narratives gathered, I was able to discern at least four overlapping but distinguishable hypothetical explanations: Communism as a belief system akin to (secular) religion—and the related charismatic bond, functionalism, cognitive dissonance, and the traumatic bond. In combination, these hypothetical explanations accounted for many of the themes that informed the content of the narratives, under such topical headings as: faith-based beliefs, the victims' perceptions of their "guilt," Party identification, the renewed (and dashed) hopes of loyalists in the Gorbachev era, the experience of children of repressed believers, and the post-Soviet resurgence of Stalin's popularity.

The Soviet example is unique in that repression held sway in greater or lesser degrees for seven decades. This study of the firsthand accounts of how it affected people who lived through it may contribute to our understanding of some of the processes by which people survive within repressive regimes and repressive regimes survive within people. For the individual, incorporating the Party's interpretive frame promoted Party loyalty by precluding contradictory evidence. For the Party, it supported a long but (in retrospect) brittle tenure.

ACKNOWLEDGMENTS

This work would not have been possible without the deeply personal contributions of a number of extraordinary individuals, who took the time to talk, listen, and think about a difficult, sensitive, and even painful subject. For this, I gratefully acknowledge: Gerta Chuprun, Elena Karagaeva, Marlen Korallov, Mariia Kuznetsova, Tania Langerova, Roy Medvedev, Nataliia Rykova, Zoria Serebriakova, and Evgeniia Smirnova. With equal gratitude, I acknowledge the memoirists whom I did not have the privilege to meet, but whose experiences are recorded and analyzed in this book. These Gulag victims and survivors were instrumental in shaping my perceptions. Arsenii Roginskii, a longtime friend, has been invaluable to this research. He advised me, debated with me, sharpened my conceptualization of this complex topic, and, most challengingly perhaps, invited and encouraged me to reflect upon my conclusions with critical Russian audiences. Semen Vilenskii has guided my understanding of the Gulag by generously sharing his own experiences, his wealth of knowledge, and his contacts since the day we met in 1995; I am richer for knowing him. Vladlen Loginov took on my task as if it were his own, providing advice, introductions, criticism, and perspective. My thanks also go to Nikita Petrov, ever ready to help when I needed it.

I would like to take this opportunity to acknowledge a number of institutions for supporting this project. In the first place, this research was most generously funded by an Innovative Grant from the Netherlands Scientific Council (NWO). Support was also provided by the University of Amsterdam, the department of East European Studies, and the Center for Holocaust and Genocide Studies of the Netherlands Institute for War Documentation. The archives RGASPI, RGANI, and GARF, in particular Dina Nokhotivich and Galina Gorskaia, facilitated timely access to hundreds of documents, even accommodating my tight travel schedule on inventory days when the archive was closed. The organization Memorial, especially Alena Kozlova and Irina Ostrovskaia, provided valuable contacts, dossiers, and photos. The International Institute of Social History in Amsterdam was most helpful in arranging for me to work with their Memorial archive. Finally, I am grateful to the Russian State Humanitarian University (RGGU)—my home in Moscow—for graciously making my stays so comfortable.

In the course of this research, I had the privilege of being invited to present my work to several different forums of experts, who helped sharpen my observations and analyses. These venues included: the Harvard Conference on the History and Legacy of the Gulag, the Hebrew University Conference on Eyewitness Narratives, the Approaches to Stalinism conference in Moscow, and the Repressed Russian Provinces conference in Smolensk. I am grateful to have had the opportunity to lecture on this research at the HL-Senteret in Oslo, the Center for Women's Studies in Zagreb, the Netherlands Embassy in Moscow, King's College of Cambridge, the Hugo Valentin Center in Uppsala, the Forschungsstelle Osteuropa in Bremen, and Lund University. The students and colleagues who attended these events asked important questions, suggested literature I had not considered, and expanded my thinking about the meaning of my findings.

Several colleagues stayed the course of this project with me. My good friend Erik Van Ree scrupulously read and critically commented on every chapter. This book benefited considerably from his informed, insightful observations. Stephen Cohen—always there when I needed him—selflessly shared his voluminous returnee archive, dialogued with me, and offered indispensable advice, support, and friendship. I would also like to acknowledge the critical remarks of Leona Toker and Alexander Etkind, who greatly improved the focus of the manuscript. Hans Blom has helped facilitate my scholarly pursuits ever since I met him. My thanks also go to Jan Lucassen and Lex Heerma van Voss for believing in this undertaking. My colleagues in Amsterdam—especially Jolande Withuis, Karel Berkhoff, Barbara Boender, Wichert ten Have, Johannes Houwink ten Cate, Selma Leydesdorff, Peter Romijn, Marjan Schwegman, Siep Stuurman, and my Veni-Vidi group—were readily available to listen and comment, and provided valuable support throughout this project. Finally, my sincere gratitude goes to Janet Rabinowitch for her drive, enthusiasm, and expert input in shaping the manuscript. Peter Froehlich, Candace McNulty, and Marvin Keenan offered excellent editorial assistance.

Last but by no means least, I humbly express my heartfelt appreciation to my family. My father, Herbert Adler, a psychiatrist and Fellow of the American College of Psychiatrists, conscientiously read and commented on every chapter. Always thinking out of the box, his unconventional, erudite observations impelled me to broaden my horizons, and added nuance to this work. My husband, Rob, and my twins, Zoë and Noah, patiently endured my frequent absences, made sure I had time to work when I was at home, visited me in Moscow, and always remained engaged in what I was doing. To them I owe the greatest debt of gratitude—I thank them for being here, and there, and everywhere for me.

KEEPING FAITH *with the* PARTY

Enduring Repression

One of the paradoxes of Soviet Communism was that a system of governance that enforced its ideology by executing, imprisoning, and exploiting the labor of groups or classes of undesirables, dissenters, alleged dissenters, and alleged associates of dissenters nevertheless retained the allegiance of some of its victims. It also maintained the conformity of the mass of its citizenry. While most secular repressive regimes do not last very long, the Soviet government did hold on to power for seventy years. Judged in terms of durability, the regime's domestic practices, including repression, could be considered to have been functional for the state. Using functionality as an informing guideline, we will assume that in some way and for some reasons the enduring allegiance of some survivors was likewise functional for them. We will look at why and how the functioning of the state and individual merged—and endured. There can be no single answer and no best perspective for understanding this complex question, but some insights may be gained by examining the individual and collective experiences of Gulag survivors. There may be similar explanations for both the regime's endurance and the steadfast loyalty of some of its victims.

The materials, including firsthand accounts, that have become available suggest a number of hypotheses regarding why some survivors remained advocates of a political system that had victimized them. The range of explanations includes the functioning of Communism/patriotism as a faith-based belief system or as a psychological defense mechanism; cognitive dissonance; functionalism; and the "traumatic bond," also labeled Stockholm syndrome. What was uniform about the repression was that these psychological and social influences affected all the prisoners. What was unique was the particular combination of each influence on individual prisoners as well as the prisoner's response.

THE STUDY

We have only the sketchiest knowledge of Gulag prisoners' attitudes toward the CPSU throughout the Soviet period and how their incarceration in the Soviet labor camp system affected their subsequent attitudes toward the Communist Party. These attitudes have hardly been explored as a separate issue in the literature. However, information about the subject has become retrievable through archives, memoirs of the returnees and those who perished,[1] and the rich but vanishing trove of information stored in the oral recollections of the survivors. An exploration of the individual experiences accessible from these sources may provide insight into the process by which individuals survived the repression and/or the repression survived in them. It may also shed light on the process by which repressive regimes maintain themselves in spite of / because of the terror they visit on their own people.[2]

The repression was always coercive, sometimes capricious, and usually beyond the power of prisoners to influence. Some prisoners maintained their opposition until the end of their lives and may indeed have paid for it with their lives. Others, as a consequence of various "incentives," professed allegiance, and were still executed. Many of the millions of prisoners did not survive their five- to twenty-five-year terms, but some of those who did emerged from their ordeal maintaining or acquiring a belief in the ideology of their repressors. This in spite of the fact that a great number of prisoners were either victims or witnesses to convictions on trumped-up charges, and were exploited as expendable forced labor.

The repression cast a broad net and imprisoned people with a variety of political histories, arrested for different reasons ranging from actual crimes, to resistance to state policy, to having been denounced by neighbors seeking to obtain their rooms or apartments. Some prisoners had themselves played an active part in the repressive operations. Their distress at their own misfortune was sometimes tempered by the belief that, although the system had erred in their particular case, the system itself was justifiable because conspiracies did exist. Roy Medvedev noted that many such repressors-turned-repressed had never recognized or obeyed any kinds of law. They violated laws and enforced the repression by operationalizing Lenin's maxim: "Bring order or implement terror."[3] An implicit evaluative judgment in this ideology is that terror, or the threat of terror, is not only a justifiable way to bring order but sometimes even the preferred way. (This authoritarian, anti-democratic approach is still relevant to the calibrated use of repression in post–Soviet Russia's attempt to achieve a civil society.) So the repressors could claim that the laws they violated were superseded by a "higher" law—the ideology that sustained the Party.

Among the survivors and victims were the dogmatists who did not lose faith in the Party but lost faith in particular leaders. They switched their devotion from Stalin to Lenin, blaming the terror on Stalinism. A memoir by Nina Gagen Torn, who spent eight years in the Gulag, described such campmates as "hardcore Leninists." They ardently clung to "Leninist ideals," a faith that allowed them to "live without breaking." They argued that the Party's tactics under Stalin discredited him, but not Communism. Hundreds of Kolyma-bound prisoners endorsed this ideology. Gagen-Torn recalled how, even as they were marched under armed guard, they sang, "You fell victim in the struggle because of fateful, selfless love for the people."[4] They sang in spite of being butted with rifles, and even when they were thrown into the hulls of the "death ships" from Vladivostok to Kolyma they continued to sing. Many were later shot, but according to this returnee, they maintained faith in *their* vision of Communism to the end of their life.

Nataliia Rykova (see chapter 3), the daughter of the Old Bolshevik Aleksei Rykov, who was executed in 1938, spent several years[5] in labor camps and exile because she was a family member of an "enemy of the people." Following her release (after Stalin's death) she campaigned to secure her father's Party rehabilitation. In our 2005 interview, when I asked her—at the age of ninety—about her attitude toward the Party, she replied with a derisive question and answer: "Which Party? That wasn't the Party we knew [and created]."[6] Nevertheless, it was important for her to strive for her father's reinstatement—even in the existing Party—"for the sake of justice." He was reinstated under Gorbachev.

The belief that the Party of Lenin would not have countenanced the repression that had become a defining characteristic of Soviet life was sometimes expressed in a "prayerful" way. Some prisoners sent their letters of complaint and appeals for justice to (the dead) Lenin, addressing them to the mausoleum, to those who were in charge of the body of Lenin.[7] They were both spurning the current regime and reaffirming their faith in Communism.

The post-Soviet opening of the archives revisited the debate regarding how many victims were repressed in what period and under which article of the Soviet Criminal Code. The range of estimates is wide because the victims include those who were incarcerated in labor camps, starved by the man-made famine, subjected to de-kulakization, deported, and killed outright. Additionally, their nonincarcerated family members effectively lived in prisons without walls. Those born in "special settlements" (exile) are not included in the category of victims of political repression, nor are those citizens who were incarcerated and sent to the Gulag on nonpolitical articles or charges such as those covered by the draconian 1941 labor laws. According to Memorial chairman Arsenii Roginskii, a review of the cases in these "excluded categories" would no less than double the number of political prisoners calculated in the Gulag statistics.[8] The accuracy of figures regarding arrest, incarceration, and release is further confounded by the fact that the statistics include rearrests and cases of moribund victims who were sometimes released only so that their death would take place outside the camp.[9] The estimates range from a few million to well over twenty million victims. There is relative consensus that in the years 1930–1956, seventeen to eighteen million were sentenced to detention in prisons, colonies, and camps.[10]

With regard to the number of returnees, there are few calculations.[11] However, using a rough approximation based on release figures in the aftermath of Stalin's death and Khrushchev's Secret Speech, it can be assumed that well over five million victims survived to return to Soviet society in the 1950s.[12] This estimate includes the former exiles and deportees. Those who did not survive the camps and did not have descendants did not, as a rule, receive posthumous rehabilitation because there were no relatives to apply for it, so there are also gaps in the rehabilitation statistics. The proportion of these ex-prisoners who requested reinstatement in the Communist Party has not yet been calculated, but available archives should allow us to investigate this question and arrive at some estimates.

We know that in 1956, the year of Khrushchev's Secret Speech, some former political prisoners who had been excluded from the Party on "unfounded political accusations" petitioned the Party Control Commission for reinstatement. We do not know the actual number of appeals for that year, but 55.5 percent were honored with reinstatement.[13] Furthermore, according to a report of the Party Control Commission, between 1956 and 1961, 30,954 Communists were reinstated, many posthumously. The report does not state how many had applied during that period.[14] Their Party and judicial rehabilitation notwithstanding, the return of these former "adversaries" had little impact on the Soviet system. The causes of this imperturbability of the Soviet system may be looked for both within the system and within its returning victims.

SCOPE, METHODOLOGY, AND LIMITATIONS

A number of overlapping and interacting determinants will be examined in this study. The changing political climate will also be considered as it influenced both the prisoners' entrance into and exit from the system. Outcomes and attitudes were in turn influenced by the prisoners' legal history, political history,[15] family history, survival history, and reinstatement history. The Gulag was populated with millions of prisoners—peasants and workers, segments of the population who were arrested by quota in 1937 and 1938, and hard-core and petty criminals incarcerated for violating labor laws. The repression targeted classes, ethnicities, minor social insubordination, deviance, and potential deviance.[16] This study reflects on the experience and attitudes of Stalin-era political prisoners, or their surviving family members, who remained loyal to the Party during and after the Gulag. The materials were chosen on the basis of this criterion. Returnees and prisoners who had no affinity to the Party were largely excluded because their sentiments require less complex explanation. The sample, or rather selection set, ranges from respondents who were the children of well-known executed Bolsheviks to lesser known returnees, and is limited to the archives, memoirs, victim accounts, and witnesses that were accessible.

Chronicling the stories of Gulag survivors may illuminate how Party loyalty was shaped and maintained, but the limitations of generalizing from a selected sample of writings and oral accounts and the selection factor of survival should be recognized. There are also the limitations of the specific group that generated their accounts—people who were educated, who may have been prominent, and who were members of the intelligentsia. They were strongly affected by a specific historical period: many of the Party faithful memoirists, even later in life, reflected the perspectives of the Thaw generation. Moreover, although we can also draw very limited inferences from interrogation protocols[17] and the publicly declared, perhaps scripted "parting words" of better known victims, much of what we know comes from survivors or their surviving witnesses. Gulag victims numbered in the millions, but we only have some thousands of memoir accounts. Thus, most of the testimony died with the witnesses, as it did with the Holocaust victims, but with this difference: the Holocaust was designed to eliminate survivors, not to have a political effect on those who managed to survive. And this difference provides a continuing record of the survival value of a political orientation—both for the individual and the system. Despite the fact that the selection set is limited and not representative of society in general, sufficient collective features have emerged from the portal of these individual accounts to suggest a commonality in the experience.

With varying motivations, some prisoners requested and received Party reinstatement upon return. Some were denied this status until the Gorbachev era. Other returnees, like longtime prisoner Lev Razgon, requested and received Party rehabilitation under Khrushchev and then left the Party under Gorbachev.[18] Still others, like Memorial member Olga Shireeva, rejoined the Party only under Gorbachev in 1988, and turned in their Party cards shortly thereafter.[19]

Two investigative approaches—a quantitative sociological survey, and a qualitative psychohistorical case study analysis—were considered. The sociological survey was impractical because of the difficulty of gathering a sample that was sufficiently large and representative to permit generalizations. Instead, the generation of hypotheses was sought by looking for common trends in a variety of individual experiences. This approach rests on the assumption that every individual experience represents a class of experiences. Thus, generalizations regarding that class can be inferred if we can accurately place the specific experience within its appropriate context.

Memory

When conducting this type of research, it is imperative to recognize that memory is malleable, and sometimes poor, inaccurate, and subject to self-censure. Personal narratives add the visceral immediacy of lived experience to the scholarly discourse of history. Because these experiences only become history as they are gleaned, contextualized, and disseminated, the history they become should be informed by their cultural, social, and historical provenance, along with their credibility, and a consideration of how they may have been changed by the gleaning process. Challenges to their credibility include the failures and distortions of memory with the passage of time, made worse by traumatic stress and compounded by chronic stress. Added to these is the unavoidable bias of their interpretive frame: all stories combine a description of what happened with an argument (often implicit) regarding how events should be construed. Political censorship prevents some stories from being told, and an overlapping self-censorship prevents some from even being conceived.

Nevertheless, despite their limitations and selective nature, the oral histories this study was able to gather from the vanishing generation of Stalin-era Gulag survivors, supplemented with the written accounts of those who have since perished, proved to be rich sources for understanding the personal and political experience of loyalty. Significant numbers, convergent and comparative accounts of similar events, verification with records and relatively objective accounts, and placing the narrator and the narrative in the correct sociohistorical context, all contribute to transforming unconditionally accepted testimony into conditionally acceptable evidence.

As with any scholarly investigation, we may believe the narrators but recognize that critical truths may be hidden from them, and only revealed, if ever, by evidence from other stories or other sources. When appropriate, we make inferences justified by our knowledge of the social context of the narratives. For example, systemic corruption, personal exploitation, and other such "unethical" antisocial behaviors occurred in and outside of the camps, but these stories are often not addressed in the loyalists' narratives. However, a more implicit theme that can be plausibly inferred from the accounts is that the repressive system sometimes made survival contingent on repressing others.

The stories gathered from oral and written sources can be viewed as narrative "artifacts" because they have been constructed by humans and can be collected, but they differ from physical artifacts because they are modified in the act of collection. Each story, no matter how true, is an edited version of the truth, and life will always be more chaotic than the stories we construct to make sense of it. It is thus critical to researching autobiographies to recognize the narratives' constitutional incapacity to be lifelike, as philosopher Louis Mink has eloquently observed: "Stories are not lived but told. Life has no beginnings, middles, end . . . [they belong to] the story we tell ourselves later. There are hopes, plans, battles and ideas, but only in retrospective stories are hopes unfulfilled, plans miscarried, battles decisive, and ideas seminal."[20]

Nevertheless, personal narratives allow us to construct a more comprehensive narrative of history, but the evidentiary basis of that reliance must be regularly reviewed. The credibility of recollected events in any personal narrative is compromised by the malleability of memory, because recollection is not a collection of past events drawn from a filing drawer of preserved memories. Rather, it is an ad hoc—for this occasion—"re-collection" and reconstruction of events.[21] Some events are inevitably lost to memory, some are falsely, if sincerely, recalled,[22] and all are selected for personal, social, and historical relevance.[23] By such means, the current personal (and national) narrative reconfigures memories of the past.[24] Furthermore, any personal narrative is just one reconstruction of what happened, and its utility is constrained by the empirical limitations of generalizing from a subset of one—unless it is typical. Support for its typicality can be provided by confirming evidence from other personal narratives that converge on similar events.

The narrator's recollection can also be biased by ideology, and this influence is especially clear when two narratives from the same person converge on the same event whose meaning has changed over time. A well-known example of how dramatically memories can change in response to new "facts" or new perceptions is the "loss of innocence of memory" experienced by Jorge Semprun, a writer, a former resistance fighter, and now a former Communist, who was imprisoned as a Communist in Buchenwald in 1943. In 1963, in a work titled *Le grand voyage,* Semprun recalled that he did not feel victimized by his camp experience, but rather empowered. His belief in the Soviet cause and Communism imbued these seeming deprivations with inspiring meaning. However, a decade later, Semprun underwent a crisis of belief after reading Solzhenitsyn's *Gulag Archipelago*. This changed his appraisal of his camp experience, now, "re-cognizing" that his experiences were different than those he had recalled in his 1963 work. He then re-remembered and re-recorded those revised experiences in a later work, bitterly reflecting on how much his Communist identity had colored—even blinded—his perception of reality.[25] As currently understood by cognitive neuroscience, both perceptions were real, for their time and place.[26]

INFORMANTS' ACCOUNTS AND EXPLANATORY HYPOTHESES

As noted previously, the hypotheses considered are not mutually exclusive, each is only a contributing determinant of behavior, they act in concert, and they overlap in their influence on the victims. The question of why their commitment to Communism had endured the Gulag was one that many loyalists did not habitually raise in public, but we could infer an answer from their personal accounts. In them, they described the meaning and fulfillment provided by the Communist Party, as well as the political, social, and material advantages they hoped to realize. At a minimum they experienced Communism as a way of making sense of their world and providing practical ways to cope with it. For some, it also had the spiritual quality of an ideology.

It can be doubly informative to approach this question through the portal of personal narratives, because they simultaneously describe what is generalizable as well as what is unique about the teller's experience. Every personal narrative is unique because each portrays the individual's adaptive response within a context. But each is also generalizable, or typical, because it represents the adaptive response of humans to particular social, psychological, political, and physical contexts. Accordingly, we can view the variety of explanatory hypotheses and models proffered by the scholarly literature as an array of the particular contexts within which the adaptations described in these personal experiences might be typical. These include: Communism as secular religion, cognitive dissonance, physical and mental coercion (Arendt's "community of violence"[27]), bonding rituals and painful initiation rites, psychological defense mechanisms, charismatic leadership, and traumatic bonding, among many others. Each of these overlapping but distinguishable explanatory factors contributes to our understanding of the individual and general effects of the repression. Those emphasized in this study are those that emerged most prominently from the personal accounts gathered, and are also widely supported by empirical evidence. Prior to discussing these hypotheses, however, it is useful to briefly address how this study approaches Communist ideology.

While the influence of Communism on the repressed was economic, social, and political, it also inculcated a faith-based belief in its ideology, evidenced by the persisting belief of some survivors, despite the evidence of the enormous scale of human rights violations they endured and witnessed. Though it can be credibly argued that their belief was supported by substantial evidence of economic development, increased literacy, social mobility, gender equality, and other promised goals, their evidentiary base fails the scientific test of inclusiveness.

All faith-based beliefs can, and regularly do, provide substantiating positive evidence, but only science-based beliefs include—even seek—negative, contradictory, and non-supportive evidence, constantly unsettling previous beliefs. The Party censored the press, and any public discussion of evidence that challenged the Party line was potentially life-threatening to participants, and even their family and friends. Without disputing any of the positive evidence supporting the belief of those who continued their faith in Communism, if that belief requires ignoring or destroying contradictory evidence, it is a faith-based belief system.

Human beings seek to find a useful meaning, or interpretive frame, for events. For science, the meaning is always derived from new events, surprises, exceptions, etc., so the interpretive frame is contingent on whether they confirmed or refuted the hypothesis. A secular, scientific system is subject to refutation if it fails to deliver as promised. Likewise, the Communist Party and other such "total"[28] institutions also provide "meaning," i.e., an interpretive frame, but unlike inclusive evidence-based systems they verge toward a religious system of infallibility because the failure to achieve goals or deliver on promises is not subjected to refutation. Adherents feel no need to do so. In his analysis of the de-conversion narratives of ex-Communists in *The God That Failed,* Richard Crossman described the emotional appeal of Communism to be in the "material and spiritual sacrifices which it demanded of the convert."[29] He maintained that the attraction of ordinary political parties was what they offered members, while "the attraction of Communism was that it offered nothing and demanded everything, including the surrender of spiritual freedom."[30] Thus invested, the Communist faithful who endured the Gulag and continued to believe in the Party did so based on faith, not outcome or reason.

Religion is also distinguished from science by its prescription of a moral code of behavior whose transgression is branded as sinful, often punishable by a supernatural power. Although the concept of "sin" is foreign to the kind of secular ideology that Communism purported to be, Stalin regularly invoked this label to vilify acts against the workers' state.[31] (We may infer that religious punishment was not Stalin's cure for these ills.) The charge of sinfulness in relation to the system itself, however, would seem a terminological mismatch. But perhaps it is not. When the Russian television station NTV announced the death of Aleksandr Nikolaevich Iakovlev on the evening of October 18, 2005, the broadcaster stated that Iakovlev was the only former high Party leader to apologize for the "sin of Bolshevism."[32] The listeners were implicitly invited to consider the similarities between Bolshevism and religion, a discussion that arose from time to time, and more so in recent years.[33] Among the ideological currents that converged within this public announcement were individual responsibility, religious confession, and a repudiation of a political ideology, now increasingly viewed with nostalgia. At the time of Iakovlev's death, this nostalgia for the Soviet era was facilitated by the decline of Russia's prestige as well as the ensuing social and economic turmoil. Even so, recasting the Soviet era in a favorable light was partly sustained by, in Iakovlev's words, "mass amnesia about mass murder,"[34] and partly by a careful selection of past events.

Aleksandr Iakovlev's ascent through the ranks of the Communist Party reflected and shaped his political horizons. He went from committed Communist and ideologue to critic of the repressive practices of the system, eventually to become a chief architect of the Gorbachev-era perestroika policies. After the collapse of the Soviet Union, he chaired the Presidential Commission on the Rehabilitation of Victims of Unlawful Repression. During his term in office he vigorously campaigned for opening the archives, for disclosure of documents on the Stalinist repression, and for the publication of victims' names. By 2001, his commission had succeeded in rehabilitating over four million citizens. In the first post-Soviet decade, Iakovlev not only denounced the former political system, but encouraged people to remember and "repent," even calling for the traditional November 7 Revolution Holiday to be renamed the Day of Agreement and Reconciliation. In a certain sense, Iakovlev escaped the gravitational field of one indoctrination—Communism—only to be drawn into another—religion.

While stalwart Party advocates may have considered Communist ideology to be "moral," if they invoked the concept of "sin" in their political deliberations it was not with reference to the Party itself. Furthermore, adherence was maintained by the very worldly system of deprivation or earthly punishment, not divine enforcement. Thus, Iakovlev's charge that the moral transgressions committed in the name of Bolshevism were sinful, wittingly or unwittingly, leads us to reflect on Karl Marx's disparagement of religion as an opium for the people.[35] To the extent that Communism can be viewed as a faith-based ideology, it is not the antidote to religion envisioned by Marx, but another opiate. However, Marx was right in recognizing the power of religion to stimulate the brain's reward centers by providing meaning and community, though he himself did not mean this quite so physiologically.[36] By design or default the CPSU appropriated this role and function in the lives of some citizens—before, during, and after their incarceration in the Gulag.

Aside from its repentant/religious aspects, Iakovlev's singular apology for his participation in official transgressions invites us to further consider other questions—for example, the extent to which responsibility is attributable to the individual or to the regime. Three features made his apology noteworthy. He was condemning a repressive regime that had not been discredited by a military defeat, he was one of its established members, and he also blamed himself. One of the important legacies of Nuremberg is that individuals are responsible for their own actions, even if carried out under orders from a regime. Most of the countries that have undertaken any efforts to deal with an onerous past recognize this principle. In Russia, however, very few officials or citizens have thus far accepted responsibility for the now repudiated acts they committed or knew of.

We approach this issue with the understanding that despite evidence of state-sponsored crimes, the Party, from Khrushchev on down, did not hold itself accountable to anyone but itself. So, what further understanding does this suggest about the ideology of the Party? While some of this imperviousness to accountability may be attributable to the self-interest of particular individuals, it appears more fundamentally grounded in an authoritarian culture and faith-based ideology. This is relevant to the seeming paradox regarding how belief in the Party persisted in spite of ostensibly contrary evidence. This seeming paradox disappears when we recognize how characteristic this is of faith-based beliefs, typified by all the religions and other total systems. Ostensibly contrary evidence is rationalized by invoking a higher, inscrutable purpose or otherworldly reward, but the basic tenet is that faith in the cause needs no proof. It is founded in the authority of a higher power and reinforced by the experience of meaning and coherence it provides to believers and/or group members who willingly make sacrifices. This may account for why and how belief-based systems can be impervious to adverse worldly outcomes.

Philosophers, concentration camp survivors who maintained their faith in God and man, and those seeking to understand the appeal of Communism have all grappled with this issue. In his poignant discussion of meaning, psychiatrist and Auschwitz survivor Viktor Frankl noted that "man is able to live and even die for the sake of his ideals and values,"[37] and Nietzsche observed that men will bear almost any "what" if they accept the "why." Catherine Merridale, reflecting on the Soviet experience in *Night of Stone: Death and Memory in Russia,* has framed this issue as "loyalty," and argued that Party membership made people feel that they were participating in a heroic, forward-focused, glorious struggle, however false that struggle turned out,[38] from an evidence-based perspective.[39]

A FAITH-BASED BELIEF IN COMMUNISM

One of the consequences of the repression was that some prisoners continued to endorse the very system of beliefs that was being used by the regime to justify their repression. Solzhenitsyn derides these entrenched "loyalists," who "fell beneath the beloved ax" and then justified it. He expresses exasperation at the fact that they did not "forsake their earlier views," even after the camp, and disdains them for begging for "forgiveness" in their petitions from camp—petitions that remained as unanswered as those of non-Party members. However, though Solzhenitsyn found them to be "pigheaded," he understood that their convictions were genuine.[40] Such Communist prisoners, who defended the Party both in camp and in their post-camp memoirs, included the writer Boris Diakov.[41] Varlam Shalamov as well railed against this group for thinking that only their own arrests had been a mistake, and Kolyma survivor Ekaterina Olitskaia simply could not understand the psychology of such fellow campmates (see chapters 1 and 2).

For the Party faithful, their belief in the CPSU incentivized their labor even within the camps, because they considered themselves to be the builders of socialism who were participating in its construction with their bare hands. The identity of a number of prisoners, along with their youthful dreams of a better life and forging a new society, merged with the Party. Their faith in the morality of socialism was largely unshaken by the repression, which they interpreted either as a perversion of an inherently good ideology or as an opportunity to "offer up," as it were, tangible physical labor in support of the ideology. André Gide justified his acceptance of "paradoxical truths" by maintaining that "the happiness of man does not consist in liberty but in the acceptance of a duty."[42] The ability to find a redeeming value in the endurance of hardships that serve a higher purpose is a widely accepted human virtue, accounting for secular heroism and religious martyrdom. Frankl drew from his personal experience but spoke for many when he wrote that "suffering ceases to be suffering in some way at the moment it finds a meaning, such as the meaning of a sacrifice."[43]

For some, such meaning had been provided by the Russian Orthodox Church before its leaders were executed or imprisoned and its property confiscated by the Soviets. In the absence of a culture of religion to satisfy the needs for revered leaders, social coherence, and meaning, Communism substituted its secular ideology and a cult of personality akin to what Weber described as "charismatic authority."[44] Under Lenin, Stalin, and their dictatorial heirs, this authority was promoted by crafting a form of "hero worship" through the combination of (real or feigned) devotion and obedience a closed system can compel.

Charisma—from the Greek *charis,* meaning "grace"—has a root similar to caring or charity. While charisma may be a somewhat imprecise explanatory factor (as are all compelling attractions, such as love), it is a powerful motivator. Weber located charisma in the personality of the leader, but it is perhaps more accurately located in the *response* of attraction elicited from adherents. Faith-based belief is primarily a cognitive, thinking process, while charisma is an emotional attachment.

Stephen Kotkin, though not emphasizing the secular religious dimension, wrote about the "new civilization" at Magnitogorsk. He described the pervasive mind-set that idealized socialist construction in the 1930s, arguing that the Great Depression made the differences between socialism and capitalism seem even more pronounced and created "greater antagonism." Thus, he observed, "No matter how substantial the differences between rhetoric and practice or intentions and outcomes sometimes became, people could still maintain a fundamental faith in the fact of socialism's existence in the USSR and in that system's inherent superiority."[45] To the extent that the individual's subsistence depended on the Communist Party, it was psychologically and politically dangerous to criticize the Party. Supplication, felt or feigned, can be in the service of self-interest. Igal Halfin has described this transformative way of thinking and acting. He cites a plaintive letter of appeal to the Party from a man who was about to be ousted from the university and presumably arrested: "I absolutely cannot imagine my existence outside the Party. . . . Though I know you will purge me—such are the times—I intend to dedicate my life to unmasking the enemies of the working class."[46] Halfin summarized the predicament of many—that a fulfilling life, and perhaps life itself, depended on being in good standing with the Party. Former oppositionist turned purge victim Georgii Piatakov described the "true Bolshevik" as having no life "outside the ranks of the Party, and . . . ready to believe that black was white, and white was black, if the Party required it."[47] When Adolf Ioffe, a Bolshevik leader and Soviet diplomat, committed suicide in 1927, his suicide note explained that there was no point in living after Trotsky's ousting from the Party leadership. He added that he could no longer serve the Party, and had lost his purpose in life.[48] With the opposition forbidden, Ioffe's life became unbearable. According to Alexander Etkind, his suicide was an effective form of political struggle.[49] Both Piatakov and Ioffe were opposition leaders, so presumably their loyalty was, as described by Nataliia Rykova (above), to the Party they knew and created.

Some prisoners went to lesser—but still great—lengths to prove their loyalty. Lev Gavrilov was arrested in 1937 and sentenced to ten years of incarceration. He spent the early war years in Kolyma, and wrote about his experiences in his memoirs. He titled his story "z/k: *zapasnoi kommunist*" (reserve Communist)—a play on words with the Russian abbreviation, or acronym, z/k, meaning prisoner.[50] In these memoirs he describes how he extracted his own gold teeth to contribute to the war effort. When he tried to give them to his interrogators, they did not want to accept this offer from an "enemy of the people." Gavrilov did not accept their assessment that he was someone who had violated his right to be a Communist, hence the title of his narrative.[51] In preserving his honor, he was simultaneously honoring Communism. It did not matter that its minions were dishonoring him. Such is the orientation and guiding ideology of the true believer.

Mikhail Trofimovich Adeev, a teacher and former Kolyma prisoner, titled his memoir "Misfortune and Bolshevik Conscience." Therein he recalls having met tens of thousands of "sons of the Party"—devoted Party members—during his years in Kolyma. Following his release in 1951, he sought not only rehabilitation (restoration of rights and the revoking of his sentence) but Party reinstatement. Like many others, he had to wait for it until after the 1956 Twentieth Party Congress. It would be nineteen years before he would regain this status. He poignantly describes the frustrations endured by him and others: "Complete rehabilitation along Party lines and reinstatement of the rights of a member of the Party was of great significance to me. To admit guilt for crimes I didn't commit would have been unfounded, to say I was repressed for nothing and groundlessly excluded from the Party could have been considered slander at the time."[52] Such predicaments were beyond the prisoners' power to remedy. They could only be resolved by the Party, as Adeev's quandary eventually was, with Khrushchev's condemnation of Stalin's criminal acts at the Twentieth Party Congress. As a result of his "complete rehabilitation," Adeev no longer had to indicate on the forms he submitted that he had been repressed. Such a disclosure carried the disadvantageous implication of culpability. Now, the number of years during which he was deprived of Party membership were added to his Party tenure.[53] His memoirs record how proud he was in 1982 to be the recipient of an award for having been in the ranks of the CPSU for fifty years.[54]

After the Twentieth Party Congress, many letters requesting reinstatement were sent to the Presidium of the Supreme Soviet of the USSR, even though the Party Control Commission was actually the body responsible for membership questions. Such pleas for reinstatement were laden with mea culpas and ardent avowals to refrain from whatever act they were accused of having committed. Golfo Alexopolous, in writing about the disenfranchised of the late twenties and early thirties, described some of their letters of appeal as "ritual laments" that chronicled the suffering incurred since their rights were taken away. Other letters were described as presenting the petitioners' "Soviet self": their personal transformation, affirmed by their abandonment of past disfavored activities; their sacrifice and demonstrable loyalty to Soviet authority; and their subsequent engagement in socially useful labor.[55] All such letters "spoke Bolshevik,"[56] as Kotkin so aptly put it in his powerful study of Magnitogorsk. They reflected the omnipresence of ideology and the pervasive fear of repression in Soviet life.[57] Jochen Hellbeck, who examined diaries and "self-consciousness" of citizens under Stalin, has addressed similar issues.[58] When access to power and community are centrally controlled, such gatekeeping can shape not only the applications, but also the applicants.

The necessity of such letters—and they were a prerequisite to attaining the status sought by their writers—underscored and reinforced the Party's censure of the victim. Some letters did say that they had been wronged by particular figures, like Beria, already an approved target. But what they did not generally say was that the petitioners were wronged by the system. On the contrary, they declared their support and asked for support from the system that had imprisoned them—and might do so again. One such letter was sent to the Presidium of the Supreme Soviet of the USSR by the poet Garnik Kazarian, whose Party membership dated from 1913. He recounts his 1940 arrest for alleged "anti-Soviet agitation," for which he was sentenced to eight years of incarceration: "Despite my circumstances, and certain that the truth would triumph, I, as a Bolshevik educated by our glorious party, did not lose heart and continued my literary activity, composing a number of poems [including] 'The March to Berlin' and 'The Strength of Communism'."[59] The poems were denied publication because of his social status. This 1954 letter closed with the request to restore his civil and Party rights, the "mighty CPSU" that "gave [him] Great October."[60] Propaganda aside, the writer was not required to write poetry about the greatness of the Party. And while a revoked sentence was essential to a relatively "normal" life, Party membership was not required.

Reinstatement in the ranks of the Party was a bestowed status, not an automatic right for returnees, not even for those who had been proven innocent of the alleged crimes. One ex-prisoner, who had been sentenced to twenty-five years in 1949 for Article 58 offences ("counterrevolutionary activities") and released under a 1955 amnesty,[61] posed this question to the Party Control Commission: "How can I prove that I am prepared to give everything to the Soviet cause, to the Soviet motherland, when all of my work since the early days of the Revolution—which was granted numerous acknowledgments and decorations—did not prevent me, guilty of nothing, from being an outcast?"[62] He concluded with this answer: "The best award for undeserved suffering would be the possibility at the end of my life to use my strength, knowledge, and experience to serve the welfare of the motherland."[63]

A PSYCHOLOGICAL DEFENSE MECHANISM

One of the consequences of indoctrination, also labeled "brainwashing," is that some victims assume a pseudo-autonomy by accepting responsibility for their unavoidable misfortunes. Robert Lifton studied the dynamics of the Chinese "thought reform" process, including the methods of coercing and creating confessions and autobiographies, and reshaping "self-consciousness." He observed how strong psychological forces were able to penetrate the inner emotions of individuals and make them shift from resistance to full participation in the reform process.[64] Endorsing the views of the oppressor, even if they are at variance with the victims' previous understandings, may have survival value within the confines of a totalitarian system. Not only can this attitude alleviate the frustration and danger of fighting a futile battle, it can make the victim feel like a winner. This process, condensed in the colloquial phrase, "If you can't beat them join them," was more precisely described by Anna Freud as an "ego mechanism of defense." She labeled it "the identification with the aggressor."[65] The victims adopt their repressors' view of them—the view they had previously opposed—and in consequence they feel almost as strong as their repressors.

COGNITIVE DISSONANCE

The theory of cognitive dissonance, developed by Leon Festinger in 1957 on the basis of his investigation of a doomsday cult, posits that people experience psychological tension when their cognitions about what is true are challenged by disaffirming evidence, and he described three overlapping cognitive stratagems by which people attempt to reduce the tension caused by this dissonance.[66] One entails reinterpreting the disconfirming evidence to make it consonant; a second, counterbalancing the impact of dissonance by adding consonant evidence; and a third, downgrading the importance of disconfirming evidence. In addition, support for the challenged cognition can be reinforced by proselytizing to increase the number of validating adherents.[67]

Examples of the reinterpretation of dissonant evidence to reduce dissonance are found in the narratives of loyalist Communists who addressed the inconsistency between their ideology and the repression by declaring that the repression was an aberration committed by errant leaders—the so-called "cult of personality" (as did Khrushchev). Other reinterpretations justified police state tactics as necessary to defend Communism from real enemies (counterrevolutionaries), embraced the work of the Gulag as fulfilling a purpose (building socialism), and maintained that "revolutions are not made with white gloves on."

Examples of countervailing consonant evidence to reduce dissonance are provided by loyalists who call attention to the industrial, educational, and social benefits provided by Communism, trumpet the scientific achievements in the name of the Party and the motherland, and laud the Party's successful mobilization of the nation's resources to wage and win the Great Patriotic War.

Examples of downgrading the importance of disconfirming evidence to reduce dissonance include Putin's (and many of his predecessors') statements minimizing or marginalizing the Gulag and Soviet repression. In recent years, Russia has largely forestalled the need to downgrade disconfirming evidence because it has been shielded from the public discourse, school textbooks, and consequently national memory (see chapter 5 and the epilogue).

Cognitive dissonance theory provides an adaptive psychological framework for understanding how the loyalists' adherence to the Party was maintained and sometimes strengthened despite such potentially dissonant challenges as the incarceration and execution of Communists, forced and punitive labor in the Gulag, and officially enforced silence about both.[68] Cognitive dissonance and related paradigms were and are instrumental to researchers trying to explain the determinants of attitudes and beliefs and the internalization of values. They may aid us in understanding how people endure repression and how repression itself endures. It should be noted, however, that Festinger's doomsday cult subjects justified choices that were their own; they had not been forced to do what they did. A violent, coercive, external power and the condition of suffering can increase the need to settle any contradictions that arise between belief and reality. Moreover, relying too heavily on cognitive dissonance theory to account for the enduring loyalty of some victims is limiting and may be misleading, because the theory posits the existence of a distressing psychological conflict caused by a relevant dissonance, while such dissonance may exist more in the preconception of the researcher than in the mind of the loyalist. For example, many people feel comfortable in employing rational, refutable evidence in choosing a car, and nonrational (which is not irrational) irrefutable evidence for choosing an emotional attachment to a faith-based belief or charismatic leader. Each way of thinking serves different purposes, and each purpose seeks a value not found in the other.

Since the 1920s, when all competing factions were banned, the Communist Party had a monopoly on power in the Soviet Union. In this climate, "fitting in" by exhibiting *partiinost'* (a sense of Party) was essential for social functioning and sometimes even physical survival. Accordingly, what might have begun as a functional, pragmatic, or coercive conformity would have a tendency to be propelled by cognitive dissonance from "adapting to" toward "adopting of" a belief system. This provides an ironic merging of faith-based and evidence-based beliefs. Driven by cognitive dissonance, the "evidence" to support an imposed faith-based belief system can be the individuals' reinterpretation of events, subjective experience, consensual validation, and real world success.

Following Stalin's death in 1953, the Presidium of the Supreme Soviet issued an amnesty that liberated 1.2 million Gulag prisoners. Subsequently, *Pravda* published the following letter from a teacher in Kishinev:

> The decree is clear evidence that we are successfully moving along the road to Communism in our country. . . . The decree is a historical document which mobilizes and inspires our countrymen to new labor achievements for the glorious goal of the complete victory of Communism, in whose name the Great and unforgettable Comrade Stalin labored to the last heartbeat. While reading this decree, I was so filled with love and devotion to our Party and to the Soviet government that I am prepared to work day and night.[69]

It would appear from letters such as this that the amnesty decree was not perceived as the start of de-Stalinization.[70] However, it is interesting to note the perspective on the issue of prisoners being released. This letter-writer does not question why so many fellow citizens were incarcerated in the first place. Nor does the letter address the fact that an even slightly greater number still remained in the camps. It takes the amnesty decree to be an affirmation of the good work of the Party and the Soviet government rather than an indictment of Stalinism. Other writers to *Pravda* may have raised these concerns and were not published, or worse—and there may not have been such a teacher from Kishinev.

Whether this letter was written by a teacher or the editors of *Pravda,* it can be understood as a cognitive stratagem for turning the dissonant perceptions of the Party as repressor into consonant perceptions of the Party as liberator. Its propagandistic success will depend on the readiness of individual readers to ignore dissonant facts. When this readiness is amplified by the psychological, social, and material influences that constrain options in a closed system, this cognitive stratagem may be incorporated by—and endure within—individuals.

In his *Gulag Archipelago,* in another context, Solzhenitsyn describes and derides the mind-set propagated in the letter. He was distressed to find such thinking in the commissioners who visited the camps in the wake of Khrushchev's Secret Speech. They had the power to release prisoners, and they did not use it wholeheartedly. He laments:

Should not the commission have stood before a general line-up of prisoners, bared their heads, and said: "Brothers! We have been sent by the Supreme Soviet to beg your forgiveness. For years and decades you have languished here, though you are guilty of nothing . . . accept our belated repentance, if you can. The gates are open, and you are free. Out there on the airstrip, planes are landing with medicines, food, and warm clothing. There are doctors on board."[71]

Had the commission reasoned the same way from the same evidence as Solzhenitsyn, they would have acknowledged that the coercive repression of the Gulag disconfirmed the ideology of the Party. Instead, their actions reflected the same view of the Party promoted in the *Pravda* publication. Instead of asking for forgiveness, the commission granted forgiveness to prisoners for acts that many had not committed. And rehabilitation—which was still a long way off for most prisoners—was granted in the spirit of a conditional pardon.[72] It would be misleading to interpret the commission's acquiescence to the repression they witnessed as an unconditional pardon for the Communist Party. In their view, this was a non-issue. The Party had, as it were, done nothing that required any such deliberation.

FUNCTIONALISM

In his discussion on "speaking Bolshevik," Kotkin writes, "It was not necessary to believe. It was necessary, however, to participate as if one believed."[73] Membership in the Communist Party, like membership in a culturally favored religion, offered instrumental social advantages for housing, job placement, and professional advancement, and it was voluntary.[74] A pragmatic incentive for professing loyalty to the CPSU was the hope that compliant behavior in and outside the camp would lead to reinstatement in the Party, which was an important, if not primary, goal for ex-prisoners.

According to Roy Medvedev, there are no uniform stories regarding how former prisoners viewed the Party, but a number of individual stories offer informative portrayals. Medvedev, the son of an executed "enemy of the people," met many Gulag survivors after their return. They felt sufficiently safe and comfortable with him to describe the repression in the Khrushchev era, and he was able to gather candid disclosures even during the Brezhnev era, when camp themes were once again taboo. He incorporated their stories in his 1971 work *Let History Judge,* published abroad, earning him both fame and the status of dissident.

Some stories began simply with the returnee's apolitical pursuit of ordinary material satisfactions that had long been denied. He described a woman who, upon return from the Gulag, said, "I am disappointed in everything and believe in nothing anymore, not beauty, not love, but I have one desire—to eat ice cream every day." The pursuit of such immediate satisfactions was fairly common among the deprived and emaciated returning prisoners. She recalled how much she loved ice cream in her childhood, how little food there was in the camp, and how the luxury of eating ice cream epitomized her image of the good life. However, in order to eat ice cream regularly she had to have a refrigerator for the ice cream, and an apartment for the refrigerator, and a pension to pay for the apartment. All of this was contingent upon restored social status, a very political goal. If an ex-prisoner could receive rehabilitated status, with Party rehabilitation, the chances of a normal civil life, including material benefits, were much greater.[75]

In recognition of this, many returnees strove more directly and self-consciously for full-fledged citizenship, with its attendant social and professional advantages. Otherwise, as one returnee stated, "it would have been even harder to adapt."[76] But some motivations were more altruistic. One returnee joined the Party in 1959, partly under pressure from her mother, an Old Bolshevik, but also with the hope that the Party needed the good influence of members such as herself in its ranks.[77]

Sometimes utilitarian behaviors that begin as an effort to convince others that the individual holds a belief can come to be internalized as an authentic belief. Some of this transformation can be accounted for by cognitive dissonance. However, there is also a functional explanation. It is what actors describe as "method acting."[78] The more the "professed" Party loyalty comes to be sincerely believed by the returnee, the more likely it is to be believed by the attendant and critical audience—the Party.

A TRAUMATIC BOND

Fear and powerlessness generally made prisoners and returnees more vulnerable to the coercive authority of the state. Stockholm syndrome, or the traumatic bond, is a recognized psychosocial process whereby forced isolation, anxiety, physical threat, and other forms of stressful conditions can lead to social bonding between jailers and prisoners or captors and hostages.[79] This phenomenon took its name from the city of Stockholm, scene of a bank robbery in 1973.[80] What stamped this incident into the annals of behavioral science was not the six-day hostage standoff but its aftermath. While the wider world was condemning their captors, the victims, even after they were freed from captivity, were defending their captors. What seemed counterintuitive to the observing public, living in an open world, became understandable when viewed from the closed world perspective of the captive–captor relationship.

Juxtaposing these different perspectives highlights the process underlying all subjective assessments. They entail the same "compare and contrast" methodology so favored by scientific valuation. During the six days of captivity, the victims came to see their captors not as people who were repressing them, but as people who were in total control of liberating them. Furthermore, ingratiating oneself to the captors—the more authentic, the more functional—could also contribute to survival. The social context necessary is a closed system, a total asylum-like institution.[81]

A similar process has been described to account for what seems to be the misguided loyalty of abused children and abused spouses. In this case the closed system is the family, and the rewards and punishments are acceptance and rejection. The Soviet state and the Communist Party were very adept at using their monopoly of rewards and punishments, particularly in the Gulag, to construct a closed system. But there must also have been an individual psychological proclivity. Otherwise, why would this constricted world view persist so long after liberation, and not in everyone?

In 2000 Eric Kandel was awarded the Nobel Prize for demonstrating, among other things, that mental experiences are *ipso facto* neurobiological experiences.[82] So we should also consider the role of neurobiology in traumatic social attachments. Fear is accompanied by the elevation of stress hormones, motivating people who are in a stressful situation to forge rapid, strong, and sometimes permanent attachment bonds to relieve the neurobiological stress. In the ordinary course of events, this is a healthy stress-reduction mechanism.[83] For some Gulag prisoners, such a psychophysiologic adaptation may have persisted beyond the prison experience, rendering it a "pathophysiological maladaptation."[84]

Witness a letter published in *Pravda* in 1953 and attributed to an ex-prisoner:

We are the children of our Soviet motherland-mother. Maybe we committed an offense, disobeyed, and mother punished us. But can we really hate her for that? She punished, but she also forgave and she once again embraces her children! . . . Let the American leaders think about whether it is possible in their country for former prisoners to leave prisons with even more love for their country and devotion to their own government.[85]

From a psychological and social perspective, such people have never left prison. They have incorporated their oppressor's belief system, they blame themselves, and they continue to seek security in reconciliation with the Communist Party— the parent.

These hypotheses—a faith-based belief, a psychological defense mechanism, cognitive dissonance, functionalism, and the traumatic bond—suggest different ways of surviving in a repressive, sometimes life-threatening environment. While conformity did not by any means guarantee safety, dissidence—actual, perceived, or suspected—could further jeopardize the lives of the alleged perpetrators as well as their families and friends. Given this pervasive threat, there was a constant motivation for conformist behavior, which in turn could lead to an unwitting adaptive strategy of conformist thinking and feeling.[86]

THE SOVIET LEGACY AND THE LEGACY OF THE GULAG

Conceptually, it is easy to differentiate the ideology of the Communist Party from the ideology of the Gulag. But, operationally, they coevolved and sometimes merged. The political ideology was reinforced by repression, and the repression purged the political system of ideological dissension and dissenters. Likewise, it suppressed the history of repression. In consequence, rehabilitation was an uneven process that often proceeded in opposing directions. At the time of Aleksandr Iakovlev's death, his commission had secured rehabilitation for most of the applicants. However, concomitantly, many discredited symbols of the Soviet system—including Stalin—were also being rehabilitated, if not officially, then unofficially, an artful stratagem in which the Party was well practiced. This affected the national remembrance of the Gulag. The fate of individual remembrance of the Gulag was more complicated, because personal and national survival are driven by different forces.

Evidence from numerous studies of Gulag survivors suggests that the consequences of the Gulag did not end with its closing under Gorbachev, nor was its influence limited to its prisoners. The Gulag, including the threat of the Gulag, pervaded daily Soviet life because it could ensnare almost anyone. Even now, in post-Soviet Russia, there is an increasing trend to repress the memory of repression.[87] This trend is reinforced by nostalgia for a selectively edited history that emphasizes the "order" and deemphasizes the "terror," that longingly recalls the superpower status of Soviet Russia and Soviet victory in the Great Patriotic War (see chapter 3).[88] To subvert Santayana's oft-quoted admonition, those who do not want to be condemned by the past should remember their history from a positive perspective.

Such recasting recognizes the role and function of *history*, whether told as a personal story or enshrined as a national story, in the purposive construction of meaning. Between the events and their *story* four sociocultural influences are interposed: attention—what is noted and what is ignored; priority—what is important and unimportant; values—what is right or wrong, good or bad; causal relationships—what causes what and how.[89] This is a template by which the present shapes the way individuals as well as nations view their past.

For many ex-prisoners and others, coming to terms with the nation's ambivalent repudiated past has required reassessing the meaning of their personal past. For the older generation who were committed to the Party, who considered themselves to be the "builders of socialism" even while in camp, a disconfirmation of their original ideology could raise unsettling questions about how they (mis)spent their lives.[90] Such unsettling questions can lead to unsettling answers. They direct us to look at how the human need for safety, meaning, structure, and social cohesion can be manipulated by the closed systems of repressive regimes and insinuated into the individual.

CHAPTER 1

The Gulag Prisoner and the Bolshevik Soul

Oksana Lazarevna taught socioeconomics at Odessa University and was the mother of two. She was also the wife of an "enemy of the people," who had been arrested and taken away. Oksana was a committed Party member, but as she watched the arrest of one after another of her cohorts, she suspected that the enemy had "penetrated the Party, and it was the NKVD."[1] One day, while Oksana was nursing her infant son, they came for her too. The NKVD agents tore the baby from her and dispatched her sons to her parents. Oksana was taken to an Odessa prison. There, the suspicions she had harbored when she was free were confirmed by what she witnessed in prison.

By the time Oksana was sent to the Gulag, she had resolved to "clear the names of honest Communists."[2] From her barracks, she began to write letters to Stalin and the Central Committee. She charged that "lawlessness reigns in the organs of the NKVD . . . it has led to the destruction of the Odessa Party ranks and many sincere Leninist-Communists."[3] Her campmates were terrified. They warned, "You will have to give these letters to the NKVD authorities in the camp. Don't you understand what the consequences will be? You will die, and you will kill your children." In her response, Oksana illustrated how the dedication to a set of values can override even so strong a human devotion as motherhood, let alone personal survival. She declared: "I am a Communist in the first place, and after that a mother."[4] Oksana was transferred, and her story, recorded in the memoirs of a campmate, ends there. The author, also a committed Party member, wrote in 1963: "In these days of the triumph of truth and justice, the complete unmasking of the cult of personality of Stalin, the restoration of the Leninist principles in life and Party leadership, I would love to know what ever happened to Oksana Lazarevna—a sincere Communist with a capital C."[5] Given the content of Oksana's letters, it is unlikely that she even made it to, or survived transport to, the camps. What is likely is that she maintained her faith until the very end.

In the aftermath of Khrushchev's Secret Speech, the great wave of return and rehabilitation was followed by thousands of requests for Party reinstatement.[6] The motivation of some applicants raises questions about the similarity between Bolshevism and religion. Because Bolshevism presented itself as a secular political movement, it may seem a terminological mismatch to couple *Bolshevik* with *soul*[7] and, further, to discern the Bolshevik soul in the grinding coercion of the Gulag. However, this linkage is justified when religion is viewed as a sociological phenomenon and religious conversion as a process that has historically been facilitated by compliance and coercion—behaviors widely evident in the Gulag. In her discussion of the former peasants who served in the Red Army during the war, Catherine Merridale similarly notes that the belief of some of them in Communism was tantamount to religious "fanaticism": "It would be unwise to assume much love for Communism among the rural population as a whole, but where the new ideas struck root, they could be embraced with a fanaticism that calls to mind the Inquisition or the new jihad. This kind of ideology was really faith, and it was ruthless and personal."[8] Lenin would not have been surprised by this phenomenon. While the revolutionary leaders, including Lenin, were atheists, they well understood the religious proclivity of the Russian peasantry and how beliefs could be exploited to facilitate the Revolution. The professed, and likely genuine, atheists of the Bolshevik vanguard produced a revolution that was, in the words of Alexander Etkind, "not necessarily secular."[9]

Religions are faith-based beliefs that provide a connection to a "higher power," contingent on adherence to a world view. In a religious context, this connection is described as the "soul," which refers to the "immaterial essence . . . the spiritual principle embodied in human beings."[10] To be sure, the frequent references among some prisoners and returnees to their "Bolshevik soul" suggest that the penchant of humans to transcend their individual, material being and connect to something greater than their *self* is not unique to religion. It is an innate property of being human—a property used and exploited by both religious and secular "total institutions."[11] Indeed, it is an ordinary part of daily human experience. Examples of this transcendent connectivity can be found in parenthood, religious devotion, patriotism, and belonging to a collective.

For purposes of discussion, this chapter focuses on and seeks to explain Gulag prisoner and returnee accounts that profess enduring faith in the Party and the Communist project. This faith raises issues concerning Bolshevism's similarity to religion, which included sacrificing the individual for the collective, self-reflection, conversion, confession, and purging. The idea that Communism was a secular or political religion is neither new nor fully explanatory, but it is one factor relevant to understanding the preservation of belief despite the Gulag.

RELIGION AND BOLSHEVISM

The success of religions in appropriating the human proclivity for a superordinate connection is evidenced by the prevalence and variety of competing religions throughout human history and across a wide array of cultures. Religions compete with each other and with secular political systems. Their popularity is especially informative because they often succeed in spite of contrary scientific evidence. Atheists regularly point out that people accept the claims of religion with less scrutiny than they would apply to claims regarding the material value of a purchase.[12] Since this is common behavior, it can be inferred that religious adherents are receiving immaterial value and relying on nonobjective evidence. The immaterial value that believers receive from religion is a connection with a "higher power" or "greater cause" that provides meaning to their life.

This perception can be more consequential than anything of material value—or any earthly connections—as witnessed by Oksana's story above. In another context, a 1787 work by the French writer Louis Sebastien Mercier offers a rich illustration of this phenomenon.[13] In an episode titled "Bringing a Criminal to Death," a jilted lover attacks and kills the man for whom his fiancée left him. He is then brought before the court, in his blood-stained shirt, "beating his chest and showing all signs of regret."[14] As he approaches the judges, he drops to one knee to kiss the Penal Code. The presiding judge tells the accused that he is not hated, and that he should ask forgiveness from God and his fellow citizens. He was given the choice of living in shame and indignity, but nevertheless living. The judge warned, however, "Thou will be looking at the sun that will reproach Thee daily because Thou robbed one of [Thy] fellow human beings of its soft and bright light . . . Thou will only see contempt in our eyes."[15] The accused did have an alternative, though: he could be "brought to death." The judge said that they would cry for him when the law had taken its course, "but death is less awful than shame."[16] The accused nodded in agreement, and he was no longer treated as a guilty man. He was encircled, given a clean white shirt, forgiven, blessed, and ritually executed. His name was reentered in the population registers. When, on the night after the execution, one of the king's advisory posts became available, it was offered to the brother of the executed man. The narrator writes, "Everyone was delighted with this choice that combined reason and charity . . . our laws lean more toward reform than punishment."[17] The lesson of this parable is that this man's death made sense. It offered him, his family, and society immaterial (and material) benefits to which they would not have had access if he had chosen to live.

All religions, as well as a secular belief system such as science, provide two basic needs—group membership with social support, and a system of beliefs that provides a cognitive frame for understanding events. These have been described as panhuman "group-system" needs.[18] What religion adds to the need for social support is access to a superhuman power, a mechanism illustrated above. While the cognitive frames of secular systems answer *what* and *how* questions, religion answers *why* questions—the purpose and meaning of events. A further distinguishing characteristic of religious systems is that their claims are not (supposed to be) questioned. As Bolshevism increasingly came to operate as a nonfalsifiable system, it merged with the practice of religion. Inconsistent empirical evidence—if admitted at all—could be interpreted as serving a higher purpose.

As noted above, because the provision of group-system needs is so necessary for social functioning, total institutions—secular (collectives, political movements, social causes, cults, etc.) or religious—can manipulate these needs for the purposes of conversion or simply adherence.[19] The immediate influence of total institutions resides in their power to compel compliance by exercising control over everything imaginable—including life, death, and suffering.[20] The long-term influence of such closed systems resides in the indoctrination/incorporation of that compliance, exemplified by the enduring belief in the Party by some Gulag prisoners and returnees. People live for belief systems, die for them, and kill for them, and as these stories will illustrate, for ardent believers, allegiance is not impaired by contradictory evidence. Some of the stories suggest that there was no contradictory evidence because the world view of true believers admitted none.

This chapter is not about the inhumane treatment of prisoners or the wretched conditions in the Gulag. That is the background. Rather, this study foregrounds the adaptive responses of some prisoners and returnees. "Adaptive" is narrowly defined as physical survival, accompanied by a functional way of processing the experience. Sometimes this entailed reframing the forced labor as a meaningful episode, akin to religious martyrdom. A relevant question—not answerable through available data and beyond the scope of the present study—is whether there was a differential survival rate that favored adherents over non-Communists and dissidents.

The Gulag has joined the tragic annals of what has been described as "man's inhumanity to man." It raised questions connected with our very being. Paradoxically, however, while the Soviet treatment of Gulag prisoners was inhumane from the perspective of secular humanism, it was all too human from a theocratic perspective. In its righteous justification by an idealized cause, in its lack of con-

tionary Russia.[28] That is not to say that Bolshevism was influenced by Orthodoxy. Robert Tucker asserts that both movements involved similar processes because they were radically opposed to the existing order.[29] Such was the prescient observation of Reneé Fülop-Miller, a Hungarian writer in the 1920s, who penned *The Mind and Face of Bolshevism*. Written only ten years after the Revolution, this early work described the visionary exuberance of a system where "the old world ceases and a new humanity begins."[30] Consequently, revolutionary language had its own explicit or implicit religious connotations. Michael Burleigh observed with reference to the language of French revolutionaries in the 1790s, "The discourse of the Revolution was saturated with religious terminology."[31] And Fülop-Miller saw the Russian Revolution sanctified in newly created names like Oktiabrina, Vladlen, and Marlen.

Fülop-Miller also recognized that the use of "red substitutes" for Orthodox festivals and rites was a political appropriation of religious practices and a political cooptation of religious beliefs. He observed: "It is precisely in this war against religion that the religious character of Bolshevism can be most clearly discerned; for the key to the understanding of all the manifestations of the Russian life and mind is the perception, important in its psychological bearings, that this apparent contradiction conceals an identity."[32]

Soviet Communism purported to be a secular political system that strove for the material benefit of—and *control by*—the masses ("dictatorship of the proletariat"[33]). However, the evidence in this study points to the conclusion that it was an ideological belief system striving for *control of* the masses. This is manifest in the loyalty of its devotees—even if they had survived the Gulag.

The loyal victim—irreverent to paradox and contradiction—is testimony to the power of belief in shaping perception. But closed systems are also powerful in shaping perception. It is difficult to challenge closed systems from within for more reasons than the brutal physical repression of dissidence or opposition. As noted in the introduction, the perceptual biases of a belief system constrain attention, priority, values, and causal relationships.[34]

The Self and the Collective

Belief in the greater good and higher laws, together with what Jochen Hellbeck describes in his work on Stalinist-era diaries as the "perceived necessity to believe,"[35] is a leitmotif in Gulag victim and survivor stories. Much of what Soviet citizens were compelled to do—before, during, and after the Gulag—was dissonant with the official version of events. Thus the sheer need for physical and mental survival could impel them to adapt by adopting and/or internalizing previously unacceptable values. Alexander Afinogenov, a Communist playwright, considered it his task to "engineer souls," including his own, because personal transformation was integral to Communist self-realization.[36] As the purge swept through his circle of colleagues and friends, Afinogenov anxiously awaited his fate. In his writing he subscribed to the official justifications, viewing the cleansing of the Party's ranks as routine and the self-criticism and public confessions as healthy. He considered individual and social purification to be intrinsically linked.[37] In consequence, he publicly reproached himself for not writing the kinds of pieces that the country "demanded." Afinogenov's success in persuasively conveying his self-condemnation may be judged from the result: he was expelled from the Party in 1937. Still, while he was subjected to interrogations and virtually lived in a prison without walls, this fate was far better than that of most of his cohorts.

In a diary entry from this period, Afinogenov compared himself to "a bricklayer who stands on the scaffolding and has trouble understanding the meaning of what he is building and its architectural form."[38] He reasoned that only Stalin, the architect, really understood the structure. In these pages, he did not blame either the Party or Stalin for his fate. He blamed himself and his "near fatal corruption," and viewed the ordeal of 1937 as a time of rebirth through this ordeal.[39] In January 1938, in the wake of the post-Yagoda purge of the purgers, Afinogenov and thousands of others were reinstated to Party membership. He continued his support of the purge campaign.

Jochen Hellbeck analyzed Afinogenov's diaries and found them to be suffused with "Christian" notions such as former self, sin, and rebirth. He argues that they were not simply the self-realization Bolshevik narratives of Communist conversion[40] that were required for those who aspired to Party membership.[41] Rather, Afinogenov's diaries described a more nuanced struggle to engage the body politic. They recounted his feelings of rejection following exclusion from a collective with which he identified.[42] His experience of merging with the collective has deeply religious overtones. Or perhaps it simply characterizes political religions, which, as Philippe Burrin has asserted, "assume most of the functions of traditional religions: social integration and legitimization, as well as functions of a cognitive, affective and normative nature."[43] Sociologist Emile Durkheim, who analyzed the connection between modern ideological movements and religion, laid out the fundamentals of this thinking.[44] He argued that the essence of religions was in group processes and rituals, and that mass movements were similar to religion because they filled the political and social functions of including their adherents in "larger-than-local" communities.[45]

The question of the religious nature of socialism and collectivism was an issue that had already been discussed in prerevolutionary Russia. Anatoly Lunacharsky, philosopher, prolific writer, literary critic, and later People's Commissar of Education, described the "religious" appeal of Marxism and collectivism. In a detailed examination of the early discussions on the concept of the collective in Russia, Oleg Kharkhordin analyzed Lunacharsky's reflections on how individuals must submit to "the species, the collective" around which they revolve. That would yield its own rewards since, in turn, "this submission to the collective resolves 'the damned issue of being' because it empowers and assures immortality, thus fulfilling the basic functions of any religion."[46] Lunacharsky went on to assert that the "human religious need" would be filled when one knew oneself to be "part of a greater whole."[47] Over time, according to Lunacharsky, socialism would supplant religion's appeal for community.[48]

In addition to the immortality attendant to belonging to the collective, Bolshevism promised a workers' paradise in this life—a promise that seemed credible because it was consonant with the Russian Orthodox belief that an ultimate paradise was achievable here on earth.[49] However, the secular hero worship promoted by the cult of personality lacked the gravitas of a divinity embedded in Russian Orthodoxy, so Bolshevism did not have an eternity to create this paradise. So, how does one account for the failure to deliver on their promise in this life? It appears that this conundrum was resolved by a combination of denial of official misbehavior or deflection of blame, discrediting dissident voices, propaganda supporting the position that the promised reward was just ahead and within reach, and the fact that there was no precisely stated delivery date.

Many of the powerless victims were offered comfort in the officially promulgated belief that their individual fate was not as relevant as the fate of the Soviet project. This sense of participation in a wholeness that transcended the individual helped some to survive, and others to face death. A number of well-known purge victims such as Bukharin and Yakir made public declarations exonerating the state for their execution. Witness Bukharin's oft-quoted parting words to his wife, "Remember, the great deed called the Soviet Union lives; only this is really important. Our personal fates are transient and pitiful."[50] Given the absolute power of the state to punish the victim's family, as well as its record of coerced confessions, what Bukharin said may have been a forced choice. However, given Bukharin's founding father status, at some level these sentiments may also be taken at face value. For believers, this declaration could serve as an affirmation of their faith in the Soviet system and Communism.

While the secular constraints of Bolshevism / Soviet Communism could not postpone the promised workers' paradise to an afterlife, it could promise a secular afterlife in the historical memory of the collective or, as historian Irina Paperno terms it, "salvation through being-in-history."[51] According to Hellbeck, Afinogenov's attitude toward death and afterlife in Soviet collective memory fits the model of "Communist self-realization, which reached its highest point with the Communist entering the pantheon of history."[52] Igal Halfin describes an earlier stage that occurs with entrance into the Party as "a clean and tidy death" of the individual, because he becomes fused with the "soul of the movement."[53] (Some view the Party entrance phase, in no less religious connotations, as a "second birth";[54] see Ol'bert below.) In Halfin's analogy, physical death was less important than the "social" death that would occur as a result of isolation from the Party. For some individuals like Old Bolshevik Adolf Ioffe (see the introduction), life outside the Party was devoid of meaning.

THE GOSPEL ACCORDING TO THE PARTY

The previously established criteria regarding personal interest, familial loyalties, martyrdom, murder, violence, and "victimization" (by the standards of secular humanism) all came to be revised and reoriented to the end of serving the cause. Olga Shatunovskaia, an Old Bolshevik who spent seventeen years in the Gulag and emerged to work for the Party (see chapter 4), addressed this issue in an exchange with her son later in life. He asked, "Mama, how was it possible that you Communists could carry out such evil as the murder of the entire family of the czar, including small children and the servants?" From the more informed perspective of the present, she replied, "It now seems like wild nonsense to me, but at the time we thought that this sacrifice was absolutely necessary for the good of the world proletariat. Revolutionary legality was higher than moral legality."[55]

In one phrase, "revolutionary legality was higher than moral legality," Shatunovskaia succinctly identified a core issue that bedeviled the Bolshevik soul. The "revolutionary legality" had become the "higher power," but unlike God, this absolute power did not reside with a remote being, located in a remote place. Rather it resided with Stalin, or Yezhov, or the NKVD, and it was always located nearby.

Entrance into the ranks of the Party was a defining moment for many, and Party dictates were accorded the authority of gospel. Mikhail Baital'skii, Party member and Trotsky supporter (see also chapter 3), was arrested and interned three times—in 1929, in 1935, and in 1950—for supporting oppositionist tendencies. In 1958, during Khrushchev's Thaw, he began writing his memoirs, titled "Notebooks to the Grandchildren." In these nine notebooks, spanning 450 pages, he records his observations on the Party, the people he knew, the system, and the camps. His wife, Eva, who eventually left him, was such an ardent Party supporter that she fainted at the news of Lenin's death. When their son was born, the couple honored the Soviet founding father by using his initials to name their son.[56] What the Party dictated determined Eva's assessment of everything, including good and evil. According to Baital'skii, the question "What would the Party think of this?" was always on her mind. He wrote: "The twenties instilled in Eva's soul altruistic love for the People and the Party (which were one and the same for her), devotion to the Revolution, and respect for science. But . . . this love became routine, reflected in the constant repetition of the words 'our Party' . . . the devotion rapidly gained a religious character."[57] Baital'skii recounted Eva's inability to imagine her life outside the Party, which "always had a capital 'P' in her heart."[58] She assumed that if the Party sanctioned the execution of its former leaders for espionage or murder, "then they absolutely were spies and murderers."[59] The Party's decision was sufficient evidence for Eva.

This confidence in the rectitude of the Party's judgment was sustained despite the arrest of a family member, the result, perhaps, of campaigns directed at breaking the traditional ties that bound families and that could compete with ties toward the state. Such exemplars as Pavlik Morozov, who denounced his father for harboring kulaks, were evidence of their success.[60] It was not unusual for wives to denounce their arrested husbands—either out of earnest concurrence with the state, or self-preservation. In the former case, the state and Stalin had become the surrogate family and father. In her work on the disenfranchised of the 1920s, Golfo Alexolopolus describes the "unyielding loyalty to Bolshevism" of a woman whose father appears to have been a deported kulak and who, herself, had been deprived of rights.[61]

The family bond was actively encouraged to be no longer sacred, because the Party had appropriated that niche. Stepan Podlubnyi, a Komsomol activist and diarist of the thirties, was a conscientious student of Marx and Lenin and an avid supporter of the Revolution. After his father had been deported as a kulak, Stepan distanced himself from this stigmatized family history. Astonished by his mother's arrest, he still did not question its grounds nor the policies that dictated it. Rather, he simply treated it as new information. He rationally wrote that the arrests did not "come as a surprise to anybody these days. But to number Mama, a half-literate woman, among the Trotskyites, that would have never occurred to me."[62]

Party entrance, expulsion, and reinstatement were personal and political landmarks. One N. S. Kuznetsov was arrested in 1938 under Article 58, but asserted his innocence. He claimed that he had been "accused of horrible things without a shred of evidence."[63] After a two-year period of interrogation, which included isolation in the Butyrka, he was sentenced to eight years of labor camp in Arkhangelsk, where he worked as a lumberman. After camp he secured work in construction, and it went well. He recalled, "everyone considered me—a 'kontri-ka' (counterrevolutionary)—to be a Communist."[64] Although the secretary of the

Party organization knew of his past, he was still invited to Party meetings, which Kuznetsov gladly attended. He had not been reinstated in the Party, because the road to rehabilitation, which had to precede Party reinstatement, was long and often led nowhere. Still, he considered himself a Party member, and more importantly, others considered him to be included in the ranks. However, in spite of working with his customary "Party passion," he was eventually fired for acting too much as if he really belonged.[65]

Kuznetsov's positive attitude toward the Party had little influence on his immediate post-camp struggle to reintegrate. One day while sitting on a park bench, he was approached by the MGB and told that he had to leave town within twenty-four hours. Kuznetsov left and went to Bukhara, Uzbekistan, where he found work, but lost it again because the local MGB accused him of violating his passport regime. He then attempted to find work in the provinces, but missed "some big job opportunities" because of his tainted past. He finally got a job in 1950, but he was underpaid because he was considered politically untrustworthy.

Kuznetsov does not explicitly address the issue of responsibility for his unjust incarceration and unfair treatment after release throughout most of his memoirs, although toward the conclusion he does refer to the "cult of personality" and its "anti-Leninist essence" (see below). In the period following Stalin's death, Kuznetsov did not expect any major improvements, but he had sufficient hope to persist in writing letters "along Soviet and Party lines" to plead for rehabilitation. He acknowledged writing a "more motivated" request for Party rehabilitation to the Central Committee after Stalin's death.[66] The CC initially answered that the charges against him had been valid—not an unusual response in 1953—but he remained hopeful. After Beria's fall, he felt certain that the "Leninist truth" would prevail, that he would return to a full life, and that he would again serve the Party and the people. Then, he predicted, the "Leninist democratization of life in Soviet society would be realized!"[67]

Kuznetsov continued to file his requests. One such letter was addressed to Nikolai Shvernik, head of the Party Control Commission. As regularly happens in the story we construct to give meaning to events, the memoir is punctuated by defining moments. Kuznetsov describes what followed this petition in epic terms. The life-changing missive arrived one day in the form of an ordinary postcard. But it was from the Central Committee, and it asked him to come to the Party Control Commission to discuss his Party rehabilitation. He immediately set out for Moscow, where he stayed at the Hotel Moskva. Kuznetsov approached the meeting "gripped with fear" that he might not be reinstated.[68] When he was told that he would be reinstated, it had the uplifting quality of a numinous experience. He writes: "I was born for the third time. The first birth was in the northern

Urals, the second in Samara when I was accepted into the Leninist Party, and the third in the building of the CC CPSU in December of 1955."[69]

Triumphant, he received his Party card—first with interrupted tenure, and shortly thereafter his status was cleared and his membership once again dated from April 4, 1917. In the seventeen years that had passed from arrest to reinstatement, his wife had died in camp (in 1943), his sister was killed in the war, and his estranged children had survived, grown up without parents, became educated, and had their own children. None of these developments disconfirmed his faith in the rightness of his Communist-Leninist beliefs. Despite his losses and those of his family, Kuznetsov was steadfast in his claim that he had retained his humanity and his Party allegiance. His faith was redeemed when the long-awaited Leninist truth prevailed. One of Kuznetsov's children became a teacher, the other a geologist. It is their fortunate education, rather than his misfortunes, that he emphasizes. He trumpets his children's success as a confirmation of the inherent transgenerational triumph of the system:

> Their employment confirms the fact that the cult of personality with its anti-Leninist essence had nothing in common with the nature of our Soviet system. In the Soviet system, even children discarded under the cult of personality to fend for themselves not only did not perish, but got an education without their parents and actively participated in the building of a new Communist society.[70]

Behavior is multi-determined, so there are many explanations for Kuznetsov's retrospective justification of events that, at the time, he may have considered unjustified. Whether or not the letter published by *Pravda* and attributed to a teacher in Kishinev is authentic or propaganda (see the introduction), it is informative of how a loyal Communist interprets official behavior. It praised the Party for the 1953 amnesty, rather than condemning it for the incarceration of innocent millions in the first place. (Of course, the amnesty followed decades of official propaganda claiming that the prisoners were not innocent, and that they were even dangerous.[71]) If there is a need to arrive at a predetermined conclusion that redeems belief in Communism, or any nonfalsifiable belief system, imaginative interpretations will find a way. One such path leads from cognitive dissonance to cognitive affirmation.

For Kuznetsov and many others, membership in the Party was experienced, profoundly, as "belonging," and acceptance into the Party was celebrated as a "birth." For true believers, such as L. A. Ol'bert, Party affiliation continued beyond the grave. As his widow recorded, just before Ol'bert's 1972 death from lung cancer, he requested that his Party card, "with which he was connected his whole life," be turned over to the Council of Old Bolsheviks. In the last hours of his life, he reminisced about what the Party card had meant to him. His dying wish was fulfilled. His wife went on to contribute his memoirs, titled "The Unforgettable" (*Nezabyvaemoe*), to the Institute of Marxism-Leninism in 1965. They were added to the collection of materials connected with the cult of personality.[72]

Ol'bert's story reveals a wide array of conflicts and resolutions that can occur between a believer and the Party. He spent twenty years in the Butyrka, Norilsk, and exile, and after another arrest he was incarcerated in Ozerlag. He was liberated in 1955 and, rather exceptionally, returned to his wife, family, and friends in Leningrad. He applied for and received rehabilitation, a personal pension, and Party reinstatement. Ol'bert writes:

> How joyful it was and at the same time painful and unbearably hard to read the lines "rehabilitated for lack of crime" after having been incarcerated for almost twenty years, having lost the best years of my youth, and not being guilty of anything against the Party or the motherland. It brought happiness, tears, and excitement, not only to me but to all prisoners who lived with a single-minded interest and hope. Everything revolved for us around the Party and the Soviet government.[73]

How did Ol'bert manage to survive the grueling years of incarceration, and more central to the issue at hand, how did his belief manage to survive? "Happiness," "tears," unjust incarceration, and a "single-minded interest and hope" were reconciled within the believer and by the Party through the ideology of Communism. This is illustrative of how an ardent belief in an ideology can imbue experience with a meaning that helps the believer adjust to otherwise intolerable vicissitudes. Even in the Nazi camps there were still some religious inmates who maintained their belief in God, in spite of their suffering—perhaps because of their suffering. Their helplessness to change their external reality may have impelled them to seek relief through belief in a supernatural power. Such relief was not available to skeptics such as Primo Levi who reacted with disgust as he observed an Orthodox Jewish prisoner in Auschwitz prayerfully thanking God that his life had been spared that day.[74] Similar phenomena have been described in some of the accounts of Gulag survival. However, a sustaining connection with a group and its belief system, if only in imagination, may have been all that was possible for many inmates.

For Nazi concentration camp believers in God, and Gulag believers in the Party, there was always the paradox of theodicy—how could the "higher power" be powerful and good, and yet permit evil? Gulag overseers propagated a simple answer: the prisoner was guilty as charged and required "corrective labor." Some prisoners reasoned that if only Stalin knew of their mistaken arrest and incarceration, he would rescue them. Others resolved the issue by assuming that their incarceration was part of a larger purpose which a wise and good Stalin was pursuing.[75] A similar resolution by Christians is found in the aphorism to the effect that the ways of God are inscrutable.

Fear and helplessness intensify the need for a belief that offers purpose and hope, and this can strengthen bonds to real or imagined beings.[76] In the Gulag, that belief system and that group could be the Party, a countervailing allegiance to divinely based religion. Sometimes, the ad hoc group was made up of fellow inmates. In the Solovetsky camps and elsewhere, many religious prisoners ended up (living and dying) in the camps for their opposition to the "Soviet Satan."[77] While in camp, they found refuge in their belief in God. A similar faith could be observed among imprisoned Communists. Ol'bert's salvation, typical of other wrongly incarcerated prisoners, rested with the hope that the Party would discover their "true circumstances" and absolve them. Then, the wrongly accused would be returned to normal life. He wrote, "This strong belief inspired many and helped them to morally endure the hardships."[78] Later, such hopes were borne out. The Party was officially presented and perceived as the savior rather than the culprit.

CONFLICT WITHIN THE BOLSHEVIK SOUL

It was not always easy to keep believing. Nikolai Makarovich Busarev, a participant in the suppression of the Kronstadt rebellion in 1921 and Party member since 1919, admitted that "belief in the Party and the Soviet system had to be held and supported" through extraordinarily difficult ordeals. He noted that many could not manage to maintain it as well as he had.[79] After reinstatement in the Party, he walked to Red Square and bowed in front of Lenin's tomb.[80] As he recognized that an accurate account of his camp experiences could have the effect of undermining the efforts of those building socialism and Communism, his Party loyalty made Busarev apprehensive about writing camp memoirs. Despite this fear, he wrote them—apparently hoping that readers would draw less than obvious conclusions about the systemic arbitrariness described in his 446-page manuscript.

There were also particular forces that strengthened the prisoners' devotion and need to believe. Ol'bert writes about the bonding experience facilitated by the war, bonding prisoners both to the Party and to each other. One benefit was that Gulag prisoners were now able to unite against an "enemy of the people" that was, blessedly, not *them*. They shared the joys of victory and the sorrows of defeat, and a number of inmates would have gladly fought for their country, but the suspect

Article 58 status stood in their way.[81] Another memoirist, Rozalia Veisman, recalls the righteous fury she felt when the enemy was at the "gate of Lenin's city,"[82] and saw this zeal reflected in the valiant heroism of the Red Army's defense of Leningrad. Such a commitment, she claimed, "could not help but penetrate the flesh and blood of each and every Soviet person." This despite the fact that her husband, who was the editor of *Leningradskaia Pravda,* had been arrested and taken away in 1937. She never saw him again. Rozalia was also arrested and suffered all the impediments attendant to her status as the wife of an "enemy of the people." Her husband was posthumously rehabilitated in 1955.[83]

Death has different meanings in different settings.[84] Patriotism aside, death in war was more honorable and, in relative terms, perhaps made more sense than death in the Gulag. In his *Generation of the Doomed,* dissident-bard Alexander Galich addresses this issue. He describes the tragic lot of those prisoners who did get to serve, and were sent directly to the frontline,[85] as well as those whose lives became "crippled" in the camps:

> Not as soldiers, but as numbers
> We died, we died,
> From Karaganda to Narym,
> The whole earth like one abscess,
> Vorkuta, Inta, Magadan.[86]

Belief in a higher purpose can imbue any experience with meaning. Clearly Galich could see no higher purpose in the Gulag. But Ol'bert, a lifelong defender of Bolshevism, merged his devotion to the state and Party with his labor in the Gulag. Ol'bert had long fought for the Bolshevik cause and had been awarded the Red Star for his underground work as a Red Guardist in undermining the forces of White Army General Denikin. His other medals included one for valiant labor, bestowed upon him on the one hundredth anniversary of Lenin's birth, and one in honor of fifty years of armed forces in the USSR. After the full restoration of his rights, Ol'bert resumed working "according to the societal guidelines of Party and Soviet work, completely devoting [himself] to the Party, the Motherland, and the project of building a Communist society."[87] To that end he delivered laudatory speeches at factories and schools and received praise and additional honorary medals from the Party and government.

True Believers

Among those who ardently believed, their positive faith was stronger than the paradox of their fate. Perhaps, for the believer, there was no paradox. According to Dariusz Tolczyk, a literary scholar, it was more "difficult for a [true believer] to renounce his belief in the Revolution in the face of imminent destruction" than to accept his own destruction. If life is only meaningful within the context of the group and its belief system, and that group is the Party and that system is Communism, then living without it is worse than dying for it. This conviction is compellingly presented in a poem written in her prison cell by a campmate of Evgeniia Ginzburg:

> Stalin, my golden sun,
> If death should be my fate,
> I will die, a petal on the road
> Of our great country.[88]

Sacrifice in the name of the greater good is a leitmotif in the memoirs of Communists about themselves, as well as in the recollections that campmates wrote about them. Mariia Moiseevna Goldberg, along with other family members, was incarcerated in Dzhezkazgan, Kazakhstan, on charges of being a "member of the family of a traitor to the motherland" (ChSIR). She described at length a Latvian campmate named Charlotte, from an old guard Bolshevik family, with whom she had also been interned in the Akmolinsk camp. According to Charlotte, her sister had carried out "legendary" underground work for the Bolshevik Party as well as for Lenin himself, and was already a Party member in 1905. While Charlotte was imprisoned, her sister was still at liberty, and her letters got through to Charlotte in Akmolinsk "thanks to the illiteracy of the censor." In these letters, her sister is forthright about the illegality of the official behavior she witnesses and is indignant about the repression of 1937. Eventually the sister was arrested and placed in a prison psychiatric hospital, where she died in 1955. Charlotte's brother had also been arrested and died either in the camps or in transit. Their mother suffered through her children's incarceration first in tsarist prisons, and then in Communist prisons. The brother's son was apparently allowed to fight in the war, and died at the front, leaving three small children.[89]

After years of back-breaking labor, Charlotte was so ill and weakened that she was no longer able to work, so she was eventually released. She survived the camps, but post-camp survival was difficult. Charlotte had no friends or family, and struggled to find work. Just when her situation was plummeting from desperate to perilous, her fortunes changed, and her request to return to Latvia was finally granted. Charlotte was eventually rehabilitated in 1955, returned to active Party work, and became secretary of a school Party organization for a number of years.

The tragic story of this "wonderful revolutionary family" was used by the author in 1962–1963 to illustrate the "fatal consequences" of the cult of personality.

Her interpretation of this misfortune stays well within the Khrushchevian framework that the terror was not attributable to Bolshevism. The memoirist concludes that "these trials did not break the Bolshevik soul of Charlotte, and she remained, as she always had been, an example of fortitude and devotion to Party matters."[90] She boasted that Charlotte represented the Bolshevik old guard, who were "raised on the Leninist truth . . . and for whom Party matters overshadowed personal harm and misfortune."[91]

If a life's purpose is embedded in an ideology, the experience of a forced labor camp may not undermine that ideology. On the contrary, a built-in interpretive bias may frame the experience in a way that reinforces that ideology. Sheila Fitzpatrick and Alf Lüdtke, in their discussion of adherents of the Nazi and Soviet regimes, refer to the fact that both stimulated "intense emotions" and the "drive to participate"; they describe the compelling attraction of "active involvement in a process of fundamental transformation of things both large and small."[92] Prophecies may fail, but the beliefs that gave them purpose may be retrofitted to maintain faith.[93] The consequences of such outcome failures can also be deflected. The Khrushchevian vision was that the Party was inherently good, and that honest Communists fell victim to Stalin's cult of personality. With the blame thus attributed to Stalin and his empowered henchmen, the Party could escape scrutiny, and ultimately enjoy impunity.

THE REAL WORLD OF THE CAMP

The stories of those whose belief in Communism survived the Gulag ordeal should not be considered as representative. Rather, they are illustrative of one functional way of processing the experience of enduring a closed system, both in the Big Zone (Soviet society) and the Small Zone (the camps). Solzhenitsyn's fictional prisoner Ivan Denisovich painstakingly laid brick upon brick and enthusiastically continued his task even after roll was called. He was a conscientious worker, he could not bear throwing out mortar, even after eight years in camp, and even at the risk of being beaten by the guards for his absence at the after-work lineup.[94] This zealousness could be explained by pride in his work, but since it "defies the camp's logic of survival," his attitude may be read as a reflection of his belief in the greater project,[95] though Solzhenitsyn presents it as a case of peasant thriftiness, reluctance to waste the prepared mortar. Ivan Denisovich aside, there were many others who clearly could not see the greater good, but could only see the persistent evil. This group did not consider either experiencing camp or having experienced camp to have any redemptive meaning. They earnestly knocked themselves out not in order to contribute to the cause, but to survive. When possible, they faked work output, but this could be risky. Ekaterina Olitskaia recalled the often futile efforts of her Kolyma campmates in the sewing factory to meet their output quota in order to keep their indoor jobs. Failure could result in transfer to an outside job in the brutal Arctic climate. When they managed to meet their quotas, the camp administration's cynical response was to create new, unattainable ones.[96]

Olitskaia spent the better part of the twenties, thirties, forties, and fifties in the camps or in exile, from the Solovetsky Islands to Magadan. She was a member of the Socialist-Revolutionary Party whose first imprisonment was in Solovki in 1924. After her arrest in the early thirties, she was sent to Suzdal. A later arrest confined her in Kolyma in 1942, and after her 1948 release she was rearrested in 1950 and sent into "perpetual exile" in Krasnoiarskii Krai, where she remained until 1960.[97] In her memoirs, Olitskaia expressed nothing but horror at the amorality of the camps and the way they reduced prisoners to "live [only] for themselves" just to survive.[98] She could not fathom the psychology of fellow campmates who supported the justice of Communism while simultaneously claiming that only their own arrests were unjustified.[99] The camp experience motivated Olitskaia, unconverted and unrepentant, to undertake the mission of telling the world her story and the story of those who did not survive to tell their own. When she wrote her memoirs in the sixties, she expressed concern that so few manuscripts were being published,[100] and tried to speak for the silent: "The survivors have been rehabilitated. Those who perished have been rehabilitated posthumously. . . . 'Human progress is built on flesh and bones,' say some, 'When you cut wood, chips fly,' say others, 'Revolutions are not made with white gloves on,' say still others. . . . And what do the people have to say about this? Ordinary people? They are silent."[101]

The people may have been silent, but many writers were not. Among them were Shalamov, who described the camps as "only making a person worse,"[102] and hundreds of lesser-known memoirists. They saw no greater good or salvation in the suffering of the camps. These eyewitnesses chronicled the workings of the system and presented abundant evidence of its abuses. Their stories are not ennobling and do not reflect religion-like devotion to the cause, but they do use terms like "hell" to characterize the experience. The harshness of living and dying addressed in these works stands in stark contrast to the heroic perspective on the camp experience depicted in literary works like *Skudnyi materik* (above). Vasily Grossman scornfully addresses this perspective in his novel *Forever Flowing*. In a telling exchange, a fictional former Party official turned inmate remarks to his fellow prisoner Ivan Grigorevich: "When they chop down the forest, the chips fly, but the Party truth remains the truth and it is superior to my misfortune. . . . I myself was one of those chips that flew when the forest was cut down."[103] The protagonist, Ivan, deftly skewers this argument by challenging the assumption that had been smuggled into the apologia: "That's where the whole misfortune lies— in the fact that they're cutting down the forest. Why cut it down?"[104]

From most of the accounts of committed Communists, the question of "why," and the issue of guilt (Die Schuldfrage), as Karl Jaspers so aptly termed it, were not much more relevant than they would be for a religious devotee. Personal misfortunes are accepted with resignation or satisfaction in the fulfillment of a greater purpose for the collective, the Party, and the motherland. After their release, some survivors, like Olga Shatunovskaia and Galina Serebriakova, continued to work within the Party organization, first on de-Stalinization, and then on "building socialism" in the Brezhnev years, when the Gulag was a non-issue. They, or their children such as Zoria Serebriakova (see preface and chapter 3), continued to work for the Party under Gorbachev, right up until the end of the Soviet Union. Others, like Lev Kopelev (see chapter 3), later turned away from the cause with the same fervor with which they had embraced it.

THE ANGUISH OF THE BOLSHEVIK SOUL

A comprehensive frame for identifying, viewing, and explaining "reality" (a Weltanschauung) common to both science and representative democratic governments is transparency and the subordination of hypotheses and policies, respectively, to independently verified data. For science, hypotheses must be supported or unsupported by inclusive data, and data must be independently verified. For governments, policies are supported or unsupported by outcome data, which is independently assessed by various empowered constituencies (the press, unions, religious institutions, academics, etc.), and governing bodies must be regularly ratified by verifiable secret ballots.

A Weltanschauung common to both religion and the CPSU is the subordination of data to irrefutable belief systems, but they differ regarding transparency. Religion is transparent about its claims because, regardless of any evidentiary challenges, its claims unapologetically rely on a "leap of faith." By contrast, while the Party propagated advances in economic development and the eradication of discrimination based on gender, ethnicity, and religion, it concealed such negative outcomes as arbitrary arrests, executions, the crimes of Stalin while he was alive (and potentially accountable), and the slave labor of millions in the Gulag. It recognized the inconsistency of these behaviors vis à vis its purported ideology, even as it attempted to rationalize the two. (Khrushchev and later Gorbachev knew that the Party had deviated from its official public declarations, but recognized that full disclosure could—and eventually did—discredit the Party.)

At one level it is an irony that Communism, which claimed to be secular and scientific, should have converged toward the same type of reliance on dogma, faith, and infallibility that characterizes religion. At a deeper level, it seems an inevitable irony because this is the very nature of total institutions. Prisoners were rendered powerless by an absolute authority, deprived of their previous social support, blamed for their incarceration, and forced to labor in grueling, wretched conditions that were termed "corrective." In another ironic convergence, the Gulag thus recreated the existential conditions for which religions have historically provided a solution. Throughout history, and even up to the present, people have had to endure unpredictable and uncontrollable catastrophes beyond the power of any human being to remedy. Religions have provided a remedy by proffering access to a supernatural power that offers meaning and a sense of security, contingent on faith and compliance.

This chapter has highlighted the association between Communism and religion, using the prism of the loyalist Gulag survivor's narrative to illustrate the similarities. The task of the narratives, like the task of the prisoners, was to process their experience in ways that enabled them to endure, and perhaps, prevail. These accounts illustrate the creativity of such efforts when the only power prisoners could exercise was over their own imagination. They sometimes idealized their suffering as serving the greater good, or viewed their persecutors as misguided, or accepted their own ignorance, relying on the wisdom of their leader or the Party, or saw the evil for what it was and found meaning in survival. Some, like Mariia Malysheva, survived and "preserved [their] sanity" by maintaining belief in the "triumph of truth." Sadly, these sentiments were expressed in a letter written by this camp inmate to her husband, who had already been executed.[105]

Devoted Communists who were Gulag prisoners had to address the issue of theodicy that also challenges the religious faithful—how could the idealized state abide evil? A common answer is that, in the larger scheme, the ways of God or the road to Communism (despite detailed theoretical maps) can seem inscrutable to the mere travelers. Another is that evil is the work of the Devil or Stalin, or Beria, or the local NKVD. If such themes bear a resemblance to religious dilemmas and solutions, they should, because they are time-honored human solutions for controlling the uncontrollable and bearing the unbearable.

CHAPTER 2

Reconciling the Self with the System

Under Stalin, in the years before the 1956 Twentieth Party Congress, simply being charged with a crime was commonly prima facie evidence of being guilty, and punishment followed quickly. After Stalin's death, and particularly after 1956, the Party officially declared that arbitrary punishment was a crime perpetrated by Stalin and his henchmen against loyal Communists and others. E. Charents, an Armenian poet who considered himself a loyal Communist, was born before 1956. "There is no crueler punishment," he lamented, "than when a man is denounced as a traitor to an idea that was sacred to him, that was in fact the only thing that made sense in his life."[1] That life, and whatever sense could be made of it, was extinguished by the terror in 1937.

When Charents was denounced, he lost his social, material, and ideological sources of support. Such victims were impelled by the belief that their predicament made sense—if only they could decipher that sense. And therein lay a paradox. The punishment made sense only if the crime made sense, but for those falsely accused, their alleged crime was a political fiction. Like Kafka's Gregor Samsa, who awoke with dismay to discover that he was a bug, or his equally dismayed Josef K., who suddenly found himself under arrest, these victims tried to make sense of their misfortune, assuming that insight would lead to a way out of the morass. The Soviet terror had created facts out of fiction for innocent arrestees, now presumed guilty by reason of arrest.

Such was the ideological quandary of those prisoners and returnees who had been Party loyalists but had been imprisoned for anti-Soviet activities, and then struggled with how they could explain it to themselves and others. In the following narratives these efforts are chronicled. The stories reveal a wide range of responses to their predicament, including resigned detachment, fatalistic acquiescence, agreement, ambivalence, anger, and compartmentalization.

The personally and politically contested issues of responsibility, culpability, and accountability for the Soviet terror, so fundamental to our understanding of the Soviet past and the Russian present, have yet to be sufficiently addressed on a societal or state level. However, individual accounts, which give voice to former prisoners, can inform our understanding of these questions. Chronicling the stories of Gulag survivors may illuminate how the self-consciousness and consciousness of guilt evolved from the thirties until today. These narratives can help us to ascertain what their experience was, how the victims perceived the Party, their Self, and their allegiance to the Party, how their allegiance was affected by incarceration, how survival was affected by allegiance, and what psychosocial and/or emotional mechanisms can account for their enduring allegiance. In consequence, the prism of how Soviet prisoners framed and understood their arrest and incarceration can offer insight into larger questions related to how repressive regimes are maintained.[2]

GUARDED AMBIVALENCE

As noted above, we approach the issues of who or what was to blame through the portal of the individual—the chronicled accounts of former prisoners. Sometimes the writers blame themselves. Sometimes they infer blame by omission and silence. Sometimes they acknowledge self-censorship. For example, one returnee, speaking for many, disclosed that, notwithstanding their belief in the Soviet courts, institutions, and proclamations, "somewhere inside, deep down, we timidly harbored doubts and disbelief in what they were saying, but these had to be suppressed, hidden. . . ."[3] How long disbelief could be hidden, and how restive were these doubts, would depend on the psychology, political history, and currently available resources of the individual.

Given that the writers of these narratives were for the most part powerless ex-prisoners, still required to conform to a closed society, it is not difficult to imagine their willingness to suspend any disbelief they might have had. Consequently, these returnees embraced Khrushchev's declaration that it was Stalin—and not the Party—who bore responsibility for the terror. He offered a simple and effective solution to their dilemma of Party loyalty, and it was quite welcome for some. The victims were no longer culpable, and the Party never was. The question of what kind of Party would tolerate a Stalin was not raised by any officials in public, nor, as illustrated by this account, by some returnees in private. Mikhail Trofimovich Adeev, a Leningrad math teacher (see the introduction), was arrested in

1937, released a few years later, and re-arrested in 1950. Both during and after his ordeal in prisons and camps, Adeev recalled, "the thought of a full rehabilitation along state [i.e., judicial] and Party lines never left me."[4] When he finally achieved this status in March of 1956, it had "great significance" because he would no longer be asked, "Why aren't you in the Party?" Like most similarly restored returnees, he credited his redemption to the Twentieth Party Congress, and this reinforced his belief in the Party.[5]

For Khrushchev and thousands of others, "Stalinism was bad because it was aimed against loyal Stalinists."[6] Additionally, not only was blame deflected to a different perpetrator than Khrushchev or the Party itself, but the victim group was also retrofitted to this vision. Contrary to Khrushchev's lament that the Party sons were the main target of Stalin's terror, those who were accused, arrested, and executed during the thirties actually comprised a broad range of the population. In fact, the principal victims of the terror were millions of ordinary citizens. However, (mostly prominent) Communists who created and built the system were certainly also singled out for purging at the height of the Great Terror. This irony was reflected in a cynical joke that circulated at that time. The dreaded NKVD knock on the door comes in the middle of the night. When the occupant asks who is there, the answer is, "The NKVD, open up!" The man heaves a sigh of relief as he tells them, "You've got the wrong apartment, the Communists live upstairs."[7]

RECONCILING THE OLD AND THE NEW REALITY

Early in the terror, it might have been relatively easy for Party loyalists to feel insulated in and by their ideology. But as the victimizations extended to friends, family, and to themselves, falsely accused Communist prisoners were faced with the emotional problem of reconciling their loyalty to a Party that vilified them as disloyal, and the cognitive problem of how to make sense of the claimed legitimacy of their imprisonment on fabricated charges. Such deliberations made the ordeal even worse. Arthur Koestler's protagonist in *Darkness at Noon* maintains that "nothing is worse in prison than the consciousness of one's innocence; it prevents acclimatization and undermines one's morale."[8] For some, the ensuing guilt, alienation, and shame attendant to being labeled an "enemy of the people" was experienced as a greater torment than the torture they had endured within the prison walls and in camp.

One such survivor, Khanna Iakovlevna Ganetskaia, neither accepted the legitimacy of her conviction nor turned against the Party. Rather, after serving her sentence, she worked within the Party for redress. She wrote impassioned pleas to Voroshilov, chairman of the Presidium of the Supreme Soviet, to protest her release on an amnesty.[9] This is her story. Ganetskaia's parents and brother were taken away in 1937, and in 1938 she was arrested. In 1943 she was released, but like tens of thousands of others in her "counterrevolutionary" category, her history of imprisonment made Khanna an automatic target for the 1949 sweep of "especially dangerous state criminals."[10] She was rearrested and sent into "perpetual exile," where she remained until the news of her release on amnesty arrived in 1954. However, she challenged this status, protesting, "I cannot agree with being released on an amnesty. I am not some alien element. I was brought up in the Komsomol, and in Soviet schools and institutes."[11] She supported her claim with evidence that she had received commendations for her Pioneer work in her youth, and later went on to head the cultural division for antireligious work at her institute. The Procuracy investigated her case and found that the only evidence against Ganetskaia had been the accusations of the other accused, who subsequently admitted that their incriminating statements were fabricated. They had been coerced during interrogation.[12] Ganetskaia's sentence was revoked, and on the basis of her new status she was permitted to apply for juridical rehabilitation and Party reinstatement.

Ganetskaia was apparently able to resolve her personal political problem without further pursuing the systemic political problem of injustice. But others could not abide this contradiction. For them, the issue of culpability was central. If the Party's verdict was just, the convicted revolutionaries had been misguided in their efforts to support Communism. If the Party's verdict was unjust, the Party had been misguided. Furthermore, the arrest of veteran revolutionaries on counterrevolutionary charges, branding them traitors, and expelling them from the Party, was the secular equivalent of religious excommunication. Like excommunication, this expulsion deprived loyalists of the sense of meaning that Party allegiance had provided.[13]

The way in which the loyalists and the Party dealt with this discordance was consequential for both, because the survival of each, in different ways, depended on the other. This question is critical to the means by which Gulag prisoners and returnees evaluated their then present, and how survivors later evaluated that past. One strategy that legitimated both the loyalists' claims of innocence and the Party's license to imprison them was to accept the imprisonment as a necessary sacrifice of the loyal Communist in the service of Communism.[14] Koestler's protagonist Rubashov, a founding father of the Revolution (presumably Bukharin), recognized his "helplessness before the latest swing of the [historical] pendulum"[15] and the mistakes in socialist theory, and he remained loyal to the Party and its goals. After brilliantly insightful deliberation, Rubashov consciously signed a false confession, concluding that "honour is to be useful without vanity."[16] He understood what had become of the Revolution, and still hoped for what could be. According to Max Weber, self-sacrifice for the "sacred goal" characterizes charismatic movements (which the Party could be viewed as representing to some) and imparts a sense of meaning to their followers.[17] Moreover, for many believers, maintaining allegiance to a cause/individual/movement even when one feels personally betrayed is a sign of true faith.

TERROR AND REVOLUTIONARY VIOLENCE: A "NECESSARY EVIL"

Convicted Party loyalists were not just criminals. They were regarded as traitors who had tainted their own and their family's moral standing. Why, then, did the accused confess to something of which they were innocent (assuming many were)?[18] The sequence leading to a false confession is typified by the experience of Lev Aleksandrovich Mankovskii. He was a philosophy professor who had been a Party member since 1919 and was a Civil War veteran. At the time of his arrest in 1938 he was serving as the rector at Gorkii State University. After initially denying the charges levied against him, he confessed, and was sentenced to ten years of forced labor working at railroad construction in Sevdvinlag. During the war he requested to be sent to the front, but his request, like that of so many of his suspect peers, was refused. He was liberated in 1948, and spent the next eight years struggling to hold on to a series of jobs, a difficult task because of his vulnerable ex-prisoner status. In 1956 Mankovskii was rehabilitated, reinstated in the Party, and granted a professorship at the V. I. Lenin Moscow State Pedagogical Institute. He owed this reversal of his misfortune to Khrushchev's Secret Speech at the Twentieth Party Congress.

That speech not only changed the political landscape; it also changed the psychological landscape of many beleaguered believers. It prompted them to judge the motives and behaviors of those who had adjudicated their guilt, and it influenced the way they judged themselves. In this post–Secret Speech period Mankovskii began to reflect skeptically on the psychology behind the cult of Stalin and its coercive methods. He recalled spending the first week of his two-week interrogation standing day and night, deprived of sleep and food. The rotating NKVD officers said little, but implied much. They read, talked on the phone, or whispered to each other, and every once in a while, in a monotone voice, asked the same questions: would Mankovskii talk and write about his counterrevolutionary activities, reveal who recruited him, and whom he had recruited. Sometimes he lapsed into a hypnotic state of hypersuggestibility. At times, the psychological torture nearly drove Mankovskii to madness. And then the solution seemed so clear and attainable. A young interrogator stated simply, "If you claim to be an honest Communist, then you should write and sign that which is asked of you. It's necessary."[19] It was necessary, but with the passage of time, he wondered more and more why it was.

This same question plagued others who had been falsely accused and forced to take part in the charade of false confessions and show trials. Confessing to crimes they had not committed might possibly spare the prisoner's family. It would certainly serve the interests of the Party. But a question that few dared voice at that time was what kind of Party required this kind of servicing.[20] An answer might be: a charismatic one. From the charismatic system perspective, adherents could argue that in the course of such a difficult and "extraordinary"[21] mission, mistakes were inevitable, as was self-sacrifice.

Coerced confessions were politically expedient and purposively public, but assessing their longer-term political consequences was long forbidden. Raising this question became a little less forbidding after the fall of Beria in 1953. An opportunity to raise this issue was occasioned by a lecture titled "The Moral Make-up of the Soviet Man," delivered to prisoners in Minlag (Mineralnyi lager, near Inta) as part of an apparently ineffective damage-control campaign. One prisoner responded, "Tell me please, citizen supervisor: since Beria has been exposed as an enemy of the people, a spy, a traitor, and a law-breaker, what does that make us—his victims—then?"[22] The Party representative avoided answering the question, but offered a cognitive framework with which to resolve the apparent dissonance. The Party boss explained that they were all only "temporarily detained," even if it was with terms of twenty-five years. (Regarding such lame deceptions, Iurii Dombrovskii, a talented novelist who had been imprisoned several times,[23] once wittily quipped to a campmate, "I'm resting at this resort as part of my twenty-five-year vacation."[24]) The Party representative then went on to boast of impending changes in the regime in the camps: the numbers would be removed from prisoners' uniforms, the workday would be reduced to eight hours, prisoners could earn some money for their labor, and other such measures would be implemented.[25] While the Party boss's response was intentionally dismissive of the issue raised by the prisoner, it was for that very reason informative. Nothing regarding prisoners' (lack of) culpability was even conceivable. They may have been convicted in the wrong way, but it was for the right reasons. Prisoners should focus on cosmetic improvements to their presumably deserved punishment.

Historical Necessity

From the sixties through the eighties, historian Roy Medvedev gathered materials from returnees and/or their family members in an effort to comprehend the meaning of the Gulag. For a number, the experience did not challenge Communist ideology. Regarding the "revolutionary violence" employed against them, some loyal Communist prisoners were unable to conceive of an alternative to Stalinism and subscribed to it as a "historical necessity" for themselves and others. According to V. Litvinov, an émigré whose father survived the Gulag, this way of thinking offered prisoners a certain "internal freedom," which permitted them to focus on other, more manageable, problems. Framed as a psychological mechanism, this might be described as compartmentalization. For example, some prisoners who worked on scientific projects in the divisions of the Gulag known as *sharashki* (NKVD-run prison workshops for specialists) claimed that their scientific creativity was not hindered by their lack of personal civil freedom. As Litvinov wrote, "This reconciliation with terror, this 'theoretical' justification of its necessity, penetrated the souls of Marxist-oriented citizens so deeply—regardless of whether they were in captivity or in freedom—that revelations on particular brutalities of Stalin did not shake them."[26]

Lennart Samuelson, who has conducted research on the sharashki, argues that it would be necessary to further examine the petitions to the Procuracy from this group of "hundreds" of prisoners in order to understand "how it was possible to live through arrests, accusations and long-term sentences for fabricated cases, and still do important work for the benefit of the people."[27] However, such behavior need not strain credulity. Rather, it is illustrative of the human capacity to survive by adjusting to adverse environments through a combination of assimilation and accommodation. Within a cognitive psychology framework, assimilation refers to prisoners' ability to change themselves by incorporating the ideology so it is conflict-free. Accommodation refers to prisoners' ability to retain their original ideological belief but change their behavior to conform to the demands of their environment. Both are adaptive, but assimilation requires less conscious effort.[28]

Most loyalist returnees had sufficiently accommodated to—if not assimilated—their political environment to censor their questions, if they asked any at all. Nikolai Busarev writes from personal experience when he describes how it felt to be a high Party official who was arrested and spent nearly twenty years in the camps. He portrays with compelling authenticity his feelings of betrayal: "The question of course arises as to how people who did so much for the Revolution, for the Soviet government, could turn out to be enemies of their party, and their Soviet state. The flip-side of this question, though, is that the arrests and judgments were carried out by our Soviet organs, our Soviet courts, in which we believed, and which deserved our trust."[29] But even though he makes a convincing case for indicting the Party, he concludes by excusing it and blaming, instead, the dead dictator. "Lenin was prescient in not wanting Stalin in the post of General Secretary," wrote Busarev. "Stalin deceived the Party. He did not keep promises he made at the 13th and 15th Party conferences to change, or to step down. . . ."[30]

Busarev's deliberations are informed by history, but they did not proceed to their logical conclusion. Missing from his deliberation is the unasked question of how such a predictable "deception" from a person with absolute power might *then* be corrected. Furthermore, in most cases, apparently those who had resigned themselves to the necessity of the process—the "chips that flew"—did not address the issue of guilt. "Apparently," however, is an important qualifier, because it was more expedient to keep such thoughts hidden.

Some victims of repression were fatalistic, accepting their lot in life with the succinct phrase "It's just the way it had to be." Nikolai Petrovich Smirnov, who served in Kolchak's army,[31] was accused of committing violent acts against Red Army soldiers, sentenced to death by an NKVD troika, and executed the next day. He was posthumously rehabilitated in 1992 on the basis of evidence from the materials in his dossier revealing that the incriminating testimony had been fabricated. The newly declassified NKVD materials disclosed that Smirnov, one of the literate few in Kolchak's detachment, had apparently been forced to serve as a clerk, but escaped at the first possible moment.

Smirnov had a son who survived the terror. He examined the files, but they did not reveal anything he had not already known, and he did not want to talk about what he knew. He neither concealed nor advertised his status as the child of an "enemy of the people." He managed to obtain work in Party and Soviet organs, but in keeping with custom he was not permitted to rise to leadership positions. A researcher asked the younger Smirnov how he could consider it honorable to work most of his life for a Party that had murdered his innocent father and deprived him of the full rights of citizenship. His answer was short, simple, and pragmatic, "That's how it had to be." After reviewing the files on his father, he wrote the NKVD authorities a letter of gratitude for their help with retrieving them, and noted that he harbored no resentment toward the NKVD agents who arrested his father. "They were carrying out their responsibilities . . . and at that time I was not the only one who suffered and lost my father. Many were repressed."[32]

At the level of the individual, the younger Smirnov's life is a triumph over adversity; at the level of the Party, it is the triumph of adversity. In order to survive in a closed and coercive society that murdered his father, he apparently resigned himself to a system he could not change, likely applied for and/or accepted a job the Party permitted, and expressed gratitude and understanding to his father's executioners. If success is defined by being alive and functioning in society, he was a success, but success required accepting egregious wrongs. It appears that his personal experience and that of his father did not influence his faith in the rightness of the cause, but we do not really know what he believed or what his motivations were. Likewise, we do not know how he really felt toward the Party, but we do know that his behavior and professed attitudes are in conformity with the Party policies. How much of the younger Smirnov's behavior might be accounted for by the accommodation of the powerless to the powerful and how much by the assimilation of the legitimacy of being powerless cannot be apportioned—perhaps even by him.

The theme that the violence was cruel but, all things considered, necessary runs through many loyalist returnee narratives. Joseph Berger emigrated from Poland to Palestine, where he became the Secretary of the Palestine Communist Party, and eventually moved to the Soviet Union and became a citizen in 1932. Berger held a leading position in the Comintern, but he was stripped of this in 1934 and expelled from the Party. In 1935 Berger was arrested and sent to the Gulag on charges of being a Trotskyite agitator. At one point his sentence was changed to a death sentence, because he did not prove to be a useful witness in the Zinoviev trial. For unknown reasons, which would probably carry considerable insight if revealed, the sentence was commuted to eight years in prison, and between 1935 and 1951 he was either in prison or in the Gulag. He was released into perpetual exile after sixteen years of incarceration, and rehabilitated in 1956. He resumed his Polish nationality, left the Soviet Union, and eventually went to live in Israel.

In his critically analytic work *Shipwreck of a Generation,* Berger ponders the question of why Communists did not do anything to subvert the policy of the purges. In the course of his deliberations he refers to a letter he received from a released campmate who had also been a Party member. She wrote, "My generation of communists everywhere accepted the Stalin form of leadership. We acquiesced in the crimes. We endorsed them. . . . The truth is that all of us, including the leaders directly under Stalin, saw these crimes as the opposite of what they were. We believed that they were important contributions to the victory of socialism."[33]

Elsewhere, in a discussion with another campmate, Berger addresses the issue of the unavoidability of terror and revolutionary violence. Their discussion took them back to terror as the modus operandi in the early days of the Soviet state (1917), and compares that terror to the later terror. As Berger's fellow inmate rationalized: "We were fighting the class enemy . . . we killed Tsarist officers, landowners, bankers. But to kill a simple, innocent peasant in cold blood—we would never have dreamed of it."[34] Berger agreed that this was the way he and his cohort of foreign Communists had viewed the terror. They were "shocked by its cruelty," but defended its necessity. Still, he imagined how horrified Lenin would have been if he saw what was happening (in the thirties).[35] If prisoners could make the distinction between the corrupt leadership and corrupted Party of Stalin and the pure leadership and pure Party of Lenin—a perception cultivated by Khrushchev and later Gorbachev—then there was no inconsistency to reconcile. (Except, of course, if one wants to consider why it had been necessary under Lenin to shoot the former aristocracy, White Guards, representatives of other socialist parties, and assorted other categories of perceived or potential opponents.)

CO-CONSPIRATORS, ENABLERS, CONFORMISTS, OR INDOCTRINATED MINDS?

Ordinary human behavior that occurs under extraordinary circumstances, viewed in retrospect and from a different perspective, can seem inexplicable even to those who lived it. Many loyal Communist prisoners who claimed that their own imprisonment was unwarranted nevertheless did not challenge the ideology of using imprisonment as a political tool. Their "captive minds"[36] were fully adapted to the political use of mass violence that had evolved into the "maintenance tool" of the Soviet system. In their support of the necessity for the violence, they shared the perspective of their captors.

After his release from the Gulag, Joseph Berger saw the movie *The Bridge on the River Kwai,* and he recalls how he resonated to one of its themes. The film describes how English prisoners of war accommodated their Japanese captors and effectively aided in the Japanese war effort by reconstructing a bridge. According to Berger's interpretation it illustrates the traumatic bond that can unite the powerless with their captors, or perhaps illustrates a nonideological automaticity of behavior. What Berger found remarkable was not that the prisoners had built the bridge—they were in a situation of duress—but the determination and drive with which their imprisoned captain had them carry the assignment to completion. It is relevant to compare the captain's determination to that of Solzhenitsyn's prisoner Ivan Denisovich, who diligently laid brick after brick, even after roll was called. That such counterintuitive behaviors occurred is clear; their explanation, less so.

More forces than the traumatic bond were at play with prisoners of the NKVD. With the dismay and bewilderment of one who has ultimately lost his faith, Berger attributed much of the prisoners' compliance to the influence of an "ingrained patriotism" to the Soviet Union: "Prisoners achieved the impossible. But why did they yield to the demands of their captors? Why did they not indulge in extensive and unceasing sabotage? Curiously enough they were convinced that everything they were doing was for the good of Russia."[37] Berger was not alone in his bewilderment regarding such compliant cooperation, including his own. His sentiments, shared by many, were succinctly recorded by Anatolii Brat, a journalist who was also the chairman of the Novosibirsk Memorial. In his reflections on the theme of sacrifice in the service of Communism, he writes the following about Nikolai Bukharin, whose (public) parting sentiments were similar to those of other Bolshevik leaders, such as General Iona Yakir:

> One of the reasons he confessed to being an enemy of the people was that he . . . thereby joined the ranks of those who accepted the conditions of the game so as not to undermine the prestige of the party, the state, and the system in front of the people and other countries. Just think: the system punishes one after another of them, and they consciously go to their deaths for the sake of preserving that very system![38]

Historian Hiroaki Kuromiya, seeking to retrieve the "hushed voices" of the arrested through their interrogation protocols, found that the accused sometimes failed to even comprehend the accusations against them, because they were so "far-fetched." Moreover, he observed, these records also reflect "traces of [their] disbelief and resistance to the absurdity of the charges."[39] Their disbelief notwithstanding, most prisoners were so broken in body and spirit by the persistent physical and psychological torture to which they were subjected that we need not look further to understand their signatures on confessions. However, that may be a simplification of the processes at work. According to some analysts, prisoners did not just sign confessions, but they actually took part in the construction of their stories of complicity in crimes. In so doing, they supported the system.

Igal Halfin has also investigated NKVD interrogation protocols; he argues that the narrative that emerges is cocreated by the interrogator and the prisoner, and that the accused is not only a subject of the dialogue, but a subject in dialogue.[40] Moreover, interrogators often invented confessions and testimonies. Halfin's earlier research found that Communist Party members went through a transforming life experience, going from "darkness to light," as their "souls" gained entrance to the hallowed organization. They had proven themselves faithful to the Revolution by such rites of passage.[41] His follow-up investigation has taken this putative conversion process a step further.

In recent research examining the dynamics of the interrogation, Halfin argues that there was a dependent relationship between the citizen and the NKVD. In this context, there was a subversive, self-incriminating subtext in the dialogue between the accused and the interrogator. The demoralized and physically exhausted accused were encouraged to infer that crimes and misdemeanors could potentially be excused if only the accused would reconstruct the Self by acknowledging culpability. Furthermore, Halfin maintains, Communist interrogators who acted with "messianic fervor" in their interrogations of Communist prisoners may not have been "othering," but rather experiencing a "radical intimacy" with the accused. The NKVD interrogator "spoke for the entire Soviet order," when he cautioned the accused, "You are undoing yourself with your obstinacy . . . if you sign, it will be a gesture of trust." The clear message was that since the Party is always right, the prisoner should hardly have to be told that this process should be embraced willingly.[42]

According to Halfin, some prisoners believed—or came to believe—that their interrogators' zealous efforts were proof that they sincerely wished to "save" the errant prisoners by a redemptive conversion.[43] Such a conversion represents a more profound change than does confession. Prisoners under duress could maintain their own ideology and justify their confession as a pragmatic accommodation to their oppressors. There were doubtless many instances when the accused gave up resisting and offered to comply by saying, "if the Party so demands, I will sign it."[44] However, the interrogator seeking conversion, which would require that the prisoner assimilate the ideology that justified the confession, would then inform him that that was not what the Party needed. The Party needed the "truth," "formulated in [the prisoners' own] words without any help from [the interrogator]."[45] The ambiguity of the perpetrator-victim relationship was sometimes subtle, subversive, and seductive. One prisoner admitted to having been "drawn to the investigator, especially in the beginning . . . [thinking] that the interrogator [could] help establish the truth, find justice."[46] She explained that this was rationalized by the fact that she was being "interrogated by a Soviet authority. The accusations came from a government we saw as no different from ourselves."[47]

In his discussion of the Communist prisoners' predicament and their ultimate willingness to sacrifice their lives for the sake of the Revolution, Halfin evokes Milan Kundera's comparison of Dostoevsky and Kafka. Whereas Dostoevsky's prisoner in *Crime and Punishment* knows the cause of his guilt and seeks punishment to relieve himself from its burden, Kafka's prisoner in *The Trial* seeks to understand the reason he is being punished.[48] Both men must depend on powerful others for a remedy. NKVD prisoners inhabited a Kafkaesque world in which the NKVD provided the punishment and it was left to the imagination of the prisoners and the creativity of their interrogators to come up with a justifiable reason for something that many prisoners simply viewed as a mistake. In the course of their interrogations, some prisoners may have become convinced of their own guilt. Halfin records how Meyerhold, the theater director, colluded with his interrogator to contrive his confession: "As [Meyerhold] became convinced of his own guilt, he found experts ready to help him build the case against himself. [Meyerhold later wrote]: 'My self split into two parts: one half searched for my "crime" while the other half . . . invented one. The investigator applied his skill and experience to help me compose [the crimes]; ours was a close collaboration.'"[49]

The merciless physical and psychological torture to which prisoners were exposed—or with which they were threatened—challenges any claim that prisoners willingly cooperated in their self-incrimination. Moreover, any claim of their volitional participation would have to question what role there could be for volition when there is a forced choice between bad and worse. While Halfin acknowledges the "appallingly polarized power relations,"[50] he still argues that the narrative that ensued was "wrought not only by mechanisms of power but also by systems of meaning that were understood, if not fully shared, by those who populated the Stalinist universe."[51] Presumably, since they shared the same values, the interrogator sometimes had to push just a little to get them past the tipping point. Halfin's research raises issues that merit further reflection regarding methods of indoctrination. We may ask, for example, to what extent prisoners saw themselves, or perhaps came to see themselves, through the eyes of the camp, NKVD, or Soviet authorities, and how rewards and punishments were manipulated to exploit the vulnerable prisoner. Manipulation is an apt descriptor, because physical coercion was so regularly employed to change behavior and belief.

One returnee, while admitting to conflicted feelings, tried to explain why she did not hate the NKVD for taking away her husband and arresting her. As she summarized, "I guess it's simple. For true Soviet people, trust and respect for the organs of state security is deeply ingrained in their blood. That trust was earned by the legendary struggle of the Chekists, the . . . unwavering glorious and iron will of Feliks Dzerzhinskii and his brothers-in-arms."[52]

Mikhail Petrovich Dabudek, an early arrestee, was sentenced to exile in Kotlas in 1934 on article 58 (counterrevolutionary) charges. During this period, he collaborated with the NKVD as an informer. He was released in 1937 and returned to Dnepropetrovsk, but passport restrictions forced him to move on to Ulianovsk. For the next two decades, Dabudek experienced the routine social and legal impediments that regularly attend returnee status. In Dabudek's case, these impediments also included the refusal of his request to join the army during the war. In a 1950 plea to the Presidium of the Supreme Soviet of the USSR, Dabudek writes: "I atoned for my guilt in the face of the Lenin-Stalin party—which expressed itself in my association with Ukrainian bourgeois nationalism—many times over. I proved my devotion to the socialist motherland in deed."[53] Presumably the deed to which he referred was the labor during exile. The purpose of the letter was to request that his sentence be revoked. Dabudek belonged to the group of prisoners (or exiles, living in prisons without walls) who had simply been released when their term was up but had not been provided with any (cleared) judicial status. This problem severely limited their prospects for housing and employment, rendering them vulnerable to rearrest. Evidently his 1950 request was successful, because in 1952 Dabudek wrote a letter to the Kiev Party authorities requesting reinstatement in the Party, and this would have required prior judicial exoneration. This request was rejected with the explanation that there were absolutely no grounds for reinstatement of his membership. In the terse words of the official, "you served your sentence . . . regained your right to citizenship, and you therefore can work honestly and justify being able to call yourself a citizen of the Soviet Union."[54] However, in August of 1956, in the wake of the Twentieth Party Congress, Dabudek's membership was restored, and so too was his tenure in the Party, dating from 1921.

Since this account of Dabudek's history has been reconstructed through memoirs and official documents, we cannot ask him if he really believed he was guilty in the eyes of the Party. We might assume that Dabudek had a fairly high degree of Party loyalty, because he served as an informer, even informing on his daughter. People like Dabudek, who, for a variety of reasons, declared their guilt, thereby exonerated the system of wrongdoing.

While the personal integrity of those who steadfastly maintained their innocence was not compromised, their public persona remained suspect. Prisoners could not be cleared of the alleged crimes unless they had been rehabilitated. But even public rehabilitation did not suffice for some who insisted on restoring their self-image. A clean biography, as Petr Sagoian, a returnee memoirist, described it, was a clear conscience. Sagoian had been arrested in 1937 on articles 58-10 and 11, sent to numerous prisons, and finally ended up in a Norilsk camp (Dudinka). Mere survival was a feat. During the grueling transport, Sagoian witnessed prisoners who were too weak to walk or even kneel. After survival, after liberation, and after rehabilitation came his quest for Party readmittance. While practical procedures would have been sufficient preparation, Sagoian described himself as attempting to achieve a mental state of purity akin to a religious experience before undertaking the application for reinstatement in the ranks of the CPSU.[55]

THE "GENERATION OF THE DECEIVED"

Anatolii Brat, the journalist mentioned above who wrote about Bukharin, compiled and edited a volume titled "Through the Eyes of Different Generations," based on correspondence sent to the Novosibirsk Memorial in the late eighties.

This work is a collection of stories by women who had been in the Gulag as the wives and widows of "enemies of the people." In a 1989 letter that accompanied the manuscript he sent to Memorial headquarters, Brat writes, "the fate of these women was repeated a thousand times over, it is the fate of the older generation, the history of our motherland."[56] Indeed, thousands of the widows of generals who had been executed were imprisoned in Alzhir, a division of Karlag, in 1937. According to many accounts, they were sustained by their faith that they would imminently be found innocent and liberated. They considered themselves patriots and valued conformity as a virtue. In camp, the women prisoners would get together and sing songs like "My Country, My Very Dear Moscow." The lyrics were suffused with praise for the potential of their "wonderful country," in which they "could not *not* believe." Many performed their forced labor with genuine enthusiasm. For example, the work of Mariia Gal'per as a lathe operator was considered so commendable that her picture was hung up on the "wall of honor" twice. (Since prisoners were not supposed to be photographed, one of Gal'per's campmate artists had painted a portrait of her.) The hopes of these women for liberation and exoneration were eventually realized, but it took twenty years. After her release and rehabilitation, Gal'per rejoined the Party as soon as she possibly could.[57] But there were dissenting voices.

Ekaterina Olitskaia, who was not a Communist but a Socialist-Revolutionary Party member (see chapter 1), found the thinking of this group to be inconceivable. Reflecting on her Kolyma years and her female campmates, she writes:

> It was difficult for me, almost impossible, to understand the psychology of the arrestees in my group. Devout Communists, who justified downright everything but their own arrests, [must have] had strong reactions to what was happening to them. Maybe they just didn't verbalize their protest. The best of them kept repeating that those in the center [Moscow] didn't know what was going on in these places, nor about the interrogation methods, nor the arbitrariness that took place during the armed escorts to the work sites. [These prisoners] painfully, acutely, felt shame, were embarrassed about themselves. I didn't understand how it was possible to be ashamed of a fabricated accusation, and not be indignant—to ask for review of their cases, rather than demanding it.[58]

Their seeming impotence also puzzled and frustrated Olitskaia. She concludes with an exhortation and a baffling question:

> After all, standing before me were not inhabitants, but fighters for the happiness of the people—fighters for justice, members of the most progressive, most intransigent party in the world.[59]

This abiding faith, despite evidence that might have challenged it, could be sustained for decades and through the vicissitudes of de-Stalinization and re-Stalinization. Anatolii Brat claimed that some survivors never changed their views in the half century between 1937 and 1989. He refers to them as the "generation of the deceived."[60] According to Brat, their deception was sustained by misplacing the blame for their fate on Stalin and his henchmen rather than recognizing the culpability of the Soviet system itself. Two convergent forces supported this deception. First, any challenge to the Party—actual or suspected—could result in imprisonment or death. Second, the socializing, normalizing influences of a closed society constrain the opinions people are permitted to voice, and even the opinions they are able to consider.[61] So there can hardly be any disconfirming evidence, because all information is systematically interpreted as affirmative.

Such influences constrained many of the repressed, but not all, as evidenced by Olitskaia and others. Leonid Furman, an economics professor, was arrested in the "anti-cosmopolitan" sweep in 1952, and sentenced to ten years of strict regime labor camp. He was released in the aftermath of Stalin's death, though not until 1955. Furman himself was not a Party member, but he had this to say about his fellow ex-prisoners who were: "The people released from jails and camps well understood who shattered their lives and they evaluated the dictatorial regime accordingly. . . . However, the former Communists, those who restored their Party membership, did not tolerate criticism of the Soviet authorities in their presence."[62] This intolerance of criticism may have been influenced by a number of psychological, social, and political forces including self-doubt, fear of entrapment, political pragmatism, perceptual bias, committed resignation, and detached resignation. In consequence, they ignored the issues of culpability and accountability.

Evgenii Eduardovich Gagen, a journalist and Party member since 1932, was arrested in December 1937 and sentenced to ten years in the Gulag, which he spent in various camps including Kolyma. He would not see his wife for fourteen years, and his confinement lasted even longer than that. With the exception of a short break in 1948 when his first sentence was completed, Gagen spent seventeen years either in camp or in exile. He returned to Moscow in 1955, and his application for rehabilitation was successful. In his nearly two-thousand-page handwritten memoir, Gagen spends little time on the groundlessness of his incarceration, focusing instead on the process of rehabilitation: "On the fourteenth of November, the *Revtribunal,* having reviewed my case, stipulated that the sentence of the Special Commission was revoked in connection with the absence of a crime. The charges were dropped. Just like that! For eighteen years I carried the stigma of being an 'enemy of the people' without having been guilty of anything. And it only took two and a half months for that to be established."[63] The Stalinist Procuracy was characterized by its accusatory bias—guilty until proven innocent.[64] Had Gagen been less of a Party loyalist, he might have reframed his perspective to recognize that it took eighteen years—and not two and a half months—to ascertain his innocence.

Armed with rehabilitation, Gagen started working on his request to the Party Control Commission for reinstatement. When his daughter, whom he had not seen for seventeen years, asked him why he was applying and what he would get out of it, Gagen answered sharply, "You don't enter the Party to get something. You do it because that is what your conscience dictates, and out of a sense of duty."[65] Initially, the review did not go well. When the chairman asked what he wanted, Gagen responded indignantly: "I was incarcerated for ten years and in exile for seven without having committed a crime. . . . You ask what I want? I want to return to the fold, and nothing more."[66] The chairman of the commission looked at Gagen's appeal and declared that it would not be possible to restore his membership because of the eighteen-year interruption [i.e., the years he was repressed].[67] The rest of the committee agreed. Eventually Gagen submitted the request to the Twentieth Party Congress for reevaluation, and it was accepted.[68] His tenure in the Party was restored and recorded as uninterrupted. After he had reentered the Party and found work, Gagen lamented that he had not yet found his place in life, a place which he defined as having his status as a Communist fully validated by his community. "I had to prove in deed that I had remained a Communist, to overcome the suspiciousness . . . that [reared its head] in some people. They reasoned that there must have been something. People are not imprisoned for nothing. In the last nineteen years many became convinced that we victims of arbitrariness really were guilty of something."[69]

Why it was that Gagen did not challenge the validity of a system that had incarcerated him for two decades for crimes he did not commit remains an open question—perhaps not for him, but for others who do not share his interpretive frame. One possible answer is provided by suggesting that the Party had preempted the same psychosocial niche occupied in other societies by religion, or the sometimes overlapping emotional niche that bonds followers to charismatic movements. If so, loyalty and commitment are grounded in faith and feeling and are not subject to challenge by real-world events.

While Party loyalty remained constant for some, there was a gradual shift, however slight, from the post-camp years through the post-Gorbachev years. Increasingly the question of accountability was being raised. In her memoir "The Tragedy of the Innocent," Galina Paushkina discusses her 1938 arrest as the wife of an "enemy of the people" and her incarceration in the Butyrka and then in

Temlag, a camp in the Temnikov region. Paushkina was rehabilitated in 1956 and readmitted to the Party in 1958; several members of her family had also managed to survive. As if describing a storm that had passed, she concluded that the vicious cycle had thus come to an end, and she felt like a full-fledged citizen of the motherland.[70]

Buttressed with a better self-image, she honored the memory of her fallen comrades. She regretted that they did not fall fighting the enemy, German Fascism, for the motherland, a privilege they would dearly have wished. She blamed their fall on the "blows inflicted by the leader of the Party and the people—Stalin."[71] She praised the Twentieth Party Congress for freeing the "innocent condemned," restoring their good names and reclaiming the lost truth. She continued, "The tarnished names of the victims of the time of the cult of personality should be cleansed." According to her, the question of how the terror was possible—and who was responsible—was sufficiently addressed by Gorbachev in his acclaimed speech in November 1987.[72] In this speech, Gorbachev revisited the Stalin question and referred to "thousands" of victims, but was no more forthcoming about systemic causes than was Khrushchev. However, he did invite those with questions to undertake the effort to fill in the blank spots in history. Paushkina was satisfied that there were no other blank spots or blind spots. At the conclusion of her twenty-three-year-long memoir (written from 1965 until 1988, largely a period of re-Stalinization) she thanked the Party "and anyone else who had the strength to wake justice up from its deep sleep."[73]

Even those who were still trying to fill in the blank spots were constrained by blind spots. Evgenii Gnedin, a Soviet diplomat and returnee whose parents were revolutionaries, anguished for decades over the question of why the repression succeeded and endured. In his 1977 *Katastrofa; Vtoroe rozhdenie, Memuarnye zapiski* (Catastrophe, Second Birth, Memoir Notes), Gnedin attempted to understand what led to this catastrophe "equal to death." He conceded that decades of deliberation had failed to answer the endless string of whys. He asked why people confessed, why they hoped against hope, why they insisted on their innocence and then admitted "guilt." Throughout his life and in his writing, Gnedin bore reluctant witness to this disillusioning reality.

Having survived, among others, the hardships of the Sukhanovka prison, notorious for fifty-two types of torture,[74] Gnedin dedicated his post-camp existence to searching for answers to these questions.[75] Though he recognized the incompleteness of the proposed answers, he failed to recognize that the questions he was posing were too limited. The consequences of the repression could not be understood solely by exploring the psychology of the leaders, their followers, and the victims. Even when such a search strategy yielded authentic information about how individuals thought, felt, and behaved, we would only discover how misleading it is to search for psychological explanations when choice and volition are illusions. When people are coerced into accepting responsibility for choices they had no power to make, under extraordinary and often violent conditions (including torture, hunger, sleep deprivation, and forced separation from loved ones), what we can learn from their explanations is that the power to compel obedience can become the power to compel explanations.

DEVIATION FROM THE PRINCIPLES OF MARXISM-LENINISM

In the post-Stalin era, some citizens, and even some officials, were venturing to raise cautious questions regarding the presumptively settled validity of guilty verdicts. A 1955 report[76] on the Moscow city courts presented to the RSFSR Ministry of Justice, for example, asserts: "Despite the great number of rehabilitated persons, neither the people's courts, nor the leadership in the Moscow City Court, asked any questions about the responsibility of the forensic investigative staff, who were guilty of gross violations of the law."[77] At this time the political climate was apparently safe enough to raise such issues, but still not safe enough to press them aggressively. This was sometimes reflected in the public's attitude toward Gulag returnees. Zoia Dmitrievna Marchenko spent three terms in various prisons, camps (including Kolyma), and exile from 1931 until 1954.[78] She survived to be rehabilitated in 1956, but her husband and brother both died in the camps. Zoia was not a Communist, but she did have acquaintances who were Party members. They did not seek contact with her until after the Twentieth Party Congress. According to Marchenko, they claimed that their Party discipline had "closed their eyes" and that the Congress "suddenly opened their eyes." In the second half of the fifties, the people in this group gradually, if sheepishly, became friendlier with Zoia. Still, Marchenko later recalled in an interview, she was socially marginalized and euphemistically referred to as a "person with a complex fate."[79] It is a classification that Kafka might have used if he were planning to rehabilitate Josef K., because it conveys both the ambiguousness of the person's culpability and the ambivalence of society toward the returnee. How much to fault the person and what fault, if any, lay with the system remained unasked questions.

The Twentieth Party Congress

In February of 1956 Stalin was posthumously stripped of his immunity by Khrushchev at the Twentieth Party Congress—in the interest of supporting Communism. There, Khrushchev provided a conceptual framework in which to place the crimes of the Stalin era. The Party leader acknowledged "a whole series of exceedingly serious and grave perversions of party principles, of party democracy, of revolutionary legality,"[80] and placed the blame squarely on Stalin and his cult of personality. This was especially egregious, he added, because "the classics of Marxism-Leninism denounced every manifestation of the cult of the individual."[81] He went on to discuss Lenin's principles and testament, and he attacked Stalin for not abiding by either. Khrushchev further pointed out that it was Stalin who originated the term "enemy of the people," and under Stalin confessions became the prosecution's chief source of evidence against the accused.

Regarding the victims, Khrushchev maintained that 70 percent of the members and candidates of the Central Committee who were elected at the Seventeenth Party Congress in 1934 were arrested and/or shot in 1937–1938 as "counterrevolutionaries," as were the majority of its delegates (1,108 of 1,966).[82] But now, he could report, these mistakes were being corrected, and rehabilitations of these and others among the "thousands of honest and innocent Communists" had already been under way since 1954.[83]

Khrushchev promulgated the Party line that the violations of law which took place under Stalin were a violation of Party principles. While he conceded that similar tactics had been used in Lenin's time, Khrushchev justified them because "there were actual class enemies," but since "the Revolution was already victorious" under Stalin, there was no need to resort to such methods.[84]

In his memoirs, Khrushchev claims to have stated at the time that he was prepared to be held responsible by the Party, if the Party deemed that all of the leaders under Stalin were also responsible. However, according to some researchers, this preparedness was only an autobiographical claim at a safe historical remove. Furthermore, it has been argued that Khrushchev did not undertake his truth-telling campaign until it appeared inevitable that the crimes under Stalin would come under public scrutiny at some point anyway. In taking the initiative of calling a crime a crime, Khrushchev could more easily circumscribe his own complicity in the system that supported Stalin.[85] In his analysis of Khrushchev, biographer William Taubman surmised that "Khrushchev practiced deception and self-deception. . . . He insisted he believed in Stalin and in the guilt of Stalin's imagined enemies [and] denied he understood what was going on until after Stalin's death."[86] Taubman correctly concludes that the political motivations for not "coming clean" and admitting his own complicity were that a more frontal attack "would have undermined the whole Soviet regime"[87] and his own political position, as he too was culpable. Instead, Khrushchev was able to deftly promote the validity of the Soviet system, while denouncing acts that had systematically taken place under three decades of Soviet governance.

Witness the testimonial of I. Ia. Vozzhaev, a former prisoner who embraced Khrushchev's explanation:

> My moral-ideological state never wavered from the beginning to the end, despite the undeserved insult visited upon me with the label of "enemy of the people," and despite having endured a severe prison regime and interrogations. I remained morally and ideologically steady and sure of our Communist Party and Marxist-Leninist teachings. I considered that the repression by the NKVD of Party and Soviet officials and the Soviet Army command was a gross perversion of the policies of the Party. And the Party will absolutely get to the bottom of this matter and correct the distortions that were admitted in the policies and practices of the Party.[88]

Notwithstanding such supporters, Khrushchev's persuasiveness depended on an audience prone to persuasion. This difficult balancing act of blaming the leader (or his NKVD) and sparing the Party was played out at all levels of society, and even in the Gulag itself.

LOYAL OPPOSITION IN THE GULAG

Stalin's death facilitated mass releases from the Gulag—mostly of criminals—but the politicals remained incarcerated for up to three more years.[89] When the post-Stalin atmosphere of liberalization was not extended to Article 58ers and other political prisoners, it stirred unrest by adding the frustration of rising expectations. This tension escalated to mass uprisings in Vorkuta and Norilsk in 1953 and, most notably, in Kengir, Kazakhstan, in 1954,[90] where the revolt, first chronicled by Solzhenitsyn, lasted forty days. Despite the paucity of sources, notwithstanding the (exaggerated) numbers of victims, most of Solzhenitsyn's account was accurate.[91] Through it all, the prisoner-strikers' ambiguous attitudes toward the Party exemplify how complex and conflicted the issue of Party loyalty was among Gulag prisoners.

In his investigation of this event, Steven Barnes calls attention to the "apparent moderation" of the prisoners' demands.[92] Their list of demands included punishment for the recent murders of prisoners, an eight-hour workday, removal of the numbers from their uniforms and the locks from the doors and windows of the barracks, unrestricted correspondence with relatives, visits, reduction of twenty-five-year sentences, and reviews of their cases.[93] Many of these requests were not for changes in policy, because they had already been promised, though never implemented, in the aftermath of Stalin's death. So the demands were not just moderate, they were conservative; they ratified the officially promulgated policy.

The prisoners' responses were (pro)Soviet.[94] They did not challenge the legitimacy of the system; they accepted it and asked for the improvements already granted but not provided. This moderate nature of their demands may have been influenced by the continued loyalty of the cohort of former Red Army officers, who had only recently defended the motherland. But it might also have reflected a strategic, realistic assessment of what was attainable by powerless inmates in a closed system. The rebellion's leader, Colonel Kapiton Kuznetsov, declared: "Our salvation lies in loyalty. We must talk to Moscow's representatives *in a manner befitting Soviet citizens!*"[95] The motto of the rebellion was "Long live the Soviet Constitution"—a theme that would later be picked up by the dissidents, and again by Memorial in the early days of Gorbachev. This common thread of loyalty to the Soviet Constitution that ran through the declaration of both the rebelling inmates and the protests of dissidents suggests that they shared a recognition that adherence to the Constitution could provide relief from repression. It also suggests that, for pragmatic and strategic reasons, the most prudent approach to the government would be to hold the government accountable to its constitutional responsibilities.

Barnes does not question the reasons for the prisoners' revolt, but aptly raises the question of why there had not been more instances of mass insurrection in the Gulag. This is especially salient, because, "Given . . . its supposedly anti-Soviet population, or at least the seeming likelihood that its inmates would become anti-Soviet based on their gulag internment itself . . ."[96] revolts should have been widespread and frequent.

Diverse groups, however, had come to the Gulag for diverse reasons and at different periods of Soviet history, and each would bring a different response to the internment experience. A number of prisoners did not become alienated from either the regime or the Soviet ideology, an outcome that led some former prisoners and researchers to conclude that the Gulag sometimes functioned as a "conserver of ideology."[97] As Semen Vilenskii, a Kolyma survivor, recalls, many of the prisoners seemed "frozen in time."[98] It was not unusual, according to Roy Medvedev, to find people who maintained the political views they brought into the Gulag. The retained political allegiances varied from pronounced nationalism to fanatic Communism. Imprisonment, torture, recurrent threats, grinding labor, and numerous other stressors did not alter such prisoners' view of the regime. However, as Medvedev also noted, the Gulag often made prisoners anti-Stalinists, but not anti-Communists.

The time of entry into the prison and camp system was an important determinant of the political outcome of imprisonment. Only after Stalin's death and Beria's arrest[99] did the burgeoning liberalization, evidenced by ambiguous but less stringent directives, create an atmosphere that could foster any hope of a successful insurrection.[100] This transitional period created an existential crisis for the Gulag. Fear of reprisals—even within the camp from the criminal element—and the futility of opposition by a cowed population could account for why discontent had only rarely erupted into rebellion—up to now.[101] Barnes points out that Soviet citizens generally did not have "alternative coherent world views." However, those who had fought in the war knew what it was like outside the zone of the USSR.[102] When they found their loyal wartime service rewarded with incarceration, ex-soldiers who had borne arms and faced death were less likely to passively accept imprisonment. This and other circumstances may have contributed to their readiness to protest, but these strikers were exhibiting neither disdain for nor struggle against the system.

Why did uprisings not occur more often? While revolting against a repressive, punitive imprisonment would seem natural for prisoners who maintained their innocence, there were a number of countervailing impediments to this course. They included (ex)prisoners' fears that they would find life in the Big Zone (the outside world) more precarious than life in the camps. But there were more fundamental issues involved. As harsh as life was in the Gulag, the prisoners who survived had adapted to it.[103] There was a correlation between adaptation to the Gulag and adaptation to the repressive Soviet system. The Weltanschauung of the prisoners, as of most Soviet citizens, was informed/constrained by Soviet ideology and continually reinforced by "speaking Bolshevik," which resulted in at least professed belief in the system. Barnes notes that the Kengir participants "declared themselves citizens, not prisoners,"[104] and their rebellion was "not against the Party, not against the Soviet regime, but in the name of the Party and the regime."[105]

Furthermore, the language of the rebellion presupposed both an acceptance of the system and an acceptance of their status within it as prisoners. The repression of the Soviet system had so intimidated and indoctrinated these Gulag inmates that they demanded not immediate liberation for their unjust incarceration, but rather an incremental improvement within their closed system. They did not dare ask for a change in the political system, nor could they, perhaps, have conceived of such. These institutionalized inmates, stuck in a closed world in and outside of the Gulag, turned to the Party for guidance, rescue, and meaning, much as do hostages who depend on their threatening captors for survival. They had faith that the Party would resolve their dilemmas, or at least be responsive. In fact, at some level this did happen—with regard to the uncharacteristically mild punishment for their acts of defiance. In the aftermath of the strike the post-Stalin authorities responded with more leniency than they had in the past, when summary executions were frequent. Of the thousands who took part in the strike, some hundreds of prisoners were transferred or given new sentences, and "only" seven were sentenced to death. The defendants appealed their verdicts, but five of them were executed in 1956. Kuznetsov had his death sentence commuted to twenty-five years, was released in 1960,[106] and was even rehabilitated.

How were the prisoner-protesters viewed in later years by the larger society? During the Soviet period, those who had taken part in the camp rebellions were considered to have acted in violation of the law, and in general were not eligible for rehabilitation. However, in the post-Soviet era, the Rehabilitation Commission struggled with the status of this group and the issue of reinterpreting the 1991 Rehabilitation Law so that they would be covered by it. They faced a dilemma. On the one hand, the acts the strikers had committed were considered anti-Soviet, which was a criminal offense, and therefore they were ineligible for consideration under the given legislation. On the other hand, within a "rule of law" system, they would simply have been exercising their rights as citizens.[107] The strikers were ultimately rehabilitated in 1992. According to Semen Vilenskii, also of the Rehabilitation commission, these individuals should have been hailed as heroes rather than simply exonerated.[108]

Kengir Survivor Marlen Mikhailovich Korallov: Allegiance to Socialism, not the Strike or the Party

Marlen Mikhailovich Korallov was born in 1925 to parents who were "Party people." Like so many others in their generation, they had participated in the Civil War and further expressed their enthusiasm for the Revolution by naming their son in honor of Marx and Lenin. Marlen's father was arrested in 1937 and executed on December 29 of that same year at the age of thirty-six. Reading his father's dossier decades later, Marlen was aghast at how his father's fate had apparently been decided in an instant (though in fact, one may conclude, probably even before that instant). According to the case file, nearly one hundred cases had been handled at the same time as his father's—in just fifteen minutes. Marlen's mother was asked to renounce her husband publicly as an "enemy of the people," but she refused to do so. In consequence, she was sent to the Gulag. Certain that a tragic mistake had been made, she maintained her Communist allegiance. Marlen's mother survived seventeen years in the Gulag and exile, and so too did her belief in the Party. She claimed that to have stopped believing would have been "spiritual suicide."[109]

Despite having one parent who had been executed and one still in the camps, Marlen managed to get a degree in philology from Moscow State University in 1947. He was not a Party member, and he viewed his parents as being part of a "tragic generation." He lamented that "this contingent of Communists had maintained ideas since their youth, despite the fact that they were never substantiated." In Marlen's eyes, Marx was wrong, but Rosa Luxemburg and Karl Liebknecht (German social democratic revolutionaries) had ideas worth building on. Between his "counterrevolutionary" ideas and his spoiled biography, it was Marlen's turn to be a political target. In 1949 he was arrested and charged with several points of Article 58, dispatched to the Lefortovo prison, and then sentenced to twenty-five years in the Gulag.

Marlen was incarcerated in various camps of the Gulag, including Kengir. He was "anti-Party," while many of his campmates believed in the Party but blamed Stalin for the repression. Although he was in Kengir during the strike, he claims he did not participate. Nevertheless, after the uprising was quelled, he ended up in an interrogation cell in neighboring Dzhezkazgan. In spite of having a legitimate alibi he was still confined to the isolator, wondering if he would ever be free again. Many in his group were resentenced under additional articles, but Marlen was released in 1955. Fortunately, an old friend of his father had risen to a relatively influential position and was able to intervene on behalf of the family. Marlen's father was (posthumously) rehabilitated, and Marlen and his mother, who was still living in exile at the time, were freed and rehabilitated.[110]

In subsequent years, Marlen wrote extensively in the "thick journals," and the forbidden theme of the Gulag was almost always a subtext. As incomprehensible as his arrest had been, he admitted that it was even more difficult to grasp the complexity of the "freedom" that was suddenly thrust upon him. When the archives became ever so slightly accessible, Marlen was finally able to read the works of the "orthodox and the renegades of social democracy" and to engage their political ideas. As a writer-philologist he struggled with "how to make sense of, how to understand, how the country of Tolstoy and Dostoevsky could produce the Gulag, and how the country of Goethe and Schiller could produce Auschwitz and Maidanek."[111] In his critical writings he aimed for a "demythologization" of the "legendary" events at Kengir, and the Gulag experience in later years. Referring to the prisoners of the sixties, seventies, and eighties (i.e., the dissidents), he concluded, "My Lefortovo was not their Lefortovo, they wrote letters, got information, got newspapers. . . ."[112]

Korallov reflected with bitterness on the missed opportunities of the twentieth century. He maintained that the ideas of his heroes Luxemburg and Liebknecht and the contributions of Clara Zetkin could have been meaningful for Russia, but came to naught—"it insults me to see what happened." However, Korallov turned insult into action. He became a founding and active member of Memorial; he continued his literary and social criticism well into his eighties.

PERSONAL AND POLITICAL NARRATIVES: MEANING AND FUNCTION

We have focused on Communist prisoners' narratives that address how they experienced being charged as "enemies" and then incarcerated. Political, social, physical, psychological, and socioeconomic coercion was omnipresent, so those who survived could do so only by finding ways to adapt to their powerlessness. This entailed a number of distinct but overlapping responses, such as: endorsing the Party and its interpretation of Communism, endorsing Communism but differing from the Party's interpretation, outward compliance with the Party and internal resistance (this risked cognitive dissonance), and outward compliance and internal detachment.

The victim's personal narratives describe how the experience of powerlessness during and after imprisonment affected them as well as their family and friends, who could at any moment be subjected to arbitrary persecution. In such a closed, coercive society, survival depended on adapting to this powerlessness, and this adaptation could include adopting the Party's political assumptions regarding itself and its victims. A particularly mind-boggling assumption was that the victims had choices and could only blame themselves for having made bad choices. With some exceptions, an implicit theme is the struggle to adapt to powerlessness. These stories could be called "survival" narratives because they recount various narrative pathways by which victims adapted to a repression that compelled them to accept responsibility for events over which they had no control.

Under Stalin, the Party's political "survival" narrative legitimized the repression because there were so many "enemies of the people." That story changed at the Twentieth Party Congress, where Khrushchev delivered a new political survival narrative: Stalin's arbitrary use of punishment was a crime, but it was a singular aberration that did not discredit the Party. Khrushchev's speech, which gave him political cover, can be labeled a survival narrative because it was crafted to ensure the survival of the Party by reconstructing its Stalinist history. A similar reconstruction of their personal history was necessary for falsely accused Communist loyalists. However, the narrative tasks of the Party and of the victims were very different. The political narrative provided the "facts"; the victims' personal narratives had to adapt to the new reality imposed by them.

Both types of narrative, the political and the personal, played a major role in the social construction of reality.[113] Whether a narrative is the official history of a Party or the personal experience of an individual, it organizes experience into a sequence of events and gives it meaning. In operation the narrative tells us, "This is what happened," "This is what it meant," and "This is how we deal with it."[114] Furthermore, as illustrated by the way the pre–Twentieth Party Congress political narrative legitimized the repression and was revised to legitimize Communism post–Twentieth Party Congress, narratives do not simply reflect an objective reality; they also construct it by selection.[115] For example, the post–Twentieth Party Congress narrative effectively unlinked Stalin from the Party.

The Party narrative is useful as a baseline for comparison because it had accompanied the acts of repression, had legitimized them, and was difficult to resist. In whatever ways the loyalist victims constructed their personal narratives, they had to adapt to the dictates of this reality. The political narrative prior to the Twentieth Party Congress described "what happened" as anti-Communist behavior (as construed by Stalin); it meant that the accused were "enemies of the people," and this was dealt with by their removal through death or imprisonment. The post–Twentieth Party Congress political narrative revised "what had happened" as Stalin's subversive appropriation of the Communist Party apparatus to impose arbitrary punishments; it meant that this singular criminal aberration did not discredit the Communist Party. This construction of reality was served by vilifying Stalin and creating a process for rehabilitating victims.

To the majority of the prisoners, their persecution and imprisonment were unexpected and uncontrollable, but they tried to regain some control over events by the story they told themselves, each other, and imagined others. In this way, the meaning of what happened could be influenced by how they dealt with it.[116] The personal narratives recounted here begin by contesting the Party's narrative, but eventually lose the contest. While denying their guilt, few of these victims took an "outsider's" perspective and blamed the Party or Soviet system for the years they languished behind barbed wire. At some point, making sense of their fate was futile. Eventually, the personal-experience narratives of many survivors reflected the shrinkage of their aspirations from "sense-making" to sheer survival, even after release and rehabilitation.

The prisoners' responses to powerlessness as reflected in their narratives took many forms, including the acceptance of their imprisonment as ideologically justified, objecting to it as the evil of Stalin or the NKVD but not the Party, and a pragmatic, resigned detachment. Further questions regarding accountability did not fit into these narratives. Most tellingly, in time many of these survivors could not think outside the assumptive boundaries imposed on their thinking from without and eventually from within. When prophecy fails, as millions of victims might attest, for true believers it was not because the belief was wrong, but because it had been perverted. When their expectations of the Communist Party failed the victims who were true believers, it was not evidence of a mistaken belief, but evidence of Stalin's villainy. Furthermore, while these loyal adherents may have encountered personally unanticipated events—including violence and imprisonment—they did not encounter contradictory "facts" because their interpretive frame did not conceive of such events as contradictory to their belief. This interpretive bias constituted one of the more consequential effects of the repression—not just that it controlled what survivors could do, but that it influenced what they could think about and the way they could think.

CHAPTER 3

Beyond Belief

Party Identification and the "Bright Future"

Mikhail Aleksandrovich Tanin had been a Party member since 1918, and by 1935 he had progressed through the Party hierarchy to become Khrushchev's assistant. However, in 1937, while serving in the Moscow Party Committee, Tanin was arrested, sentenced to (the notoriously euphemistic) "ten years without the right of correspondence," and executed. Meanwhile, Tamara, who had been his childhood sweetheart and later his wife, was advised to leave Moscow because the wives of "enemies of the people" were being picked up. She did not heed this advice, because she accepted the official explanation that if these women were arrested they must have been guilty. At the very least, they were probably complicit in their husbands' offenses. Tamara later cursed the "blessed simplicity" that had misled her. In her memoir she reflects, "Later, through my own experience, I understood the 'guilt' of the overwhelming majority of arrestees in those years. The real enemies, well masked, wishing to weaken the Party and undermine its authority, snatched its best members and simply physically destroyed them."[1]

It is unclear what Tamara's criterion was for "best members," but many memoirists described themselves as such. This may suggest that they considered the educated intelligentsia to be the Party's best members (i.e., the Party elite, or those—like themselves—sufficiently literate to write memoirs). In 1938 Tamara was arrested, sent to the Butyrka, sentenced to eight years, and dispatched for two months' transit to the women's camp Alzhir.[2] Her ensuing eighteen years were spent in camp or exile. As often happened, the arrest of a family member had negative consequences for their relatives. The Tanins' son was expelled from school, began drinking, and spent years in and out of jail for various infractions.

On release from incarceration, Tamara resolved to transform her personal experience of repression, as well as her husband's fate, into a tale of hope for their son. Writing her (six-hundred-page) memoir in the early sixties, Tamara declared that her goal was that these stories would "reveal before his eyes one vivid page in history, acquaint him with people long gone, who were building him a bright future in difficult conditions, while battling known and masked enemies of all that is advanced and progressive in the struggle for Communism."[3] Such an adversity-driven positive reframing has been described as "benefit-finding,"[4] a process of infusing adverse events with redeeming psychological, social, and spiritual meaning. Employing a positive appraisal can provide an adaptive buffer against distress.[5] A similarly positive interpretive bias is reported by the historian Jolande Withuis in her study of the Dutch postwar Communist Women's Movement. Many of these women had endured incarceration in Ravensbrück concentration camp as a result of their participation in the resistance during the war. The war, and their survival, strengthened their sense of sisterhood and allegiance to Communism. Withuis observed that they regularly cast their sacrifices during and after the war as heroic. She concluded that this positive spin was facilitated by a belief system that allowed them to inhabit their own "mental world" of "higher ideals" and camaraderie.[6] These prisoners were actually in opposition to the system that incarcerated them, so their experience was different from that of the loyalists who landed in the Gulag, but similar mechanisms of positive appraisal were at work in both cases.

The Tanins' son apparently adopted his mother's interpretive frame of events. By 1962 he was finishing his dissertation, and his son was enrolled at the university. In some pages from his personal experience appended to his mother's memoirs, he concluded with the following: "I love my country; I love the Communist Party and am grateful to it for being able to reveal and eliminate all of the bad things that happened under Stalin." He went on to express gratitude to Khrushchev for returning his father's good name and for his initiatives toward restoring happiness to their "innocent suffering family."[7] Empirical evidence suggests that positive illusions are correlated with increased happiness and well-being.[8] However, various studies also found that the long-term effects of an overly positive perceptual bias can interfere with personal growth and problem solving.[9] Perhaps similar positive and negative effects may also apply to the political system. To the extent that individuals such as Tanin and his mother identified with the political system, self-preservation and Party loyalty merged.

Identification has been defined as a "largely unconscious process whereby an individual models thoughts, feelings, and actions after those attributed to an object that has been incorporated as a mental image."[10] Depending on the individual, that object can be a person, a group, a system, a political party, an ideology, or an ideal. Identity along with loyalty and patriotism are powerful forces that enable (in the broad sense of the word) enduring commitment to a person, a cause, or a country, even in the face of great challenges to that belief. The life stories chronicled in this chapter offer a variety of ways in which individuals interpreted their experience of Party allegiance, and how their victimization affected it. The common outcome of their life story was an enduring support of the Party despite their personal hardships. Their accounts explain how they arrived at this conclusion.

Thus far we have viewed the loyalists' commitment to Communism as largely a faith-based belief and considered how this belief influenced victims' assessments of the culpability assigned to them. This chapter will look more closely into the narrative explanations of how loyalty developed and how Communist identity was maintained among better known as well as ordinary returnees. Additionally, the effect of the war on loyalist inmates and returnees will be examined. Approaching this question from the perspective of identity combines the survivors' psychological coping mechanisms with the triumphal coping mechanism of "mother Russia" during the war, where self-image often merged with national image. On the whole, the convictions of true believers endured the challenges of the Gulag and prevailed for decades. The following narratives attempt to explain how this was possible.

LOYALTY

So far the term "loyalty" has been used as a rather generic description of commitment to the Party. However, a 1952 Harvard study introduced useful nuances. The categorizations it identified on motivation for loyalty are different from but related to those already outlined in chapter 1. In the course of this pioneering investigation, researchers looked at what the stories of Soviet refugees revealed about the Soviet social system. They distinguished three types of loyalists: "the value-oriented idealist, the system-oriented conformist, and the self-interested careerist."[11] Though one orientation was usually dominant, some combination of these orientations could also be found in every individual.

Most of the cases investigated in the present research involve value-oriented idealists, because while many of these returnees largely dissociated themselves from the regime and leadership under Stalin, they were still strong supporters of the Party and even the system itself. Their support was sometimes grounded in their early history/identity with the Party, and it endured in spite of, or even *because of,* the hardships of the Gulag.

In a 1959 letter to Khrushchev published in *Pravda,* one woman wrote: "We do not have 8,366,000 Communists. This is not an entirely accurate count. We have immeasurably more Communists, because there are many who 'carry the Party membership card not in the pocket but in themselves.'"[12] She hastened to explain that she was not a Party member because on the eve of her planned entrance, her father was arrested. She thanked the Party for his posthumous rehabilitation. As noted earlier, Stephen Kotkin has convincingly argued that belief was essentially not all that relevant if people knew—or had internalized—how they were supposed to act, or what they were supposed to say. In that vein it is not surprising that many of the published, or publicly professed, statements "spoke Bolshevik." While we may assume that when such letters were published in *Pravda* they had been selected to boost the Party, similar sentiments could also be found in the less public domain of memoirs and correspondence.[13]

In case citizens wondered how to frame the Gulag experience, solutions were readily provided. A "heroic past" and a "bright future" were useful constructs that allowed the faithful to ignore feelings of betrayal, circumvent issues of culpability, and maintain their identification with the Party. After all, they were taking part in something "extraordinary," much larger than themselves. Those who were willing could adopt the official line, which was widely disseminated. For example, in a play from the early sixties, witness the prescription for attitude writ into the remark of a young woman when asked how she felt about the Soviet government and the Party in view of all she had come to learn about the repressions. Without hesitation, she replied: "I did not apply for dismissal from the Komsomol. Why are you asking me this question? Even people who carry the weight of all of these horrors did not lose faith in the Party! How could I possibly do so, now that the truth has triumphed, and all the innocent people have been freed."[14]

This redemptive affirmation was propagated throughout the channels of public discourse, especially political discourse. A March 1956 report from the Leningrad Provincial Committee of the CPSU describes the "unanimous approval" by its members of the Secret Speech in which Khrushchev provided a Party-preserving way to interpret the Stalinist past. While open dissent was hardly a viable option, the authentic enthusiasm that pervaded the majority of official proceedings suggested a combination of relief from the old, approval for the new, and the promise of stability going forward. The report notes two points in Khrushchev's assessment of Stalin that generated applause—his description of Lenin's stance on the cult of personality and his emphasis on the "unconditional observance of norms of Party life and collective leadership." But the most fervid applause was in response to Khrushchev's description of Soviet economic and cultural successes and the victory in the Great Patriotic War. Finally, there was an extended round of applause when Khrushchev reported that those who had "innocently suffered in the so-called 'Leningrad affair' were now rehabilitated and the honor of the glorious Leningrad Party organization was restored."[15]

One Cherniak, however, a delegate who had also attended the Seventeenth Party Congress and subsequently spent seventeen years in prison, sounded a more critical note. She was disappointed that Khrushchev had not addressed a number of other important issues—for example, the pervasive anti-Semitism, which Lenin firmly opposed. She recommended that theoretical reports be written on the role of the individual in history, and on Marxism's views on this issue. In addition, Cherniak argued that the facts of what happened should be revealed. "Then there will be no distortions. That means everyone should read the report of N. S. Khrushchev!"[16] In conclusion, even those who raised questions largely endorsed his approach.

Still, while criticism was more tolerated in the public sphere, it could be an impediment to Party membership. One reinstatement application up for review was that of P. I. Gudzinskii, a Party member since 1919 and senior engineer at the Aviation Research Institute. In the course of the Commission's deliberations, it was reported that Gudzinskii had made "anti-Party statements" during a Party meeting devoted to discussion of the results of the Twentieth Party Congress. The Party Control Commission report records the following: "[Gudzinskii] slanderously maintained that in the course of thirty years the party and the country experienced a dismal period in the history of its development and this history was not judged at the Twentieth Party Congress, and the report on the cult of personality at the Twentieth Party Congress 'taught the Party nothing.'"[17] While no longer punishable by imprisonment, such criticism was discouraged in other ways. Gudzinskii's exclusion was upheld.

Blaming past political transgressions on the cult of personality required the Party to perform a delicate historical and political balancing act. On the one hand, it wanted to account for the repression as a consequence of Stalin's misappropriation of power; on the other, it did not want to be held accountable for permitting one man to appropriate so much power and participating in repression. In a June 1956 report on the Party's effort at "overcoming the cult of personality and its consequences," P. N. Pospelov, its principal writer, asserts that the cult of personality "without a doubt inflicted serious harm on the Communist Party and Soviet society, but it would be a grave mistake to draw any conclusions with regard to changes in the social structure of the USSR, or to look for the source of the cult in the nature of the Soviet system based on the existence of the cult of personality in the past. Either of these approaches would be absolutely wrong."[18] He further claimed that no cult of personality could change the nature of the socialist government, "which is based on the union of workers and peasants, and the friendship of the peoples."[19]

A focus on the cult of personality was a relatively safe strategy for relocating the repression to the past. This label, but not this stratagem, had been used three years earlier by Malenkov in discussing Stalin's legacy with a select group of elite Party members. During the discussion, Malenkov had criticized the Party for corrupting Marxism "by letting the cult of personality flourish."[20] In the ensuing three years the focus shifted away from the Party's role and responsibility. Stalin was a singular aberration, disconnected from the socialist system. This stratagem worked because those in power wanted the investigation of the repression to be limited to Stalin, and wanted to answer questions raised about the repression with "Stalinism." The cult of personality perspective was considered such a useful way of (not) dialoguing about the past that it was recommended for export to Chinese Communists. In 1967 one Old Bolshevik provided his Chinese comrades with both a diagnosis of their malady—the cult of Mao—and a prescription to cure the Party of Mao's legacy. He hoped that the Chinese people and the Chinese Communists would come to understand how harmful the Mao cult was to their cause. He hoped they would have the strength exhibited by Soviet Communists to "unveil and liquidate its consequences."[21]

In the ensuing years, as Leonid Brezhnev amassed more and more Hero medals and Victory orders,[22] the CPSU proudly proclaimed its success in overcoming the cult of personality. In conformance with a Politburo resolution of September 1979, *Pravda*'s lead article in its December 21 issue was devoted to the hundredth anniversary of Stalin's birth. It provided an assessment of his accomplishments and failings, underscoring the assertion that the Party had judged Stalin and quickly overcome the cult of personality and its consequences. A further attempt at distancing was the claim that "the cult could not change the nature of the socialist system, or turn the Soviet people away from the road to socialism."[23]

This stratagem was readily accepted by those who wanted (needed) it to work. Olga Andreevna Slavianina-Olbinskaia, an Old Bolshevik, was arrested in 1937 as the wife of an "enemy of the people." She spent seven years in the Ufa prison and Temnikov correctional camp. Her husband was executed in 1939 at the age of forty. In her memoir, written between the 1960s and the mid-eighties, she provides this assessment of the Stalin era:

The cult of personality of Stalin was created not by the people, but by Stalin and his lackeys. . . . Though the Soviet people lived in forced silence, they never lost faith in tomorrow. That's why the whole Soviet people rejoiced when it was told the truth about Stalin and his abuse of power. The Leninist Central Committee of our Party has been restored to Leninist principles of Party life and Soviet governance. And the truth, expressed straightforwardly and decisively, helps us to correctly orient ourselves in our assessment of the past.[24]

Slavianina was eventually rehabilitated and reinstated in the Party, and she proceeded to work for the Party. In concluding her memoir, she notes with satisfaction that she had fulfilled her obligation to her husband, to the Communists who suffered and died with him, and to their wives, "who all believed without a doubt until the very end in the sacredness of Lenin's idea and the ultimate victory of justice."[25] For her, as for the Party, the repression had been compartmentalized: it was not the Party's fault. The cult of personality—an abrogation of Party policies—was to blame, and all of that was now relegated to the past.

WHAT EXCLUSION AND REINSTATEMENT MEANT

With the Party now clearly separated from the past bad leadership, thousands of applications for reinstatement poured in.[26] The stories shared common themes, but each was individual. Successful applicants were overjoyed by acceptance into the Communist community. Such a reaction to an approved application was epitomized by one case reported in a memorandum by A. B. Aristov to the Central Committee. The applicant was Bakhish Mekhtiev, a former lieutenant colonel in the Soviet Army. During the war, while Mekhtiev was in command of a rifle regiment, he was wounded three times and sustained other injuries. For his role in the defense of Stalingrad, he was awarded fourteen medals. Subsequently Mekhtiev took part in the Victory Parade in Moscow. However, his status as a hero was short-lived. Allegedly Mekhtiev confided to friends that Zhukov and not "the other one" deserved the title Generalissimo. In 1947 voicing such an opinion warranted a ten-year prison term for anti-Soviet agitation. Two years later additional charges of treason were brought against Mekhtiev, and his term was increased to twenty-five years. When the commission informed this returnee that he had been approved for rehabilitation (and presumably reinstatement), according to Aristov, "he took a long time to collect himself, sobbed like a baby and vowed that he had never in his life had any bad thoughts about the Soviet regime and his beloved Party, that he was branded an 'enemy' by the real enemies in Beria's gang, and he requested that his sincere gratitude be conveyed to the government and Central Committee of the Party for their just decision."[27]

As also noted in chapter 1, the moment of Party reinstatement became one of the epic moments of a returnee's life. Some were dumbfounded—literally speechless, upon hearing the news of a positive decision. Others could only weep. Moisei Aronovich Panich had struggled long and hard and vainly for reinstatement. In 1962, he was called to the Bureau of the Provincial Party Committee, and expected to be re-questioned about his past, his present, and his *partiinost'*. Instead the provincial Party secretary simply proposed that Panich, "who had lost his Party membership in 1938 as a result of the cult of personality and was subsequently rehabilitated," should be reinstated. The secretary then asked if there were any objections from Committee members to the approval of this applicant. There were none. In Panich's words: "All of this excited me greatly. I stood up, wanted to say something about the victory of the Leninist Truth over the arbitrariness of Stalin's times, etc. But tears started streaming down my face, my throat closed, and I couldn't utter anything. No one asked me any questions."[28]

Grigorii Ivanovich Chebanov was incarcerated from 1939 to 1954 and spent ten of those years doing hard labor in Kolyma. Chebanov's wife was sentenced to fifteen years, but her term was reduced to eight for health reasons—a rare exception. While in camp, Chebanov secretly kept a diary, scribbling notes on cigarette papers and sewing them into his coat collar. He wanted to be sure he would accurately chronicle his experiences in the camps, so he could reveal them to others after liberation. His memoir details mistreatment, cruelty, torture, and daily human misery of the camp. In addition to the standard grueling conditions of Kolyma, Chebanov was placed in a *kartser* (punishment cell) for twenty-two days. In the course of his years of internment, Chebanov lost 40 percent of his hearing and seven teeth. He did not, however, lose his faith in or identification with the Party. One determinant of his enduring allegiance to Communism can be found in his strong Bolshevik credentials, including his armed defense of the cause in the Civil War. In 1952, at age sixty, he wrote to Stalin from camp. He complained about the false charges, for which he had already served thirteen years; he also expressed his fear that he would die without seeing his loved ones, but most of all, he stressed that he did not want to die in disgrace with the Party.[29]

It was Stalin's death, rather than Stalin, that helped Chebanov. In the post-Stalin climate of reform, Chebanov was released within a year. He received judicial rehabilitation in 1956 and Party rehabilitation in 1959. The years of deprivation did not undermine his loyalty to the Party. While awaiting approval for reinstatement Chebanov was apprehensive: "I could not imagine spending the rest of my days outside of the Communist Party."[30] He experienced "utter joy" when Party Card number 0851496 was handed to him on June 28, 1959.

Party reinstatement not only required determination to get through the process on the part of the applicant, but that determination was also subject to measurement. As with so many other government operations, acceptance or rejection of an application was dependent on the whims of particular officials at particular times. Witness the following cautionary tale. Orest Ivanovich Shamaev was a senior lieutenant in the Red Army when he was wounded in action and taken captive in 1943. He went through transit prisons in Stalino, Zaporozhe, and Kirovograd in Ukraine, then through Chenstokhov in Poland, ending up in a stone quarry in the Alps, not far from the Austrian city of Bad-Ishl. After liberation by the Americans in May of 1945, Shamaev was repatriated to Russia, where he was arrested for counterintelligence crimes and incarcerated in a transit camp. There he was subjected to a grueling interrogation from June until August 1945. Exhausted, demoralized, and weakened by torture, Shamaev finally signed the interrogation protocol.

In a fifteen-minute trial in August of 1945, he was accused and convicted of economic espionage that entailed divulging state secrets on the location of strategic bases in the Soviet Union. These crimes fell under a sub-point of Article 58 ("counterrevolutionary crimes"). However, the authorities claimed that they were showing leniency because of his youth, sincere repentance, and service to the motherland. They sentenced Shamaev to ten years of correctional labor camp and three years of deprivation of rights.

After serving nine years in Perm, Shamaev was released in 1954 in the aftermath of Stalin's death and Beria's execution. In 1958 he was rehabilitated, his former military rank of senior lieutenant was restored, and his POW and Gulag prison terms were counted as service to the armed forces of the Soviet Union. However, none of this entitled Shamaev to automatic Party reinstatement. When he applied, the chairman of the Party commission charged with preparing materials for the Bureau proposed the following: "To the extent that comrade Shamaev did not apply for Party reinstatement immediately upon release, but more than three years later, he transgressed the term stipulated by the Charter of the CPSU."[31] Protocol, whim, and legality dictated that he was not only required to apply anew, but his special privileges and Party tenure (i.e., credit for his years of membership) were voided. He had no opportunity to protest. Shamaev felt so crushed by this decision of a Party to which he still owed allegiance that it "inflicted a heavier psychological and moral trauma than did the illegal repression that I had endured." In later years, when the shock of this rejection had passed, he considered returning to the Party but did not think he was any longer capable of active political Party work. In the Gorbachev era Shamaev apparently changed his mind. In a 1988 Memorial questionnaire, when asked what kind of assistance he required, Shamaev requested help—"if it was not too late"—with Party reinstatement.[32] Now, forty-three years after his false arrest, torture, and imprisonment, he still longed for Party membership.

Exclusion from the Party and the long, uncertain struggle for reinstatement were recollected by some survivors as more consequential than their incarceration. One memoirist, Mariia Moiseevna Goldberg, described her experience of Party exclusion as excruciating.[33] Another returnee with similar sentiments characterized her exclusion as "political death" and wondered whether staying physically alive even made sense.[34] In 1938 Goldberg had been charged as a "family member of a traitor to the motherland" and sentenced to an eight-year prison term. Years later, Goldberg writes that she still wonders why she did not "go mad" from the whole experience. Quite the contrary, despite her circumstances, she maintained her sense of dignity. The strength she drew from her hardship is epitomized in a poem about Communists written by one Tikhonov: "You could make nails out of these people, but there wouldn't be a nail in the world that was stronger."[35]

As loyal Communists, Goldberg and her fellow campmates in Akmolinsk had to reconcile a special set of issues. They all agreed that nothing was more sacred to them than their socialist motherland and the Leninist Party,[36] but they found themselves convicted by the system for crimes that neither they nor their husbands had committed. In time, they concluded that it was an illusion to think that Stalin was ignorant of the Gulag, and in blaming Stalin, they themselves were apparently able to resolve the paradoxes that confronted their belief system. But how could they explain their imprisonment to their children, who had been raised to believe in the Party and to be good Soviet citizens? Now, many of their children had been dispatched to orphanages and been given different surnames because their parents were "enemies of the people." The potential crisis in belief for their children was harder to remedy. They had been raised to believe their parents, but they also believed the Soviet state. Goldberg concluded that the only way of rationalizing this dilemma was to fall back on the adage: "When you cut wood, chips fly."

Goldberg had been released in 1945 and was not rearrested, as were so many of her peers. Still, prior to Khrushchev's reforms, she lived in continual fear that it would soon be her turn. Even as that fear subsided, Goldberg remained uneasy about her spoiled social identity and her non-Party status. This was mitigated, however, even prior to her rehabilitation, because she had the good fortune of being reintegrated into her group "without the shadow of suspicion." Goldberg recalled her relief at the effortless meetings with Komsomol and Party friends and comrades, who blamed neither her nor the Party, because "apparently they viewed me as one of the chips that flew when the wood was being cut. To my Party comrades I had remained a Communist, who had experienced a great misfortune that did not get the better of me."[37]

Goldberg felt validated by their acceptance of her and their willingness to let her reincorporate herself into their world. For her, and for many returnees, the Party was the only world in which she had ever found meaning—or ever would. Like other loyalist returnees, she attempted to blend back into the Party, combining her personal story with the authorized Party story so that her own authentic narrative authenticated the Party line. Once restored to the political and social acceptance of her comrades, Goldberg and other survivors reframed the physical hardships of the Gulag as an unfortunate chapter in the history of the Party. Incorporating the Party's official story of itself into their personal story of themselves minimized cognitive dissonance and completed the work of the repression. When the survivor's story is a reinforcing version of the Party's story, then the Party need not censor a description of the hardships of the Gulag—so long as it controls its meaning.

YOUTHFUL IDEALS

"My dream of a better life in my early youth led me to the Party," explained Mariia Karlovna Sandratskaia.[38] She was "proud and happy to take part in realizing its ideals."[39] In May of 1937, her husband Vasilii Ivanovich Gorb, a military man, was falsely charged and arrested for "counterrevolutionary, Trotskyite, diversionary, and espionage activities, and attempting to assassinate Voroshilov." At the time of her husband's arrest, Mariia was pregnant with their fourth child. The baby was born in August—the same month in which its father was executed. In October of that year Sandratskaia was arrested as the wife of an "enemy of the people." Along with her nursing infant, she was sentenced to eight years in a special women's camp. As was the custom, her older children were sent off to orphanages or juvenile detention centers. One of them was so severely beaten by the other children that he lost his hearing in one ear. Sandratskaia was released in 1947, and in 1955 she wrote that the Party restored "the good names of the true fighters for Communism who died in 1937, felled as victims of the repression of the period of the personality cult of Stalin." Gorb's case was one of the privileged few to be examined prior to the Twentieth Party Congress. He was posthumously exonerated, and subsequently Sandratskaia was rehabilitated and reinstated. She exulted: "And so after eighteen years of expulsion I was returned to life."[40]

There is no more compelling explanation for her devotion than the one she offered. From the beginning to the present, the Party was her life. It taught her to live and work, and to "be actively involved in the realization of the precepts of Vladimir Ilich Lenin." When her children and grandchildren reproached her, as a Communist, for failing to prevent the tragedy that befell them, she explained that they believed in Stalin at the time. She no longer believed in Stalin, but her belief in the Party endured. She insisted that her only remaining desire was to live the rest of her life in a way that would be "necessary and helpful to the Party and the country."[41] Sandratskaia claimed that she experienced "an inextinguishable love for life, and an undying feeling of faithfulness and devotion to the Party and the country."[42]

Another returnee, whose husband was executed in 1937 while she herself was shipped off to Tashkent, fondly recalled their activities in the Communist Youth League (Komsomol). Her sentiments captured those of a generation: "We both dreamed of quickly building socialism, considering Party and state affairs more important than family and personal matters. We were prepared to go to Kolyma to take part in the developing of this far rim."[43] Most ended up doing just that. Apparently it was indeed a task for which they were prepared, as attested to by their survival and that which survived in them.

The Party's appeal in the 1920s was sometimes contagious. The Italian ex-Communist Ignazio Silone explained it thus: "The spectacle of the enthusiasm of Russian youth in these first years of the creation of a new world, which we all hoped would be more humane than the old one, was utterly convincing."[44] Ultimately disillusioned, Silone left the Party but recalled the day he did so as having been "a sad one, it was like a day of deep mourning, the mourning for my lost youth."[45] Still others hoped to regain what they lost through Party reinstatement.

Aleksandr Ivanovich Milchakov

For many young people the 1920s was a heady era, because the Party embodied their youthful idealism and aspirations for forging a new society. The story of one of the better known returnees, Aleksandr Ivanovich Milchakov, who personified youthful devotion to the cause, is informative. In the 1920s, Milchakov had served as General Secretary to the Central Committee of the Young Communist League. He gradually rose in the Party hierarchy, and in 1937 Milchakov headed the chief directorate of gold for the People's Commissariat of Heavy Industry. By then, however, friends, neighbors, and colleagues began to disappear. Milchakov was the sole former first secretary of the Central Committee of the Komsomol to still be free.[46] That was not to last. The next year, in December of 1938, on Stalin's birthday, he was arrested. His memoir does not state the charges, but they were apparently tied into his work in the Commissariat.

In 1939, Milchakov was sentenced to fifteen years of imprisonment and five years of deprivation of rights. Together with twenty other prisoners he was sentenced to labor in Norilsk. However, the authorities apparently had a much harsher sentence in mind. Not long after their arrival Milchakov and his campmates were led to a location eighteen kilometers outside of the city to be executed. There the doomed men agonizingly awaited their fate for the next two weeks. Then, unexpectedly, A. P. Zaveniagin, the head of the Norilsk construction site, spared their lives, returned them to Norilsk, and compelled them to dig foundation pits under a large metallurgical factory.[47] After ten years at hard labor, Milchakov was transferred to Magadan and placed in a penal camp with a strict regime. He survived that terror too.

In 1954, after fifteen and a half years in the Gulag, Milchakov was released. One of his former campmates, Evgeniia Ginzburg, described—both derisively and with some admiration—the simple and effective attitude that permitted Milchakov to resume, in 1954, the idealism that had been interrupted in 1937: "He had knotted the two ends together securely, joined up '37 and '54 and thrown away everything in between."[48] Milchakov was one of the very few returnees who were able to attain judicial rehabilitation during this period of "silent de-Stalinization."[49] As soon as possible he returned to Moscow and to the Party fold. Neither the threat of execution nor the years of grueling labor under inhumane conditions had alienated Milchakov from the Party. The Order of Lenin, which had been bestowed on Milchakov prior to the repression, was apparently well deserved, although it did not spare him from imprisonment. Speaking for many, one of his comrades described the enduring zeal that Lenin had inspired. They had all "connected their fate with the Bolshevik Party in the early years of the Revolution. The first Komsomols tried to work, live, study, and fight as genuine Communists, in ways that Lenin would approve."[50] They had been taught that if they wanted to become Leninists, they had to learn to serve the cause of liberating the workers, the cause of Communism.[51] They had to understand that their personal lives were not separate from their public lives.[52] Their duty was to serve the cause. As soon as he arrived in Moscow Milchakov applied for reinstatement, and it was granted. When the Order of Lenin, of which Milchakov had been stripped, was returned to him by Voroshilov, the chairman of the Presidium of the Supreme Soviet reportedly shed a tear (of joy) when he signed off on it, because it was only at that moment that he found out Milchakov was still alive. Such was the arbitrariness of the repression that someone as celebrated as Milchakov could disappear, and someone as powerful as Voroshilov would be ignorant of his fate.

In February of 1956 the Kremlin was abuzz with rumors of impending de-Stalinization, and deputy premier Anastas Mikoyan invited Milchakov to come meet with him there. Mikoyan told him that he had spoken with Khrushchev about Milchakov's return, and asked if he needed anything. He responded that he did not: "My Party card was returned, my decoration was returned, I was given an apartment, medical treatment. . . ."[53] This modest response reflected the priorities of a true Party man. However, beyond granting him reinstatement and rehabilitation, Mikoyan had a prestigious invitation to offer.

Early in their discussion, Milchakov raised issues of political concern. He inquired as to whether Lenin's testament would be read at the Twentieth Party Congress. This turned out to be more contentious than Milchakov had anticipated and attested to both his idealism and political naivete with regard to the surviving entrenched Stalinists in the Party. Mikoyan informed Milchakov that Khrushchev had considered reading the testament, but the safe in which it was kept could only be opened by unanimous decision of the Central Committee. This was problematic, he explained, because many of those who would attend the Congress had been educated and promoted through the ranks under Stalin; most of the Leninist cadres had been destroyed. This explanation was not convincing to Milchakov. He asserted that there could be no movement forward without a discussion that addressed the arbitrariness of Stalin's reign, and how it violated Lenin's principles. He further argued that it was necessary to "restore trust in the government." This assertion apparently went beyond the safe limits of the discussion. Mikoyan excitedly retorted: "Don't the masses trust us?" Milchakov, realizing that he had not been sufficiently cautious, shifted his approach by suggesting that such a discussion would serve to "strengthen trust in the government."[54]

Their ensuing exchange illustrated the core belief that sustained many survivors: Leninism was pure, Stalinism was a corrupt aberration, and we continue our struggle to achieve Lenin's vision. Mikoyan outlined his strategy for "liquidating the consequences of arbitrariness and repression." He told Milchakov about the commissions that would be traveling to the camps to expedite the process of rehabilitation.[55] Each was to have one "rehabilitated comrade" in its ranks, and he invited Milchakov to take part in a commission. Milchakov was apprehensive about accepting this honor. He feared that those oppositional Stalinists, about whom Mikoyan had warned him, might interfere with their work. "They may disturb the rapid restoration of Leninist norms in the life of the Party and government."[56] Mikoyan assured him that such resistance would be overcome, because they had already removed a number of generals and colonels from the MGB and MVD who had supported Beria. Mikoyan's promise and Milchakov's apprehensions were both realized by ensuing events. The commissions did fulfill their task of freeing prisoners, but they often did so within the framework of a "forgiving Stalinism" rather than an affirming Leninism. The commissions acted as if they were granting conditional pardons for crimes that had actually been committed.[57]

Milchakov attended the Twentieth Party Congress in eager anticipation of witnessing the necessary political change, but he was unpleasantly surprised at the changes in the attendees. There were very few familiar faces—only Shatunovskaia, Snegov, and a few others had survived. On the eve of the last day of the Congress (when the Secret Speech was about to be read), Milchakov suffered a heart attack that prevented his attendance. But afterwards, Snegov brought him a copy of the speech. As he recalled, "I read, I was excited, and I was overjoyed at the triumph of justice and the discrediting of unheard-of malice."[58]

Subsequently Milchakov was unable to continue his official activities, but he continued his political mission by authoring a memoir about the first decade of the Komsomol, "to fulfill his Party duty to the memory of the many who died in the years of Stalinist tyranny."[59] In it he described his satisfaction that, by the early sixties, the Party had exposed and punished Beria's "criminal band," but also his disappointment that other accomplices of Stalin, such as Yezhov, Beria, and Kaganovich had not been properly judged.[60] Absent from his accusations were the names Khrushchev, Voroshilov, Mikoyan and others, who had blood on their hands and feet. Milchakov apparently accepted—or adapted to—the post–Twentieth Party Congress political narrative and he praised the delegates of the Twenty-second Party Congress for demanding the expulsion of Kaganovich from the Party.

Milchakov titled his memoir *Bright and Tragic Youth,* an apt description of the unfulfilled and yet fulfilling aspirations of his generation. The book was published in 1988, under Gorbachev—at a time when the "glory" of those days was regularly revisited. Such attempts at restoring sufficient belief in socialism to strengthen the Soviet system were ultimately unsuccessful (see chapter 4).

INSIDERS' DELIBERATIONS ON THE OLD AND THE NEW

Many loyal Communists believed that individual human suffering was justified if it furthered progress toward achieving the goals of Communism. Consequently, returnees who had participated in the work of the Party in its formative years were not only constrained in their judgment of the system, but some were even reserved in their judgment of Stalin. Writing in 1966, V. N. Lazarev provided an ambiguous explanation and an ambivalent assessment of Stalin:

In the world there is a constant struggle of the new against the old. Stalin decided to become the midwife to receive the birth of the new. I do not want to judge if Stalin was right or wrong. I am certain and fully expect that in time the Party Central Committee and historians will have their say in this. I don't judge Stalin, who fought for something new and saw this struggle as necessary, but I do judge his insolence and coarseness in carrying out these measures.[61]

As both an ex-official and an ex-prisoner, Lazarev saw the terror from both sides. An early believer in the cause, Lazarev joined the Party in November of 1917. In 1930 he was given "certain assignments" to round up people and send them to Central Asia. He claimed to have been "troubled" about doing this, but did it anyway.[62] During the several years in which he served as secretary of a cell of the apparat of the Central Committee, he occupied an apartment in the elite House on the Embankment in Moscow. He was accorded the honor of being elected by the deputies of the Kzol-Ordinsk district to attend the first session of the Supreme Soviet of the USSR in December of 1937. By then, virtually the entire leadership in Kazakhstan had been "renewed," leaving Lazarev as the only one still free, but not for long. He was soon called in for interrogation, and when told to hand over his Party card, he later disclosed, "I was ready to kill myself."[63]

Lazarev's interrogation lasted all night, and additional pressure was applied by arresting his wife for "knowing that her husband was an enemy and withholding that information."[64] Like thousands before and after him, Lazarev signed the requisite confession, and then spent the next year in a Moscow prison. At the end of 1939 he was sent off to Tashkent, and subsequently to various other points of the Gulag where he spent time in an isolation cell, had to build his own barracks, and was forced to harvest timber. In his memoir, Lazarev complained less about his forced labor than about his indignation—apparently unaware of the irony— of serving in the labor brigade under a kulak. Lazarev attempted to call Stalin's attention to this inequity by sending him the following letter: "When I was working locally in the Party central committee, I fought honestly and with all my might against kulaks, and now I have been given a kulak just to mock me."[65] The letter went unanswered, and surely unread. But since the "kulak" had been incarcerated on the same kind of trumped-up charges as this Party man, what could Stalin have said anyway?

In 1946 Lazarev was released, and after negotiating the complicated bureaucratic process of reentry, he was able to register to live in Kazan. He even found a (low-level) job, but he was rearrested in the terror wave of 1949 and sent back into the system—first to Krasnoiarsk, and later to the Arctic. This time around

Lazarev contracted tuberculosis and was admitted to a prison hospital. The illness provided a certain benefit, because hospitalization often contributed to prisoner survival. After a year Lazarev was released with limited rights. His place of residence was largely determined by the authorities until 1954, when he was called into the MVD and issued a passport. In November of 1955, Lazarev was granted rehabilitation and immediately contacted the Central Committee to apply for Party reinstatement. He and a group of others from Kazakhstan were reinstated and "personal pensions" (extra privileges) were even arranged for them. Housing at that time remained quite scarce, and returnees were very low on priority lists.[66] Lazarev wrote to Khrushchev requesting help in obtaining an apartment in Kazan. The letter brought results. Within a couple of days he received a call from an official asking on which floor he wished to live.

Lazarev was able to maintain his allegiance by selective attention to his personal history and selective editing of the Party's. Reflecting on the good and evil, right and wrong, done in the name of the Party and whether all of the sacrifice of so many was ultimately redemptive, Lazarev maintained that he never thought that Stalin had been misled by Yezhov and Beria, nor did he think that Stalin behaved with malicious intent.[67] Rather, Stalin was sincerely engaged in building a new society. To bolster his assessment, Lazarev drew on Lenin's belief in breaking down the old. The Bolshevik leader had also maintained that it would not always be necessary to destroy, it was also necessary to create.[68] Notwithstanding the question of how much destruction was "necessary," for Lazarev and a host of other loyalists, the ends justified the means.

Chekists, NKVDers, and Party Identity

Suren Gazarian considered himself an "honest Communist" who started his career in 1921 working in Tiflis as a "proud chekist in Dzerzhinskii's iron guard of the Revolution."[69] He was arrested in 1937, accused of plotting and espionage of the NKVD apparatus. Despite being subjected to severe torture during interrogation, Gazarian refused to sign anything.[70] Even so, he was sentenced to ten years of incarceration. He was released in 1947. Throughout his life, Gazarian struggled to reconcile his conflict between Party loyalty and justice, a dilemma vividly portrayed in his 1961 memoir. As a loyal Communist he felt obligated to obey Party orders, but when his NKVD colleagues obeyed their orders to arrest him, he felt betrayed. Beria was the chief target of his anger because Gazarian believed that he, along with a "band of criminals," had usurped power.

Gazarian spent a good deal of time during his ten years of incarceration trying to come to terms with his feelings toward the Party. On the one hand, maintaining his innocence, he wanted to return, and to return to a privileged position, and that could only be done through the Party. On the other, the torture he had endured and witnessed in the Gulag turned him against Beria, Stalin, and the coercive apparatus of the NKVD, of which he was once a part. Like many former prisoners, Gazarian returned a broken man, but it was his spirit, not his health, that had been broken. He suffered the anguish of trying to reconcile his deeply felt allegiance to the Party with what he felt the Party had become. Gazarian reconciled this conflict by embracing both Khrushchev's attack on Stalin and his glorification of Leninist traditions. After their release, Gazarian and a number of his peers, who had persecuted "enemies of the people" before their own arrests,[71] were now willing to forgive both them and themselves. By so doing they hoped to restore their self-esteem, as well as their elite social privileges.[72]

Gazarian describes his relief, when he was restored to the status of a "full-fledged Communist," that he was finally back in society.[73] Still, his memoir reflects his uneasiness with the Stalinists who remained in the KGB. He had known these people well in the 1930s and was apprehensive about their influence, although some had led the de-Stalinization campaign. In the absence of judicial or other proceedings, such concerns were to preoccupy the next two generations. For now, however, Khrushchev's approach had earned Gazarian's gratitude and support.[74]

Many NKVDers loudly proclaimed and probably sincerely experienced Party loyalty. A review of the 1955 appeal to the Presidium of the Supreme Soviet by G. Zhukov, a twenty-seven-year Party veteran, will be useful to our understanding of Party identity. Unlike the other subjects of this study, Zhukov was not a Gulag returnee. Rather he was appealing the revocation of his Party card on charges that he had allowed abuses by fellow NKVD agents in 1937 and 1938. After twenty-five years of service in the "organs," Zhukov had been fired from the KGB in October of 1954, briefly arrested and detained, and in November was stripped of his military rank of General-lieutenant. He found this deprivation acceptable, but the deprivation that was "equal to physical death" was the Party Control Commission's revocation of his membership. Zhukov could not "imagine [himself] outside of its ranks."[75] In his defense, he claimed to have acted properly by administratively reprimanding four colleagues for falsifying evidence and employing illegal methods of investigation. He had even sent one to court.

Zhukov also claimed that any efforts to rein in his subordinates should be overlooked because it would be naive to think that anyone could have done more in those days.[76] Still, he admitted that he should take responsibility for his mistakes and accept a Party penalty. After all, he contended, "the Soviet authorities do not have vengeance as a goal. They even correct hard-core criminals. There is a reason why they pronounced two broad amnesties after the war."[77] Zhukov argued that his mistakes and crimes were logical consequences of the circumstances that prevailed at that time. He pleaded for a reconsideration of his case because the most valuable thing in the world had been taken from him—"the right to call myself a member of the Party, which I love like my own mother."[78] (The correspondence in the case file stops there. It is likely that Zhukov's exclusion was upheld, given the prevailing political shift toward de-Stalinization at the time.)

Many of those who had served the Party by working in and for the Gulag justified both the need for the Gulag and the appropriateness of its treatment of the prisoners. Some Party members never admitted that mistakes had been made. One such was an (anonymous) official who had been employed by the Gulag for fifteen years in Siberia, the Urals, and on the Volga. He presented his point of view in an anonymous letter sent to the Party Central Committee in March of 1964. In it he criticized the influential poet Tvardovskii's praise of Solzhenitsyn's *One Day in the Life of Ivan Denisovich.* He hoped that his critique would be included in the deliberations regarding whether this work deserved the Lenin Prize. He claimed that, as a rule, the camps were filled with real enemies of the Soviet authorities—traitors, bandits, and other criminals. He wondered where these miscreants were to be found in Solzhenitsyn's book. He also described how the Party and MVD organs had given such "serious attention" to the selection of staff in the camps. He wrote that "for these places they tried to find the best workers from the Komsomol, members of the CPSU, and non-Party members, many of whom had been worthy participants in the Great Patriotic War."[79] However, he did allow that there may have been some isolated cases in which the camp staff was not up to the high demands and may have permitted some heavy-handedness.

The official then undertook a point-by-point refutation of Solzhenitsyn's characterization of particular people, places, prison terms, prison tasks, and so forth. He insisted, for example, that prisoners were never sent out to work in temperatures below minus 40 degrees (centigrade), for fear that they could get frostbite. He also maintained that lockups of more than 3–5 days in the kartser were virtually unheard-of. Moreover, he hastened to add, the regular inspections by the Gulag and NKVD supervisors, and even the Procuracy, assured that arbitrariness did not take place. The letter-writer also argued that the staff—especially those stationed in the inhospitable Arctic climate—deserved special appreciation because they and their families had to live and work in the same places as the prisoners: "They put their labor into the implementation of serious tasks for the Party and the state such as the construction of highly important industrial and defense objects, about which the story writes nothing. Quite the contrary, almost all of the camp staff is portrayed as 'parasites, boneheads, beasts, and bribe-takers,' while the prisoners are characterized only from a positive perspective."[80] The author identified himself as "a member of the CPSU." We discern in this official's narrative the two self-preservative themes found in the prisoners' personal "survival narratives"—"I/we are honorable" and "I/we have acted properly." For some, loyalty and Party identity meant not seeing or perceiving that mistakes had been made.

Lev Kopelev and Raisa Orlova

"We believed that the cult of personality was an illness that could be cured by restoring health to a socialist society," explained Raisa Orlova, dissident and wife of returnee/dissident Lev Kopelev.[81] Like many others, their devotion to Communism inspired them to work within the system to improve it. Like some others, also, they found their ideals increasingly discordant with those of the Party. Kopelev's political history has been fairly well publicized, so this study will not elaborate at great length on his case. His biography is, however, particularly noteworthy in our context, because he remains one of the best-known instances of a profound identification crisis with the Party. Kopelev had been a Party propagandist in the thirties and participated in the "heroic tragedy" of collectivization. He explained his justification at the time as follows: "We were raised as the fanatical adepts of a new creed, the only true *religion* of scientific socialism. The Party became our church militant, bequeathing to all mankind eternal salvation, eternal peace, and the bliss of an earthly paradise."[82] Kopelev maintained that the Party was always right, and its ends justified its means. Accordingly, he did not mind propagandizing the confiscation of bread from starving peasants because "instead of fate, as in the days of antiquity, historical necessity ruled and [he] believed in it unconditionally."[83] Decades later he bitterly recollected his participation in this murderous campaign and lamented that no "victories" or "mitigating circumstances" or "intellectual emotional factors . . . be they explained or predetermined by sociohistorical objectivity"[84] could exonerate him.

Kopelev had joined the Red Army in 1941, and by 1945 he was serving in East Prussia as a major in a propaganda unit with the frontline troops when he was arrested. He was accused of lack of vigilance, insubordination, and leniency in his dealings with the German population in the early stages of the Russian occupation. His superiors were especially distressed by his criticism of the atrocities committed by Soviet troops as they raped and pillaged their way through occupied towns. By the next year he was exonerated, but shortly thereafter his case was reconsidered, and this time Kopelev was sentenced to ten years of imprisonment and five years of deprivation of civil rights.[85] Nevertheless, his incarceration did not undermine his faith in the Party. Following his release in 1954, Kopelev sought rehabilitation and reinstatement in the Party and obtained them in 1956.

Throughout this ordeal, Kopelev and his postwar wife Raisa remained convinced that the Party provided the right—and only—horizontal and vertical framework within which to move forward. They applauded the Twentieth and Twenty-second Party Congresses for allowing the release of millions of prisoners and lifting restrictions on censored literature. They were certain that the Party's shift away from Stalinism was irreversible, so that they could work within the Party to affect change.[86] However, the persecution of poet Joseph Brodsky in 1964 and the trial and incarceration of Andrei Siniavskii and Iulii Daniel in 1965, together with other instances of re-Stalinization, caused them to reconsider their Party allegiance.

Kopelev and Orlova could reconcile neither with the renewed repression nor with the increasing reversal of de-Stalinization. The Party, in its turn, could not accept their outspokenness. By 1968, Kopelev was ousted from its ranks and fired from his job. He was expelled from the Writer's Union in 1977; three years later the Kopelevs were forced to emigrate to Germany, and then he was stripped of his Soviet citizenship. Thus ended an ideological journey, begun with youthful idealism, renewed by the hope that the Party had reformed when he reentered society in 1956, and now burdened by an enlightened disillusionment regarding the nature of the Party. In recounting his life, Kopelev deeply regretted the "ideological blinders" that predisposed him to favor the Party, even while in camp. He subsequently devoted himself to supporting those who campaigned for human rights. Such histories personalize questions regarding the origins of Party loyalty, its persistence in spite of the failure to deliver promised material and civil benefits, the limitations of loyalty, the tipping point that leads to disillusionment, and the consequences of renunciation.

Unlike Kopelev, some prisoners and returnees never wavered in their allegiance to the Party, neither upon arrest and incarceration, nor later during the camp and post-camp period. Indeed, committed believers interpreted their arrest and imprisonment, even on fraudulent charges, in a way that reinforced their commitment to Communism. These difficulties were viewed as a necessary and justified sacrifice. But such a view may sometimes have been influenced by the Party's employment of coercive psychological practices. From his studies of Chinese brainwashing, Robert Lifton eloquently argues that cognitive and emotional responses can be incorporated into people by forcing them to adapt to a controlled milieu, such as a prison, labor camp, or closed authoritarian society. The vital need to adapt to inescapable events can result in what Lifton describes as thought reform:

the "penetration by the psychological forces of the environment into the inner emotions of the individual person is perhaps the outstanding psychiatric fact of thought reform." This can shape one's "sense of inner identity" along with one's relationship to others.[87] Lifton illustrates this by recounting the experience of a student activist who had worked closely with the Communist Party, but had been arrested by the Kuomintang police and threatened with execution. Instead, he was imprisoned, but his dedication to Communism persisted. Indeed, it was reinforced by a similar dedication he found in his fellow prisoners. The student recalled: "We were there together and had no horror of death. We felt that we were being sacrificed for a great cause, that our deaths would have a purpose. . . . Some of us felt that we were so young and our greatest regret was that we could not do more work for China."[88] When this inspiring declaration is compared with that of Nathan Hale, the twenty-one-year-old American revolutionary hero who regretted that he had only one life to lose for his country,[89] it can appear more admirable than misguided. Hale and the Chinese student activist share the quintessentially human ability to transcend individual needs for a social cause. The triumph of social causes depends on such devotion, but their successful achievement of promised goals also depends on the critical monitoring of its devotees.

As attested to by the personal narratives of Gulag prisoners and survivors throughout this study, they likewise subscribed to the justification of means by the Party's ends. However, ideology aside, those who were forced to adapt to a closed, coercive system would find it expedient to strive for reinstatement in the Party. Even so, outward conformity need not reflect inward conformity, as illustrated by Aleksandr Aleksandrovich Baev, a molecular biologist who survived seventeen years in the Gulag by insulating himself "with a kind of autism."[90] As evidence of the success of this strategy, he rejoined the scientific world after release and advanced to a high position. Baev was hired at the Institute of Molecular Biology of the Academy of Sciences in 1959, became a corresponding member of the Academy in 1969, then an Akademik, and under Gorbachev Baev became advisor to the Presidium of the Academy.

IDENTIFICATION WITH THE PARTY: DISTINGUISHING BOLSHEVISM FROM STALINISM

Galina Serebriakova

Long tenure in the Party, especially if it began as youthful idealism, tended to be associated with an enduring commitment. However, such endurance required either making the distinction between the Party then and the Party now, a willingness to disregard the increasingly draconian methods adopted by the Party, or an acceptance of sacrifices of individual rights because they are justified by a just cause, even if it is a loved one who is sacrificed. Galina Serebriakova struggled to reconcile these issues. "We tried very hard to convince ourselves that those who were being arrested were apparently guilty, because the law enforcement authorities would not make mistakes," writes Serebriakova in her literary memoir *Smerch*.[91] She was referring to her reaction to the arrest of Leonid, her first husband, in 1936. Leonid Serebriakov had been a Bolshevik founding father and occupied a high position in the government as First People's Commissar for Auto Transport[92] when he, along with Piatakov, Radek, and Grigorii Sokolnikov, were arrested on charges of participation in the "Trotskyite-Zinoviev gang." Serebriakov was sentenced to death and executed in 1937. Sokolnikov (Serebriakova's husband at the time), also a high official, was sentenced to ten years in prison, where he was killed in 1939.[93] As Galina anxiously awaited the imminent arrival of the "black raven" car that picked up arrestees, she wrote a letter to Stalin and Yezhov. In it she acknowledged that if the Party "sacrificed a man such as my husband, there must have been weighty grounds, but I myself never noticed anything suspicious or non-Party in his behavior. . . . What should I do? The shadow of political damnation is now hanging over me."[94] Apparently, Serebriakova was not successful in convincing the authorities that she really believed that there were "weighty grounds." After some time, she was called in to the Lubianka, where she was politely greeted by Yagoda and his deputy, Agranov. On that day, *Izvestiia* had unleashed a particularly virulent campaign against her.[95] The interrogators wanted to know "everything," but what Serebriakova was telling them was not what they wanted to hear. She explained to them, "There is not a trace of guilt in the people I have been talking about. Otherwise I would have told the Party about it. The people around me were always Soviet and Party in words and deeds."[96] At the time, Galina Serebriakova had been recognized by the Party as a talented, promising writer whose credibility was attested to by a long Party history and service at the front in the Civil War.

Agranov and Yagoda approached her interrogation by claiming that they were trying to rescue her from a horrible fate. However, this rescue required that she admit to things that were blatant lies. She could not. They permitted her to go home, but the investigation continued day after day, and sometimes night after night. On the fourth or fifth day, Yezhov joined the interrogation, and the questioning became increasingly antagonistic. Yezhov darkly informed Serebriakova that "we want to keep you as a writer. You are standing at the edge of an abyss. If you give the right testimony you will not be arrested. In a few months we will restore your Party membership, and you can return to literature. You can remarry

. . . your children will grow up in humane circumstances."[97] Serebriakova resolved that death was not the worst thing that could happen, and dying would be better than slandering herself or her friends. Still, the interrogators continued to press Galina to admit that she had overheard her father and husband discussing the preparation of a terrorist act against Stalin on December 10, 1934.[98]

At home again, Serebriakova felt she was losing her mind. She attempted suicide, but was unsuccessful. The "organs" left her alone for a while, and she was admitted to a hospital. Before she was able to recover, Serebriakova was picked up in the hospital and taken to an internal prison of the Lubianka, then was moved to the Butyrka. There Galina was subjected to torture alternated by isolation. At one point, she thought she was becoming delirious. She started to ask herself: "What if my husband was just pretending, and he really was a conspirator? Then neither my country nor the Party was hurling me into the abyss, but rather the betrayal of a person close to me."[99] For the time being, that issue remained unresolved. Betrayal by the Party was an unacceptable conclusion, and so too, ultimately, was the version of events that placed her husband in the role of conspirator.

More time passed. Galina was told that her husband had been tried and sentenced to ten years in the Gulag. She was released from custody and returned home to her mother and daughter. In June of 1937 Galina was sentenced to five years of exile in Kazakhstan. Her thirteen-year-old daughter Zoria was placed in an orphanage, and Galina set out for Semipalatinsk. Thus began her twenty-year sojourn, where she alternated between exile, arrest, interrogation under torture, camp, hunger strikes, and severe solitary confinement. Despite the abhorrent circumstances in which she existed, Galina maintained her Party loyalty, and sought and found like-minded campmates. She recalled how once while she was in the kartser she found a rolled-up cigarette paper in her daily bread ration. It had been put there by one of the prisoners awaiting the execution of his death sentence. He pleaded for Galina to survive so that she could convey to the world that they died innocent, and true to the Party. He wrote: "We were and remain Communists. The enemies penetrated the government and deceived the Party. In court I told the truth, but they believed them, not me. Communism is the truth and it will triumph. To die young, and in this way, is horrible, but we have found courage because we are innocent . . . Hail to Communism."[100] This was one of many such stories—one had even been written in blood—that Galina records in her memoirs.[101] She also sympathizes with the interrogators, who were forced to act as they did in order to advance their standing in the Party ladder and yet were depressed by their assigned tasks.[102]

Galina was finally released in 1955 and was rehabilitated on the first day of the Twentieth Party Congress. She maintained that Stalin's cult of personality was alien to the Party. Writing in praise of Khrushchev in *Pravda* in 1961, Serebriakova claimed that she did not "lose faith in our Leninist party or in the strength of the all-conquering teaching of Marx and Lenin."[103] She called Khrushchev a "true Leninist" for whom she had "deep respect." Galina returned from the camp an active propagandist for the Party. She wrote a manuscript describing her camp life, but voluntarily withdrew it from publication, and protested its publication outside the Soviet Union in the Brezhnev era. Serebriakova was apprehensive that such disclosures about the Gulag would jeopardize the Party's standing and her standing in the Party. Her apprehensions were informed by the consequences of Solzhenitsyn's *Ivan Denisovich*.[104]

Zoria Serebriakova

Galina Serebriakova's Party loyalty was shared by her daughter Zoria, who joined Galina in exile in Semipalatinsk after her release from the orphanage where she was too old to remain.[105] Zoria continued her schooling in Semipalatinsk from 1945 to 1947, graduated, and married in 1948. While Galina was being shifted between prison camps and in and out of exile, Zoria was arrested on charges that she had corresponded with two "enemies of the people." One source was a letter to Solkolnikov, her stepfather; the other was a photograph of her father, Serebriakov, although the fact that these "enemies" were her stepfather and father respectively was not mentioned in the case file she read decades later.[106] Zoria initially spent two months in isolation, while her nursing infant was sent to an orphanage. Later that year, her charge was reclassified from article 58 (counterrevolutionary terrorist) to the lesser offense of 7-35 (family member of an "enemy of the people"). For this charge, she received ten years of exile, and she could take her son with her. She was released in 1955 and returned to Moscow.

Zoria pursued a career as a historian, defending her candidate dissertation under Khrushchev and her doctoral dissertation under Gorbachev. She argued that the liberating process initiated by Khrushchev was unprecedented in its humanity. She knew of no other case in history where so many people received freedom as a result of the actions of one person (see introduction). She praised his courage, because he knew what danger he braved. Reportedly, when Khrushchev entered the Twentieth Party Congress, he told one of the delegates, "I may not return."[107]

Zoria was passionately critical of those who criticized the Party. For example, when the long-awaited monument to victims of Stalinism was finally erected in Moscow by the organization Memorial in 1990, the event was a difficult experience for Zoria. She never visited the monument after that, because she resented the fact that at the unveiling ceremony, the participants inveighed against the Bolsheviks and the Communist Party and accused the Soviet regime of crimes. She reproached perestroika figures such as Afanasiev, Razgon, Yeltsin, and Sakharov for failing to limit their criticism of the repression to Stalin. The only speaker with whom she could identify was Yevgeny Yevtushenko, who recited his famous 1961 poem "The Heirs to Stalin." This poem hailed the removal of Stalin's body from the mausoleum, but cautioned about his spirit escaping. At the unveiling of the Solovetsky stone Zoria saw Anna Larina, widow of Bolshevik founding father Nikolai Bukharin. Disappointed by the light in which the revolutionaries were cast, Zoria lamented to her, "Where did we end up?"[108]

Zoria's public and private assessments of Soviet history reflect her enduring adherence to the Communist Party's self-assessment, namely that Stalin bore chief responsibility for the repression. Consequently, she did not agree with several arguments in my 2002 book on Gulag survivors, for example, that the Soviet system was adapted to repression, or that returnees in the post-Stalin era struggled to reenter Soviet society. In our 2006 interview, Zoria, reflecting on the beginning, the middle, and the end of the Soviet Union, disclosed her disappointments, and kept returning to the exclusive culpability of Stalin. She pointed out that since Stalin's signature was on forty thousand death sentences, "it is tendentious to put a stone at the place they died without using his name. Crimes must be called crimes, and guilt should be properly attributed." In addition, she defended Feliks Dzerzhinskii, head of Lenin's secret police. Zoria explained that the monument to Dzerzhinskii (hauled away in 1991) was built in 1958, after the Twentieth Party Congress, as a symbol of socialist legality. "There was no mass repression then. They did not shoot one Menshevik. They sent scholars on a boat to well-fed, warm Europe. Pardon me, that was not terror," she argued. She added that Dzerzhinskii supported the New Economic Policy of the twenties and provided for the support of orphans. "How can you make a revolution without putting down revolts? Then there is no revolution," Zoria contended.

Zoria believed that perestroika was a successful alternative to Stalinist and post-Stalinist totalitarianism, because it permitted the Soviet government to remain in place as its reformed variant, socialism with a human face. She claimed that the previous fifteen years (1991–2006) had proven that this model was better for the country. She buttressed her claim by reminding me that there was not one political prisoner under Gorbachev. Moreover, at that time the past was more open than ever to scholarly inquiry. As a consequence, many of Lenin's comrades, including Zoria's father, Leonid Serebriakov, and her stepfather, Grigorii Sokolnikov, received posthumous rehabilitation and Party reinstatement under Gorbachev.[109]

Zoria's views are not representative of all Communist loyalists, but they do highlight two complementary Party assertions: criticism should have been much more limited, deflected from the Party to Stalin, and Lenin's place in Soviet history is sacred and should be insulated from scrutiny (see also Kuznetsova's comments, chapter 5). Zoria's outspokenness was sometimes problematic in the post-Soviet era. She alienated some by disagreeing with the Belovezh Accords that dissolved the Soviet Union because the treaty "did not speak for all the peoples." While she lost her job at the prestigious Institute of History of the Russian Academy of Sciences under Yeltsin in 1992, she became a consultant for the Gorbachev Foundation.[110] At the conclusion of Galina's memoirs, she adds a special section for Zoria about her father. In it, she salutes "these people whom I knew, for whom I was responsible," and points out that they "hated violence, loved people, and died for the idea of good."[111]

As noted in the introduction, those who do not want to be burdened by the past seek to remember it from a positive perspective.[112] Zoria's views of the events that befell her family and shaped her country are informed by the meaning that Communism provided for her parents, their comrades, and herself. They were among the builders of socialism. Compelling visual testimony from those early, formative memories is preserved in a picture that still hangs in Zoria's dacha in Nikolina Gora, just outside of Moscow. It portrays her father and Lenin together, brothers-in-arms.[113] After release from two decades in the Gulag, Zoria's mother spent the next two decades polishing the Party's image in her writings on Marx and socialism. As for Zoria, her memory of events selectively attends to "release" over "incarceration" and "rehabilitation" over "execution." For Zoria and her like-minded cohorts, the troubled Russian present reminds them of their noble aspirations which, they maintain, were just short of being realized.

Zoria and others like her identified with an idea for which they made great personal sacrifices. They prioritized the Party even when it erred over their familial ties. Other families faced with similar predicaments chose a different path. Additional prominent examples of intergenerational Party membership and incarceration include the Bogoraz-Daniel family, the Yakirs, and the Bonners. (The political history of these families differs from that of the Serebriakovas because the loyalty of the first generation was succeeded by dissidence in the second.)[114] Some who lost faith did so because they came to believe that the Party had changed.

Nataliia Rykova

Nataliia Rykova's family had a long history of commitment to the Party, but the repression undermined it. Aleksei Rykov was an Old Bolshevik, a member of

Lenin's Politburo, and a close comrade of Bukharin. His wife, Nina Semenovna Rykova, had been an active Party member since 1903, transporting underground literature to Russia and carrying out other orders from Lenin.[115] Rykov was arrested in February of 1937, sentenced to death, and executed in March of 1938. Nina was arrested in July of 1937 and executed at Butovo on the outskirts of Moscow in August of 1938.[116] And, in the meantime, their twenty-one-year-old daughter Nataliia—who had grown up in a Kremlin residence in the Hotel Natsional[117]— began her Gulag sojourn on January 1, 1938. In our 2005 interview, Nataliia, then age ninety, reflected on her parents' devotion to the Party. For her father, the Party was simply "sacred," though Stalin was not.[118] Political discussions were so central to her family's life that it might have been expected that they would continue in the camp. They rarely did. Nataliia explained, "We already understood everything; it was clear so we didn't need to talk. What could we have done anyway? We hoped that the Party would get better, but we saw that the camp supervisors were also Party members."[119]

With a futile shrug, she said these were questions for historians. For prisoners, the problem was simply to try to survive until the end of each day. According to Nataliia, her family already knew and understood what was happening in 1928 and 1929, and her father did not want to work with Stalin.[120] In a 1961 plea to the Twenty-second Party Congress for Rykov's Party reinstatement, Nataliia wrote to the Presidium that her father knew that Stalin was planning to kill him, and he knew why. It was not for alleged treachery to the Party's cause, but because Stalin had reason to doubt Rykov's devotion to him personally.[121] Apparently Stalin's suspicions were accurate. Nataliia's mother, on the eve of her arrest, entrusted her with this truth about her father, and implored Nataliia to reveal this to the Party in twenty or thirty years.[122]

Nataliia survived camp (Vorkuta) in part because of special treatment—in quite a literal sense. A few of her campmates, who were medical professors turned prisoner-doctors, suspected that she had developed cancer. Consequently, she was offered, underwent, and survived two difficult mastectomies in the camp hospital within a year of each other. She survived the cancer and the Gulag, but with no desire to be a Party member. Nor did she feel the need to join the dissident movement.

Nataliia recalled that for a long time before their imprisonment her family had already come to recognize that the Party was becoming repressive. During her years in camp, Nataliia had reconciled with the realization that the Party was no longer the same one for which her family had gone through the Revolution and the Civil War. She described some campmates who still lived for the "beauty of the idea" of Communism, but when they applied for reinstatement, they were motivated by more immediate needs—recognition, self-confirmation, and justice. And so, too, did Nataliia—not for herself, but for her parents. Nataliia's mother, Nina, suffered as heavy a punishment as her husband. Unlike the fate of many wives of "enemies of the people" who were shipped off to the Gulag, Nina was sentenced to death and executed. Through Nataliia's efforts, Nina Rykova received judicial rehabilitation in 1957, but "no grounds" were found for her Party rehabilitation. Rykov (and by extension his family) had been accused of being the Right Deviation, and the Party's policy at that time was clearly stated in the journal *Kommunist:* "The Party never has changed and cannot change its attitude toward trends hostile to Leninism."[123] Nataliia protested the Party Control Commission's decision in a 1961 letter to Khrushchev. She wrote, "My mother was arrested with her Party card in hand. . . . She had a thirty-four-year unsullied Party record, fourteen of those years were underground. For me, her daughter, she was a Communist in everything she did. The judicial rehabilitation of such a person— without Party rehabilitation—is not rehabilitation."[124]

Nataliia later wrote that she was not going to seek a review of her father's case, because she was convinced that "dead or alive Aleksei Rykov belonged to and belongs to the Party."[125] She added that when the Party needed it, she would tell them what only she knew. Nataliia's request with regard to her mother was honored in July 1961 when Nina Semenovna Rykova received posthumous reinstatement.[126] In spite of her earlier reluctance to pursue this course, Nataliia subsequently began the long lobbying effort for the reevaluation of her father's case.[127] This request, too, would eventually be honored, but it took nearly three decades. Rykov, along with Nikolai Bukharin and Mikhail Tomskii, was rehabilitated under Gorbachev in 1988.

In her memoirs, Bukharin's widow, Anna Larina, who spent almost twenty years in the Gulag, recalls how she and Nataliia Rykova persisted in writing new appeals. Prior to every Party Congress, they would phone each other for encouragement in what seemed a futile task. Finally, they appealed to Mikhail Gorbachev at the Twenty-seventh Party Congress and succeeded. At the news of Bukharin's Party reinstatement, Anna Larina reflects, "It is difficult to convey my reaction, my excitement and delight. . . . Although I believed the truth would triumph, it was detained too long on the road. I had already lost hope that I would live to see the rehabilitation."[128]

As for Nataliia, she did not appear embittered by her Gulag experience. Decades later, she did not recall even such details as the year of her release from the Gulag. (It was 1946.)[129] She did, however, recall hearing the news of Stalin's death from her husband at their home in exile. They did not mourn. Nataliia had no investment in the Party—either wanting to join it or criticize its injustice. But her family had created it and provided her with a Bolshevik upbringing, so securing Party rehabilitation for her father and mother was a daughter's gift, an attempt to redeem their Truth.[130]

Mikhail Baitalskii

The camp experience did not shake the faith of some Party veterans—especially those who could separate the Party from Stalin. Another prominent example of enduring faith in the Party and the ultimate triumph of socialism was Mikhail Baitalskii (see also chapter 1). Early on he joined the Komsomol, and then the Party in 1923. His faith was distinguished by his support of Trotsky's proposals, and he participated in the circulation of Lenin's testament with its warning regarding Stalin as General Secretary. Baitalskii was arrested in the sweeps of 1929, 1935, and 1950, and ultimately released and rehabilitated in 1955. Despite the years of incarceration, Baitalskii emerged a supporter of the Revolution. After his release, he spent twelve years writing a memoir titled "Notebooks for the Grandchildren." In this voluminous work he compiled the camp experiences he endured and witnessed, with the conclusion that they confirmed the tenets of Lenin and Trotsky. By 1970, when he had completed his work, it could only be circulated in samizdat because the successors of Lenin had proscribed a forthright discussion of this subject.[131]

IDEOLOGICAL AND PRACTICAL REASONS FOR PARTY MEMBERSHIP

That a camp past left a political and vocational stain was a practical truth of daily living for returnees,[132] made worse by the bureaucratic obstacles to Party reinstatement. This predicament continued for decades after Stalin's death. From 1954 on, a flood of requests applying for a change of status poured into the Presidium of the Supreme Soviet. The applicants beseeched the officials to provide a favorable ruling on a variety of justifying grounds. A number of the letter-writers professed that their motivation was to be able to raise the next generation to be good Communists. One such came from Boris Iakovlevich Teper, who had been exiled from Kiev in 1937. Seventeen years later he wrote the following plea for release to Voroshilov:

> Remaining a Communist in my soul, though my Party card was revoked, I tried all these years to expiate my guilt. The work characteristics that I am including attest to how I did this. However, there has still not been a change in my circumstances. I have four children. I want to raise them as full-fledged

builders of Communist society. But for that it is necessary that the fate of their father does not drag them down, and does not stand in the way of their normal growth and development.[133]

Teper's request was granted. The paper trail stops there, but it is likely that he then applied for and received judicial rehabilitation and Party reinstatement. Such letters, of which there are many, highlight how returnees—and not the Party—were suffering from a tarnished image. Reinstatement was fundamental to repairing the spoiled standing of Gulag survivors and their families. Teper's letter only hinted at the vocational and educational issues, but they were omnipresent considerations in a closed society.

As noted earlier, many Communist prisoners were not uncritical about ending up in the Gulag, but they repaired their self-image along with the Party's image by concluding that their incarceration was a mistake, that the Party would come to realize this and then correct the mistake. One prisoner who worked on the Kotlas–Vorkuta railway claimed that if the Party had asked her to go there voluntarily, she would absolutely have done so, but then she would have taken her son along. Her like-minded brigade-mate maintained that she too had dreamed of great construction projects and would have been happy to volunteer, but as a free person.[134] Through this psychological strategy, some prisoners were able to extract a modicum of self-determination and merge it with the goals of the Party. Even in the face of involuntary servitude they could identify themselves as "builders of socialism."

Zakhar Isaakovich Ravdel, an engineer, joined the Party in 1929, and by 1933 he had worked his way into the Central Committee of the Komsomol in Ukraine. Ravdel had hoped to further pursue his scientific career, but he was informed that he was needed by the Party to "organize the mastering of new technology among millions of young Soviet people."[135] To overcome his hesitation, they appealed to his dedication to Communism, pointing out that "as a Communist, you should play a leading role in this."[136] Ravdel readjusted his aspirations and placed the Party's wishes above his own, affirming that he was indeed "above all a Communist." Even so, he was arrested in 1937 and sentenced to fifteen years of incarceration. Ravdel was sent to the Solovetsky camps, isolation cells, and the Arctic north of Norilsk and Kolyma, as well as the horrors of the "death ships" and transports that hauled prisoners to and from these hellish destinations. After his release, Ravdel again became active in the Party and was reinstated following the reforms instituted by the Twentieth Party Congress. Ravdel's early and continuing commitment to the ideology of the Party gave him a sense of self-worth and meaning, even—perhaps especially—during his ordeal. He explained that this was not so for everyone, and unflinchingly reported how the Party undermined the self-worth of innocents:

> Right in front of my eyes, as soon as they were arrested on fabricated charges, people who had occupied high posts and had availed themselves of all kinds of privileges were prepared to sign any self-incriminating slander when they got wind of the horrors of "interrogation." And then when they landed in the prisons and camps, many of them lost their self-confidence, humiliated themselves for an extra portion of *balanda* [thin gruel] or a drag of *makhorka* [tobacco substitute].[137]

Ravdel counted himself among the "many others" who accepted their servitude in the proud spirit of dedication to the motherland. This group, according to Ravdel, "faced their hardships with courage. In the camps, during hard labor with meager rations, in the cold with threadbare clothing, they did not grumble, did not grovel . . . and they did the task they were assigned, remembering that the work done by them would be for the good of the motherland; they believed in their right to self-respect and full rehabilitation."[138] Ravdel claimed that such people comprised the majority of arrestees, who, like him, were incarcerated in the thirties. For them, the Party provided a source of meaning that justified immediate sacrifice, albeit with the expectation that such sacrifice would eventually be recognized and valued.

Evgeniia Borian was arrested in 1937 for being the wife of an "enemy of the people" who had been the first secretary of a provincial committee. She received an eight-year prison sentence, but was sent to the Gulag in the middle of that term. After her release, Borian was rearrested and sent into eternal exile. Writing in 1967, she expressed the following sentiment: "In all my years of imprisonment [1937–1954], I never lost faith in the cause of our great Communist Party and the hope for the restoration of the truth and my good name as a Communist and fighter for the Soviet government."[139] The dissociation from Stalin that started in the Khrushchev era had validated the legitimacy of the Party and reaffirmed the convictions of returnees like Borian. However, during the Brezhnev era, a number of ex-prisoners found it difficult to reconcile their allegiance to the Party with allegiance to a newly repressive Soviet government.

THE LOYAL OPPOSITION OUT OF THE GULAG

A number of returnees believed in the future of Communism but were skeptical about the post-Khrushchev leadership's interpretation of the Party line, with its shift toward Stalinism. Such passionate figures as Aleksei Kosterin, Sergei

Pisarev, Lev Kopelev, Petr Grigorenko, and a host of others championed the dissident movement, but all of them were—or once had been—ardent Communists. While Kopelev rejected the Party, others, like Kosterin and Pisarev, maintained their faith in the Party—right up until the very end.

Aleksei Kosterin

Aleksei Kosterin had solid Bolshevik credentials. He spent three years in tsarist prisons, joined the Party before the Revolution (in 1916), and fought in the Civil War. He was arrested in 1938 and spent eighteen years in Kolyma. The rest of his family, caught up in the various waves of Soviet terror, met a tragic fate as well. Kosterin's father died of starvation in the winter of 1931–1932, his older brother was arrested and executed in 1936, and his middle brother was excluded from the Party, fired from his job, and threatened with arrest; subsequently, he drank himself to death. Kosterin's mother turned in her Party card when her oldest son was arrested, claiming that she could not be in a Party that allowed such injustice. When her middle son died, and her youngest son, Aleksei, was arrested, she died of heart failure. In spite of Party efforts to supersede family loyalty, what most ex-prisoners wanted most was a reunion with their family. But by the time Aleksei emerged from the Gulag, there was no family left. Absent family and religion—the usual sources of community and meaning—he rejoined the ranks of the Party.

After Kosterin received rehabilitation and reinstatement in the Party, he embarked on a spirited advocacy of Marxism-Leninism and other pre-Stalinist-era values. His open protest of the 1968 invasion of Czechoslovakia, among other conscience-driven activities, cost Kosterin his Party membership. However, he resigned before being expelled, justifying his departure by stating that "this is not the Party that I entered, and for which I fought in the Revolution and the Civil War; therefore I do not want to be counted among the ranks of this party and be responsible for its acts."[140] While renouncing the Communist Party's policies, Kosterin identified himself as a loyalist. With a conviction grounded in his ideological roots, he declared, "With the Party card or without, I was, I am, and I shall remain a Marxist-Leninist, a Communist, a Bolshevik. This is my life from early youth to the grave."[141] Two weeks after turning in his Party card Kosterin died, but his funeral brought together hundreds of people and became a rallying point for the opposition. Even though it was violently broken up by the KGB, the gathering became the first "open meeting." At a more personal level, Kosterin exerted a deep influence on Sergei Pisarev, his friend and fellow dissident.

Sergei Pisarev

A fanatic Party loyalist, Sergei Pisarev had a long history of recurrent clashes with the Party that might easily have challenged that commitment. He had been expelled from the Party eight times for, among other things, defending his repressed comrades, was interrogated forty-three times, severely tortured during thirty-eight of these sessions, and incarcerated twice. Pisarev accepted the punitive consequences of challenging the Party, but not without criticism of their methods. For example, he successfully campaigned against one of his interrogators who was then kicked out of the Party and fired from the KGB. In 1953, as the Doctors Plot unfolded, he wrote a letter to Stalin criticizing the secret police for fabricating this new wave of terror. The response to his whistle-blowing was imprisonment in the Leningrad Special Psychiatric Hospital. There he began to gather evidence on the political misuse of psychiatry. Still, as one of his friends observed, "despite all of that, he preserved his belief in a 'just Communism.'"[142] Throughout his adult years, Pisarev continued to write letters to the Central Committee and state organs in an effort to unveil abuses and abolish abusive institutions. Pisarev's campaign was unsuccessful, because the number of Special Psychiatric Hospitals only increased. However, Petr Grigorenko, who assumed his mantle, wrote, "Pisarev continued to believe in the Central Committee and wrote to it right up until his [1979] death."[143]

THE CRUCIBLE: THE "GREAT PATRIOTIC WAR," THE PARTY, AND STALIN

The abhorrent presence of the Nazis on Soviet soil, and the death and destruction wreaked by their aggression rallied Soviet citizens, prisoner and non-prisoner alike. The propaganda machine worked overtime to equate the defense of Mother Russia with Party loyalty, and with success. Even in the midst of the war, some soldiers took the occasion to apply for Party membership.[144] Letters from the front contained such messages as: "You cannot defeat a people who are led by the Communist Party."[145] Some praised Stalin.[146] Kopelev and his comrades, long Party devotees, first joined the Party during the war, motivated by an "emotional, patriotic impulse."[147]

Such impulses visited those in the camps as well. More often than not, accounts from Gulag prisoners describe their frequent requests to serve the motherland. From within the Gulag itself, or the special settlements, it was reported that one member of every family was applying to go to the front.[148] Their motivations varied from patriotic to practical. They saw service in the Army, as noted by one memoirist, as a chance to "prove their devotion to the Party, to socialism, and to Comrade Stalin himself."[149] Committed Communist prisoners might not have seen any inconsistency in being a devotee *to* and a political prisoner *of* the Communist Party. And ardent patriots often found it preferable to risk their lives in combat for Mother Russia than to die of overwork in a labor camp. Those whose requests for military service were rejected sometimes found a newly discovered advantage to being in the Gulag by recognizing that, in the words of Georgii Shelest, "This camp is Soviet, after all, not fascist!"[150]

When permission to serve was granted, the political prisoners were sent right to the front line, but the majority of these applicants were simply rejected for their "insincerity to the Party."[151] These wholesale rejections may have cloaked the Party's strategy for avoiding two major risks. On the one hand, if these prisoners were truly "enemies of the people," how could they be trusted to serve? On the other hand, if they could be trusted to serve, their potential disclosures about the Gulag to fellow soldiers might jeopardize the army's trust in the Party. Perhaps sending political prisoners directly to the front, where life expectancy was very short, was a suitable compromise.

Stuck in the Gulag for the duration of the war and forced to increase their productivity under even harsher than usual conditions, prisoners succumbed more quickly to disease, which led to a high mortality rate. In 1942 alone, every fourth prisoner died of exhaustion or illness. But even "doomed as they were by the Stalinist regime to die behind barbed wire," wrote one analyst, "when the question of rescuing the motherland arose," they were ready.[152] This was probably not paradoxical to prisoners who had little trouble distinguishing patriotism from Party membership, and less trouble choosing a heroic over an abject death.

Lev Gavrilov (see the introduction) survived eighteen years of "ostracism, and being cast out," prisons, camps, and exile. He endured ten prisons, among them Butyrka, Lubianka, Lefortovo, Magadan, Krasnoiarsk, and ten camps including those of Kolyma, followed by exile in Norilsk.[153] Whenever he felt daunted by the need to make sense of the "dark and criminal arbitrary rule" to which he had been subjected, he turned to the remedy available to all believers—faith. Whether that faith is in a generic "higher power," religious "mystery," or the secular dogma provided by the Communist Party, it answers the otherwise unanswerable question of *meaning*. While evidence-based faith may be weakened by hardship, faith-based beliefs are frequently strengthened. However, as was so often the case, Gavrilov's allegiance to the Party had little influence on how its officials viewed him. He tried to join the army and was rejected, as were his campmates. "How can that be?" they exclaimed, "we are Communists! How could we not be included in the ranks of the defenders of the Motherland?"[154] Ultimately, Gavrilov made a unique contribution to the war effort—his gold teeth.

The request of another patriotic prisoner-applicant was accepted because the military had come to realize how much more it needed military than political skills in its combat units. Vladimir Vasilievich Karpov, whose story is rather extraordinary, had just finished his studies at a Tashkent military school and was about to receive the rank of lieutenant when he was arrested in May of 1941. The reason: when he was reading a brochure on Lenin's "What Is To Be Done?" he had underlined Lenin's name in red and Stalin's name in blue, and then showed the brochure to a fellow student. Karpov, then nineteen, was accused of insulting the leader; he was labeled an "enemy of the people" and sent to Tavdinlag—where he timbered in temperatures that dropped to 50 degrees below zero. The Gulag experience did not diminish Karpov's patriotism. On the contrary, he was so eager to serve that he regularly wrote letters to M. I. Kalinin requesting to be sent to the front. Then, in 1942, quite unusually, Karpov's request was granted. He took part in highly risky operations for which his troops were poorly trained. Of the 198 scouts in his regiment, only eight survived.[155]

Karpov was apparently not a Party activist, but he was a loyal patriot who advanced quickly from the rank of ordinary regimental scout to that of captain. Along the way, he was thrice wounded and received numerous military decorations. After the war, he attended the prestigious Frunze Military Academy, and still later he turned to writing, ultimately changing professions. He went on to become the First Secretary of the Writer's Union. In a 1995 interview, Karpov told *Pravda* that he ranked Stalin's leadership right along with that of Roosevelt and Churchill, but he considered Stalin even "mightier" because he was the "Supreme Commander in Chief." He acknowledged that Stalin "visited a lot of misfortune on our people, I was one of the repressed, but we can never forget his achievements. He rescued the country."[156]

Did Stalin, and/or the Party, offer light in the darkness, or did they primarily reflect a light that was thrown on them by events? Historian Catherine Merridale described the desperate need for solace felt by millions of young soldiers as they faced death—their own and their comrades'. In this time of need, Stalin, the embodiment of Mother Russia, evolved into a totem. The need created the remedy from the material at hand. Merridale writes of Stalin: "He was a talisman, a name, a hollow image that some privately abhorred. But it was better, in this darkness, to find something to believe in than to die in utter desolation."[157] As attested to by numerous firsthand accounts, and evidenced by psychosocial research correlating distress with religious conversion experiences, anxiety increases vulnerability to interpersonal influence.[158] Moreover, by saturating the public sphere with pro-Party propaganda and embedding *politruks* (political advisors) into the Red Army, the Party increasingly "wrote itself into the war,"[159] capturing all the leading and supporting roles.

Some of the deep-seated roots of belief were planted in the war, the legacy of which extends to identity issues even today (see chapter 5). According to Merridale the war was "the crucible in which a new mentality was forged."[160] Hitler's invasion provided Russians with a clear, non-contrived, *external* enemy of the people, against whom they could unite as one people, find heroism in the common man, and fashion Stalin as a heroic counterweight to Hitler. For some, it also validated previous Party and state policies that were claimed to be preemptive. The victory was framed, perceived, and loudly trumpeted as a triumph *of* and *for* the Stalinist state. Such newly burnished credentials buffered the Party from the recurring accounts of the surviving victims of the Gulag's state-sponsored terror, as well as the recurring stories about its non-survivors.

For an entire generation, the war was the "defining event of their lives. [It gave them] greater purpose" and the sense that they as individuals could make a difference in the "destiny of the nation."[161] Even Article 58ers who had not been permitted to fight largely perceived the defeat of the Nazis as their triumph. "When this day came," recounted one returnee, "the joy of victory was coupled with our feeling that we in the camps, if even on a small scale, also worked toward that victory."[162] The war was a symbol of the pride and power of the Soviet empire. Especially in less proud and less triumphant times, the memory of the wartime valor and sacrifice of citizens imbued their later existence with some sense of meaning.[163]

It was also the case that the sheer determination to avoid Nazi destruction and survive may have been a greater driving force than either belief or loyalty. Since behavior is multiply determined, the motivation for professed belief can be elusive, and that again raises the issue of the lack of alternatives. In a closed system there are not many safe, viable options with regard to belief. One interviewee who took part in the postwar Harvard refugee project, now safely situated in the West, asserted: "If the people of Russia were assured of a better, more democratic and representative government, they all would fight against the regime. Even the Red Army would surrender by the thousands . . . in order to destroy the Bolsheviks."[164]

The Party was not always successful in merging the patriotic fervor aroused by defending the beleaguered motherland with a similar zeal for defending Communism and idealizing Stalin. There were veterans who claimed they did not want to be associated with support of Stalin. One memoirist, for example, who was able to take part in the war only by concealing the fact that her parents had been repressed, resented any accusation that veterans supported Stalinism. From what she observed, the vast majority of frontline veterans were in fact anti-Stalinists.[165] Since patriotism often merged with allegiance to the Party or Stalin, it is difficult to verify the accuracy of this assertion.

The place of Stalin in the history of the war necessarily conflates what he did with what the Red Army did in his name. The linguistic battle of Stalingrad (then) vs. Volgograd (now) is refought every few years in the arena of public opinion. In 1961, in the post-Stalin surge of anti-Stalinism, Stalingrad, the city named for him, was renamed Volgograd. However comforting this was to anti-Stalinist sentiments, there never had been a decisive battle of Volgograd to which veterans and a grateful nation could return for inspiration. In consequence, veterans who might not necessarily have supported Stalin supported restoring his name to the city.[166] Now, decades later, when veterans recount their wartime stories, Merridale found that they still use the "language of the Soviet state, talking about honor and pride, of justified revenge, of motherland, Stalin, and the absolute necessity of faith."[167] The wartime experience and the memory of it reveal the enduring power of belief, even for non-Party members. The "necessity of faith" describes the transformation of despair by hope for a brighter future. Any leader or system of belief that provides that remedy would be compellingly attractive.

Their war experience, however, also made many veterans into more informed skeptics. Some experienced a postwar disillusionment with Stalin because seeing the material benefits capitalism had provided made the material benefits of Communism seem less praiseworthy.[168] Furthermore, they questioned the government's use of scarce resources to build oversized monuments to Stalin instead of houses for the people. This issue was portrayed in a short novel published in one of the "thick journals" during the Thaw.[169] Though it was fictional and conformed to the Khrushchevian ideological revision of Stalinism, the novel nevertheless raised the question of the extent to which promised improvements were realized. According to the story, in the new era, these promises were fulfilled. The protagonist was a camp returnee and a frontline veteran. Disturbed by the construction of monuments instead of houses and the continuing "class struggle," he wrote a letter to Stalin. In it, he asked Stalin to explain why the class struggle was supposed to be increased in a country where socialism was triumphant. He did not venture to address the terror or the camps. The response came in the form of arrest and imprisonment. He was released and rehabilitated only after 1956.[170] The story ends with the veteran-returnee, a Party supporter if not a card-carrying member, now happy that he has no further ideological conflicts. For those who might have experienced any crisis of faith in the Party, the plot reassures the reader that the Party had returned to Leninism, that houses were being built, and that there was no class struggle in the USSR.

ALLEGIANCE: THE TIES THAT BIND, BUT NEED NOT BLIND

Identification with an ideology, a religion, a cause, an organization, or an individual can have deep nonrational roots—universally and cross-culturally. It is not difficult to understand loyalty to the Communist Party when it delivers on its material and political promises, or the withdrawal of loyalty when it reneges, but how can we better understand an allegiance that continues despite unfulfilled promises and even after the Party's attack on the loyalist? An answer may be found by considering the immaterial, nonpolitical, emotional benefits provided by the experience of a social bond with the Party—similar to religious affiliation. As with religion, an intrinsically positive outcome requires only belief, although a Party career also required concrete work. Belief is not invalidated by unanswered prayers, and contradictory evidence can be processed in a way that does not cause a crisis of faith. Belief may even be reinforced by penance and punishment for "sins." Communism officially eliminated institutionalized religion as a competitive provider of the basic human need to find meaning by connecting to a higher power—however defined.[171] The satisfactions derived from familial bonds were also undermined by the Party—leaving the field to itself. All of the narratives in this study powerfully attest to the fact that identity with and belief in the Party was not dependent on outcome. One life story, a little different than the others that we have been exploring, expressed this particularly eloquently.

Jo Langerova and Oscar Langer did not explicitly frame their familial and political struggles as a competition for Oscar's "heart," but it is implicit in Langerova's memoir, titled *Convictions: Memories of a Life Shared with a Good Communist*.[172] In this memoir Jo Langerova describes how an idealistic couple, devoted to each other and to Communism, participated in the evolution of the Slovak Communist Party. Langerova poignantly conveys the anguish of her loss of faith, allegiance, and love as she saw her loyalist husband maintain "truths" that she no longer found convincing. Jo and Oscar had married in the thirties, she writes, "when our notion of life in the Soviet Union—our Utopia—was not based on the current reality but on an idealized view of what it had been like in the early twenties."[173] Like other idealists of their generation they were drawn to the egalitarian vision of the Party of the twenties. This vision might have been especially appealing because Jo and Oscar were Czechoslovakian Jews who would have perished after Hitler's Anschluss in 1938 had they not fled to the United States. Their families who remained met a tragic fate; they were killed in pogroms, or in Theresienstadt and Auschwitz.

Oscar was an economist and an "ardent Communist" who eagerly anticipated the end of his "temporary exile" in the United States so that he could return to serve his native country and his Party. In 1946, eight years after their exodus, a letter arrived stating that the Party needed his services. Oscar was ready; Jo was not. By then, she had grown wary of the Party because she "knew too much about Russia not to have doubts about socialism."[174]

Nevertheless, they answered the Party's call and returned to Czechoslovakia, where Oscar began working for the Central Committee as an economist. In time he was promoted to a leading position in the Slovak Ministry for Food Production and Distribution. As they became more involved with the Party's operations, they noticed how Party policy could change from one day to the next, sometimes overlapping with and sometimes contradicting the previous policy. The political situation at that place and time is beyond the scope of this work, but what is relevant is how a Party loyalist viewed the increasing victimizations of his colleagues. Jo's efforts to make this issue a major concern for Oscar revealed a difference in their understanding of political morality, strained their relationship, and introduced the Party as a third party in their relationship as well as their conversations. Publicly, that is, while speaking with Jo in a room where the walls may have had ears, Oscar would tell her that the repression's infringement of individual rights was justified by security needs. It was "much better if a dozen people are arrested, investigated, and released if found innocent than if a single enemy goes free."[175] Privately, he disclosed his authoritarian ideological justification for the infringement of individual rights—condensed as "chips fly." "Try to look at it this way," he exhorted. "These men are perhaps not guilty in the everyday sense of the word. But just now the fate and interests of individuals are of secondary importance"[176] because nothing less than the "future of mankind" was at stake. Oscar was also confident that if mistakes were committed by the Party, those who were falsely accused would inevitably be released.

Jo had difficulty accepting that "morally wrong" actions could be justified by the claim that they were "politically right."[177] And try as he did, Oscar was unable to justify the Party's policy to Jo's satisfaction, because, as she came to understand his position, the Party's mission was justification for any of its policies. At that time Jo did not understand why Oscar did not see how far the Party had strayed from the ideals that had attracted them to the Party. She would eventually come to recognize that Oscar could not be swayed by her rational reasons because he was already swayed by the overriding nonrational, emotional satisfactions of Party allegiance.

Meanwhile, the Langers' fourteen-year-old daughter, Susie, developed her own sense of identity with the Party. She became a founding member of the first young Pioneers organization in Bratislava. This group of aspirants were preparing themselves for a life of service to the Party, and their hero was Pavlik Morozov, the boy who denounced his father for harboring kulak neighbors during collectivization. Susie was a devout Pioneer; she had even called Moscow to convey her congratulations to Stalin on his seventieth birthday.[178] Against this background, Jo was apprehensive about how Susie would react to Oscar's arrest in 1951. Apparently Susie chose family ties over Party ties, because she abandoned her beliefs after hearing this news.[179]

While under arrest, Oscar was forced to appear as a witness against Rudolf Slansky in the notorious Moscow-backed eight-day show trial of the Czech Communist Party leader in 1952.[180] Later, at his own trial, Oscar confessed to charges that Jo knew to be untrue; he was sentenced to twenty-two years. Oscar's imprisonment was the ideological tilting point for Jo. She was no longer in doubt about her assessment that the Party was morally corrupt. The solace she found in her talks with other wives of arrested Party members validated her victimhood, if not its value. Most of these wives regretted their marriages, because they had been doubly deprived. Not only were they now deprived of their husbands' presence, but they previously had been deprived of their husbands' companionship because "Party members were like monks who had decided to devote their lives to a faith. So they ought to live like monks . . . [and be] absolutely forbidden to take wives and make children."[181]

Oscar's imprisonment apparently did not alter his assessment of the Party's moral standing or his allegiance to the Party. Despite the risk to his health caused by mining uranium and the general harshness of prison conditions, Oscar wrote to Jo, "I too see the mistakes, but I know they are temporary ones which the Party will overcome, and that they are outweighed by the good the Party has done."[182] True to his principles, Oscar refused to be released on an amnesty, since he had committed no offense. Jo was skeptical. She reasoned that it was not realistic to expect justice from the very people who had imprisoned him. And she was right. So, also, was Oscar. But each was dealing with different domains of realistic expectations. Jo's were instrumental, contingent on the delivery of promised reforms. Oscar's was the intrinsic satisfaction of devotion to a higher calling.

Once released, Oscar vigorously sought and was eventually granted rehabilitation. But his health had been compromised by his ten years in prison, and he died within a few years of his release. While Oscar did not live to see the Prague Spring, Jo briefly considered that his sacrifice was, perhaps, redeemed by Dubcek's reforms. But she soon concluded that this was a vain hope. She saw through the new Party's misleading condemnation of the old Party's "violation of socialist legality," "mistakes," and the "cult of personality." This new socialism was "only skin deep," because the Party was still being portrayed as "infallible."[183] The political play was the same. Only the actors had changed.

In 1968, five days after the Soviet tanks rolled into Prague, Jo fled with her younger daughter, Tania, first to England and then to Sweden, where Susie was performing as a singer. They became refugees, abandoning their homeland again, but now no longer inspired by a Communist ideology Jo mistakenly thought she shared with Oscar. By considering Jo as representative of a secular, evidence-based belief in Communist egalitarianism and Oscar as representative of a faith-based belief in Communist authoritarianism, we bring their irreconcilable assessments of the repression within the scope of daily human experience. Imprisoned loyalists were as aware of the repression as devout Christians would be of a catastrophic earthquake that brings a church roof down on the heads of worshipers. Like a faith-based believer, Oscar recognized the repression as tragic, but irrelevant to the Party membership that provided meaning to his life. On the other hand, like an evidence-based believer, Jo recognized the repression as both tragic and relevant to the Party's claim on her loyalty. We need invoke neither a state of denial[184] regarding the true nature of their Party, nor selective attention to account for the enduring allegiance of devout loyalists. Oscar died believing in the Party, which may have been its own reward. Moreover, one might even say his hopes were borne out, however temporarily, shortly after his death.

THE PROMISE OF COMMUNISM

At the conclusion of her memoirs, in 1962, Tamara Tanina (see beginning of this chapter), looking at the then present and the future, expressed pride at the accomplishments of Iurii Gagarin and the Twenty-second Party Congress, which "confirmed the program for building Communism in our country." She then predicted that in twenty years the young and middle generations would live under Communism,[185] as she and her late, repressed husband, Mikhail Aleksandrovich Tanin, had imagined it would be. In fact, by 1965, within three years of Tamara's optimistic forecast, the Gulag had slipped out of public discourse, while new political prisoners were slipped into its confines. Twenty years later entirely new—albeit smaller—cohorts of political prisoners had been in and out of the camps. (Perhaps she was right, and that was Communism.) Still, loyal victims often continued to believe that the repression they suffered did not invalidate the promise of Communism. They viewed their suffering as an acceptable sacrifice for the fulfillment of their youthful and unflagging ideals. The repression changed loyalists' expectations of the present, but not their hopes for the future they were building.

Some ideological pioneers achieved a second Communist life after they emerged from the Gulag. Such veteran Communist officials as Olga Shatunovskaia, Aleksei Snegov, and the lesser known Valentina Pikina, who had been secretary of the

Central Committee of the Komsomol, put in their eighteen years in the Gulag, and then served in Khrushchev's rehabilitation apparatus. All three of them became members of the Party Control Commission, and all were convinced that they could stay in the Party and improve it. The rise of Gorbachev gave many such figures a sense that these hopes would be fulfilled. One less prominent survivor, M. N. Kuznetsov, had been convicted under several points of Article 58 and interned in the Gulag from 1937 to 1947. After his release, he was "deprived of rights" for over five years. All in all, Kuznetsov spent eighteen years in Kolyma. He eventually achieved rehabilitation and Party reinstatement. Kuznetsov blamed Stalin, and looked forward to the day that the archives would open. He concludes his 1987 memoir with gratitude and praise: "Those of us who survived those years are grateful to N. S. Khrushchev for his courage to give us back our good names. . . . let us go back home, and return to public, social, and Party life. We are also grateful to Gorbachev . . . for offering new evaluations and approaches so that the Party and scholars can restore the genuine and correct history of our Party and Revolution."[186] Kuznetsov spoke for the many surviving loyalists who hoped and believed that if they stayed in the Party, they could improve it.[187] Those who died during the Gorbachev era arguably saw that hope borne out.

Belomorkanal (White Sea Canal), the building of mooring dikes, 1932; from the collection of the Karelian State Regional Museum. *Memorial archive.*

Camp fence, Vorkuta, 1956–1957; from the collection of T. Kizni. *Memorial archive.*

The remnants of Marx, Engels, and Lenin under the steps of the former Institute of Marxism-Leninism (today RGASPI), Moscow, 1997. *Photo by Nanci Adler.*

Fallen idols, under the stairs of the IML, 1997. *Photo by Nanci Adler.*

Фамилия _Гальпер_ Имя _Мария_ Отчество _Максимовна_

СВЕДЕНИЯ НА МОМЕНТ _1937_ АРЕСТА[1])
(указать, какой по счету арест)

Место жительства _Москва, Лопуховский пер, д 2,"А" кв 19, ком 3_
Место работы _завод им. Орджоникидзе_
Должность _револьверщица_   Профессия _до 1936г. переводчица_
Партийность (не только КПСС) _КПГермании 1925-1931, с 1931 до 1937 ч.е. 1956 до к.г._
член КПСС

А Р Е С Т
Дата ареста _25.10.37_ Место ареста _г Москва_
Обстоятельства ареста _приглашение в паспортный стол на 40 мин_
Ваше мнение о причинах ареста _письмо из-за границы 2го мужа, подписывала_
В. Кнехель

С Л Е Д С Т В И Е
Продолжительность следствия с _не знаю_ по _____
Место проведения следствия _Бутырская тюрьма_
Следственный орган _____
Фамилии и звания следователей _____
Краткое изложение предъявленного обвинения _Участие в контрреволюционной_
деятельности не подтвердилось, недонесение на 1го мужа с кото-
Кто еще проходил по тому же делу _рым разошлась в 1931г_

СУД ИЛИ ЗАМЕНЯЮЩИЙ ЕГО ОРГАН И ПРИГОВОР
Продолжительность суда с _не было_ по _8 февраля 1938, решение_
Место суда _Москва_
Судебный орган _Особое совещание при НКВД СССР_
Приговор или заменяющее его решение _лишение свободы как_
член семьи изменника родины
Дата вынесения приговора _8 фвр 1938_ Статья _7 СИР_   Срок _8 лет_
Поражение в правах _____

ОТБЫТИЕ СРОКА
Продолжительность отбытия срока с _25.10.37_ по _август 1946_
Место отбытия срока _Карлаг, Долинка_
Род занятий _до 1940г общие работ лагерный номер 2 хим токарь_
Лица, отбывавшие срок в том же месте _А. Лисовская, Д.М.Дмитриева,_
Н.Д. Данилова, Э.С. Паперная, Ф Шебеко и др

О С В О Б О Ж Д Е Н И Е
Дата освобождения _25.10.45 или 25.08.46_ Причина освобождения _окончание срока_
Дата реабилитации _02.09.56 г_   Реабилитирующий орган _Воен. трибунал Моск.воен.округа_
Причина отказа в реабилитации _____
Реабилитационное определение _дело о ней производством прекращено_
за отсутствием состава преступления справки Н-1295

1) Если арестов было несколько, то сведения о каждом из них
   заполняются на отдельном листе

Memorial questionnaire on the repression, Mariia Gal'per, Karlag survivor,
Party member, late 1980s. *Memorial archive, f. 1, op. 1, d. 989.*

майора из камеры, дней через десять был
получен перевод на 27 рублей. Нам стало
ясно, что наш соратник был освобождён.

Моё морально-идеологическое состояние,
несмотря на нанесённое мне незаслуженное
оскорбление, занесение меня в рубрику врагов
народа и перенесение тяжестей тюремного
режима и следствия не поколебалось, я от
начала и до конца оставался морально и
идеологически устойчив и верен нашей Ком-
мунистической партии и марксистско-ленин-
скому учению. Я считал, что репрессии
органами НКВД по отношению к руково-
дящему составу партийно-советского аппарата,
а так же и по отношению к командному
составу Советской Армии является грубейшим
извращением политики партии, И что обяза-
тельно партия в этом деле разберётся и
исправит допущенные извращения поли-

Excerpt from the memoirs of I. Ia. Vozzhaev. *RGASPI, f. 560, op. 1, d. 7, l. 15.*

Marlen Korallov,
in camp, early 1950s.
Novaia gazeta,
October 31, 2008.

Nataliia Rykova, outskirts
of Moscow, 1954. *From
the personal archive of
T. I. Shmidt, Moscow.*

Above. Oscar and
Jo Langer at home in
Bratislava, 1934–1935.
*Photo courtesy of
Tania Langerova and
Susanna Klanger.*

Right. Evgeniia Shtern
and her husband,
Vladimir Markovich,
with their daughter
Evgeniia (Smirnova),
Moscow, 1936.
Memorial archive.

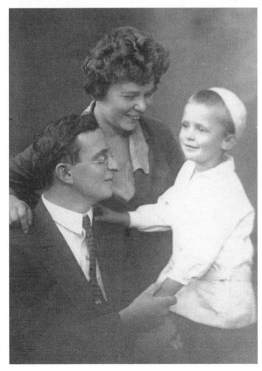

Ilin family: Mariia, Ilia, son Vladimir, and daughter Mariia
(Kuznetsova), Kiev province, 1936. *Memorial archive.*

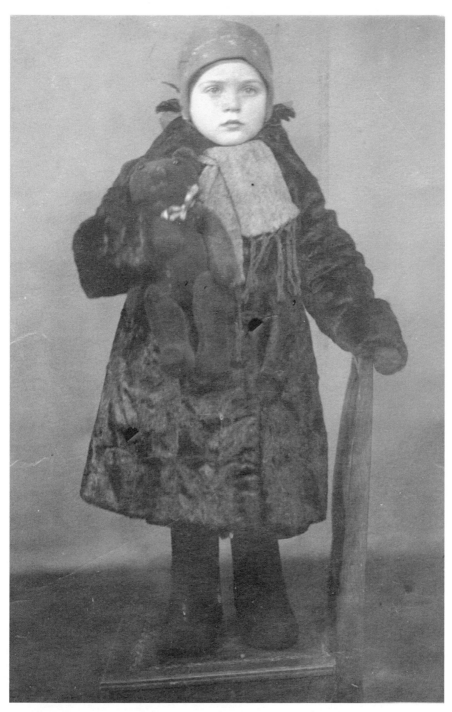

Mariia Ilina (Kuznetsova); taken in an orphanage, 1930s. *Memorial archive.*

Gerta Ioel'son-Grodzianskaia (Chuprun),
Moscow, 1939. *Memorial archive.*

Dina (Evdokiia) Sidorovna Ioelson Grodzianskaia (mother of Chuprun)
with son Alik, Moscow, 1930s. *Memorial archive.*

Punishment cell along the Igarka-Salekhard railway, 1989.
Photo by Alexander Vologodskii; Memorial archive.

CHAPTER 4

Striving for a "Happy Ending"
Attempts to Rehabilitate Socialism

It is a historical irony that those loyalist returnees and the family members of non-survivors, who had lived into, but not beyond, the Gorbachev era, died with the assurance that their faith in Communism had been redeemed. Their belief had survived the camp experience, the post-camp experience, and the post-Khrushchev period of re-Stalinization, during which the Gulag had once again become a tabooed theme. Despite the repression they had suffered, it appeared that there was a "happy ending"—for them and for the Party. Having survived and endured, the Party was now reinvigorating itself with glasnost and perestroika, as it officially embraced the broadest efforts hitherto to fill in the blank spots in history and rehabilitate and reinstate those who were eligible. If these returnees survived the Gorbachev era, they witnessed the end of the CPSU and the Soviet Union itself.

Under Khrushchev and, decades later, under Gorbachev, a number of privileged returnees were empowered to acknowledge the repression, reinstate their comrades, and restore faith in the Party and the Soviet system. This chapter will review the motives and efforts of these individuals, consider the position of the dissenting socialists, revisit the issue of Party loyalty, and consider the impact of the Gorbachev-era policy regarding public access to the history of the Gulag. Throughout, we will witness the enduring triumph of belief over contradictory evidence and despite a failed prophecy.

TRYING TO REFORM THE SYSTEM FROM WITHIN[1]

Those returning prisoners who had survived the physical harshness of the Gulag now had to deal with the psychological and political challenges of the complex and uncertain process of rehabilitation and, for some, Party reinstatement. In the post-liberation period, most former prisoners were at the mercy of grudging officials who allowed or even facilitated impediments at every stage of the complex bureaucratic process. Very few ex-prisoners were ever able to advance to high positions. However, a select number of Party veterans who had survived the camps were recruited by Khrushchev to work within the apparatus, to personally ensure the success of his de-Stalinization policies. Stephen Cohen has argued that these returnees—"Khrushchev's zeks"—influenced his "moral awakening."[2] Ultimately, they learned that they had a very limited mandate, but a few lived long enough to see new efforts emerge under Gorbachev.

Aleksei Snegov

Aleksei Snegov had occupied a variety of Party posts in the 1920s, and in 1930 he worked briefly with Beria as the first deputy of the Transcaucasian regional Party Committee in Tbilisi. He then worked for the Party in Russia, but ultimately, like many of his peers, he was arrested in 1937. He was briefly released in 1938. Snegov quickly returned to Moscow to seek help from deputy premier Anastas Mikoyan but did not heed his advice to go to a sanatorium in Sochi. As Snegov, years later, told Sergo Mikoyan, son of Anastas, his father had been concerned about Snegov's welfare because he had presciently worried that the wave of liberation would not guarantee against subsequent "unpleasantness." Snegov adamantly refused to leave for Sochi until his Party card was returned. As he waited to be seen by the head of the Party Control Commission, he was approached by two NKVD men who ordered him to follow them. Mikoyan had been right. As Snegov recounted, "I ended up back in the same place that I had by some miracle only just gotten out of, and this time it was not for one year, but for seventeen."[3]

After Stalin's death, Snegov apparently smuggled a letter out of camp to Mikoyan and Khrushchev, offering his services in the trial of Beria.[4] Snegov's help was deemed necessary to implicate Beria for his activities as first secretary.[5] So, after seventeen years in camps and exile, and an extensive search, he was tracked down and brought directly from the camp to the Kremlin. There he not only provided evidence against Beria but also revealed the horrors of Kolyma and the torture to which he had been subjected. It seems that Snegov was sent back to the Gulag after his testimony, but he was ultimately released and rehabilitated in 1954.

As noted, Snegov was no ordinary returnee. He was an old acquaintance of Khrushchev, and the Soviet leader recognized the importance of his firsthand experience, as well as his knowledge of how the Gulag operated. Having been on the inside and being now on the outside, Snegov, a firm believer in working within the system, offered suggestions for improving it. For example, according to Roy Medvedev, in the period prior to the mass liberations Snegov did not go so far as to request release for a cohort of women prisoners in Vorkuta and Kolyma, but rather tried to better their conditions and fit their forced labor to their abilities. He informed Khrushchev how inefficient it was to have thousands of women, who were too weak to break the frozen Arctic earth with ice picks, laboring in these northern camps. Medvedev claims that Khrushchev then ordered that these women be dispatched to southerly camps in Kazakhstan.[6] Snegov also promoted the idea of special commissions for releasing prisoners.[7]

Sergo Mikoyan recalls that when he saw Snegov in 1954, he found him neither downtrodden nor broken; quite the contrary, he was a virile and energetic man who had triumphed over his "torturous masters."[8] Furthermore, he had gone into and come out of camp a committed Party man; "He not only did not become an enemy of socialism," wrote the younger Mikoyan, "but all of his concerns and criticisms [centered on how to] restore . . . the belief of the people in socialism and in the party of Lenin."[9] Of course, he conceded, they were all confronted with the fact that this Party was different from that which Lenin had created, because Stalin had destroyed that Party. For Snegov, the Party had filled the "meaning" niche so eloquently described by Frankl; suffering may have been viewed as no more than sacrifice for his ideals and values.[10]

Khrushchev later acknowledged that when such figures as Snegov and Shatunovskaia were arrested, at first he really believed they had been connected with enemies. That changed immediately after Beria's crimes were exposed by Khrushchev and others. They were then freed and reinstated. However, Khrushchev believed that they and "thousands like them" would need an explanation, so that they would not have an "unhealthy attitude toward the Party and its leadership."[11] But for Snegov and Shatunovskaia, such explanations were unnecessary. According to Mikoyan, "They did not demand an explanation, they understood a lot themselves, and most importantly, they were pleased that finally, after many years, the 'mistake' with regard to them was admitted."[12] Nevertheless, they recognized that there were millions of Party and non-Party members who would need an explanation.

Snegov was a powerful advocate of de-Stalinization and played a prominent role in bringing about the Secret Speech at the Twentieth Party Congress. He reportedly argued to Khrushchev and Mikoyan: "If [you] don't discredit Stalin at this Congress, the first since the tyrant's death, and do not tell about his crimes, [you] will go down in history as his willing accomplices. Only by exposing the role of Stalin can [you] convince the Party that [you] were involuntary participants."[13]

Snegov passionately embraced the release process in the aftermath of the Congress, urging the utmost haste because he feared that "every day's delay would bring about the death of many people."[14] He also undertook an active advisory role regarding the composition and functioning of the commissions that ultimately liberated millions of prisoners. After the Twentieth Party Congress, Khrushchev appointed Snegov to be deputy head of the political department of the Gulag in the slightly revamped MVD (Ministry of the Interior).[15] He accepted the posting reluctantly because it required him to revisit the camps, but it placed Snegov in the unique position of being able to influence the pace and procedure of rehabilitation. Snegov maintained this function until 1960.[16]

In subsequent years, during the era of renewed repression (1965–1987), this "committed Bolshevik" devoted his efforts to researching and writing an anti-Stalin book. His authorship was a part of his battle against the rehabilitation of Stalin and Stalinism. During this period, he became acquainted with Roy Medvedev, whose housekeeper also came to work for Snegov. As it turns out, she informed the KGB regarding the literary activities of both of them. Consequently, his access to the Party archives became difficult. Looking back at Snegov's accomplishments, Sergo Mikoyan argued in 2006 that if he and the other "*shestidesiatniki*" (sixties generation, otherwise known as the children of the Twentieth Party Congress) had been able to continue their pursuit, "in which they were hindered by the Party bureaucracy, they would have broken the backbone of Stalinism and that same bureaucracy back then."[17] The younger Mikoyan concluded that if that had happened, things might have gone differently for the country. Mikoyan, Snegov, and others like them willingly accepted the Party's narrative—first espoused by Khrushchev—that disengaged it from Stalinism.

Olga Shatunovskaia

Olga Shatunovskaia was another early Party functionary who spent seventeen years in the Gulag and emerged to become an important participant in the de-Stalinization and rehabilitation apparatus. According to her 1955 autobiographical statement to the Central Committee, Shatunovskaia was already an active Bolshevik in Baku in 1916, at the age of fifteen: "From that time my life has been uninterruptedly bound to the life and struggle of our Party."[18] After the 1917 Revolution she joined the Baku Party Committee, and when the Soviets lost Baku in 1918 she went underground. When the Turkish authorities took over in September of that year, Shatunovskaia was arrested and sentenced to death by hanging, but her death sentence was commuted at the last minute. Subsequently she managed to escape to Georgia, where she resumed her underground activity.

Shatunovskaia spent the next decade helping establish Soviet rule, mostly in Baku. From 1929 to 1931 she studied Marxism under the aegis of the Party Central Committee, and from 1931 until her arrest Shatunovskaia worked for the Moscow Party Committee, where she met and worked with Khrushchev. In 1937 she was dismissed from her position and arrested—"at the enemy-hand of Beria and Bagirov."[19] Shatunovskaia was first taken to the Lubianka, from there to the Butyrka, then through a number of Moscow penitentiaries, and finally to the Krasnopresnensk prison. After being sentenced to eight years of hard labor for "counterrevolutionary activities," she was sent to Kolyma.[20] She survived all of that and returned to Moscow in 1946, only to be picked up again in the 1948 sweep, which was aimed at those who had already served prison or camp terms. This time she was dispatched to Central Asia, where she was arrested a year later and sentenced to perpetual exile.

Comparatively speaking, Shatunovskaia's return was no less than heroic, and she remained a dedicated Communist. In May of 1954 her sentence was revoked and she was completely rehabilitated. By July of that year she was reinstated in the Party, and in January of 1955 she was appointed to the Party Control Commission. At Khrushchev's request Shatunovskaia took part in a committee investigating the circumstances surrounding the murder of Sergei Kirov. The accumulated documents were voluminous—sixty-four volumes, to be exact—but Khrushchev decided not to publish them, a crushing disappointment for her.[21] However, Shatunovskaia, together with Snegov and others, played a key role in the preparation of a draft of the Secret Speech for Khrushchev.[22]

Shatunovskaia was also successful in her efforts to reform the entrenched repressive apparatus. For example, she suggested that the liberation commissions travel to the camps in order to accelerate the process by releasing prisoners on the spot. She also lobbied successfully to have the membership of each commission include one rehabilitated Party veteran. As so often happened, however, this provision was not consistently implemented. Another triumph of Shatunovskaia's reformist efforts delegitimized the status of perpetual exile. In theory anyone who had been sentenced under this 1948 decree should have been released immediately.[23] In practice, the process was beset with bureaucratic obstacles, but eventually millions were liberated from their prisons without walls.

Even during the Thaw, it was risky to advocate for the rights of illegally incarcerated fellow citizens. According to Antonov-Ovseenko, Shatunovskaia was under constant surveillance and her mailbox was frequently broken into. It can be assumed that many letters petitioning for release were intercepted.[24] As part of her investigation into the crimes of the thirties, Shatunovskaia prepared the cases of Bukharin and Rykov for rehabilitation, but her efforts were foiled by their political ramifications. To have rehabilitated Bukharin at that time could have required a rehabilitation of his ideas regarding, among others, the preservation of elements of a market economy. Openness to such possibilities at that time was offensive and would remain so for another three decades. Despite, or perhaps because of, Shatunovskaia's determined efforts to expose the crimes of the past, she was kept away from Khrushchev, who had decided that it was politically too risky to publish her material on the trials. As Khrushchev explained to her, "If we were to publish this material at this time, it would discredit us, we'll return to this in fifteen years."[25] Shatunovskaia feared that Khrushchev's political tenure would not last that long because he was not "surrounded by Leninists."[26] In fact, he was ousted just two years after that exchange, and the rehabilitation of Bukharin and other prominent figures was not accomplished until 1988 under Gorbachev. In the decades between Khrushchev and Gorbachev, the rehabilitative efforts of Shatunovskaia and Snegov were officially not appreciated. Witness Brezhnev's scathing assessment of their work on the Solzhenitsyn case in a 1974 confidential meeting of the Politburo: "Solzhenitsyn was incarcerated, served his term for *gross violation of Soviet law* [my italics] and was rehabilitated. But how was he rehabilitated? He was rehabilitated by two people—Shatunovskaia and Snegov."[27]

A quarter of a century later, Shatunovskaia bitterly reflected on those times: "Those eight years of work in the Party Control Commission were more difficult than the seventeen I spent in the destruction [*istrebitel'nye*] camps. . . ."[28] (Her choice of words is noteworthy, because while many survivors have referred to Kolyma as "Auschwitz without ovens," generally few ex-prisoners—and fewer scholars still—use this particular terminology with reference to the Gulag.)[29] Nevertheless, Shatunovskaia endured Brezhnev, her belief in the Party survived Brezhnev, and she resumed her work under Gorbachev. In 1988, she petitioned Politburo member Aleksandr Iakovlev to reopen the investigation of Kirov's murder. She also publicized her research that revealed the following KGB statistics on repression: between January 1, 1935, and June 22, 1941, 19,840,000 "enemies of the people" were arrested, of whom 7 million were executed in prisons. According to the document she was citing, the majority of the others died in the camps.[30] These figures were significantly higher than others, and it is not clear how they were derived. Writing in 2006, Grigorii Pomerants revealed that he had met with Shatunovskaia shortly before her death. She was still completely lucid, and she still insisted that she had seen such evidence. Pomerants expressed his bewilderment at how she could have come up with figures that exceeded official findings by such a large margin.[31] Shatunovskaia claimed that this documentation was located in the Politburo archives, along with the rest of the material she had compiled into sixty-four volumes. She further questioned why the investigations that ensued after she was forced out of the Party Control Commission in 1962 maintained that there was not enough information to implicate Stalin in Kirov's murder.[32]

In a 1989 letter to Iakovlev, Shatunovskaia wrote that an official from the Party Control Commission had come to consult with her in June of that year. It seemed to Shatunovskaia that a "historical forgery" had been committed by the Stalinists surrounding Khrushchev. A number of key documents—including those citing repression statistics and documents implicating Stalin—had disappeared from Shatunovskaia's Party Control Commission investigation files. And if this new commission based its findings on falsified materials, the product of their work would undermine the Central Committee's commitment to reevaluate the trials of the thirties. She concluded that their preliminary conclusions "dealt a blow to the prestige of the Party in this crucial period of perestroika."[33] In 1990 Iakovlev requested that the Politburo commission looking into the crimes of the thirties return to the Kirov case. After a further investigation, they reported the following: "In the process of further study of the tragic event of December 1, 1934, it has been reliably determined that there was no conspiracy with the goal of murdering S. M. Kirov and this crime was committed by Nikolaev alone."[34]

In a 1991 memorandum to the Central Committee, N. Katkov reported on the conclusions of the 1988–1990 investigation into Shatunovskaia's claims: all of the individuals who had been implicated in the Kirov affair were rehabilitated and reinstated, with the exception of Nikolaev. Katkov noted that Shatunovskaia's figures purporting that there were nearly twenty million arrests were contradicted by the figure of two million that she herself had reported to the Central Committee in 1960.[35] Shatunovskaia died in 1990, so she did not live to read this final conclusion of the investigation to which she had devoted so much of her working life. She would not have agreed with the report's findings. However, in her lifetime she was able to witness that this discussion could once again be raised and devoted serious official attention in the Soviet Union.

Valentina Pikina

Like Snegov and Shatunovskaia, Valentina Pikina was another Party veteran turned zek turned reform official. Before her arrest and imprisonment in the Mordovian camps, Pikina had been the secretary of the Central Committee of the Komsomol. She was subjected to a number of interrogations, but did not sign any confessions. After years of incarceration she was released, rehabilitated, and reinstated in the Party, and she became a member of the Party Control Commission. According to former dissident Iurii Gastev, she had "tons of assistants, subordinates, telephone lines, and other privileges commensurate to her rank." Quite atypically, her husband, a general who had denounced Pikina after her arrest, survived his own eighteen-year sentence and they reportedly reunited after their return from camp. Pikina embraced the spirit of the Twentieth Party Congress, but also viewed it as simply a matter of course. The Party was carrying out its work, so that now the truth would be told. Pikina referred to the crimes of the past as "the mistakes of the cult of personality."[36]

Following Khrushchev's ouster, most of these former prisoners found that their positions of influence were short-lived. Politically, the rehabilitated had gone out of fashion,[37] and many feared that their ex-prisoner status made them vulnerable. Gastev (who was eventually forced to leave the Soviet Union in 1981) remembered meeting Pikina in Mordovia when he landed there himself. He knew of her through his mother who had been incarcerated with Pikina years earlier in the Lefortovo. They were in touch with Pikina again after liberation, but Gastev recalled gradually losing contact with her in the Brezhnev era, either because she toed the Party line or because she was afraid. Gastev characterized Pikina as an honest, dedicated Communist who "always considered her privileges to be payment for her 'service to the people.'" He concluded that she had been able to maintain her original ideals, despite the persecution under Stalin and the corruption under Brezhnev and Andropov, by disregarding all such "interim leaders" between Lenin and Gorbachev.[38] Such cognitive dissonance, or compartmentalization, permitted Pikina, like Milchakov (see chapter 3), to "knot the two ends together" and throw away everything "in between."[39]

COSMETIC CHANGES

One of the characteristics of Khrushchev's Thaw was that a lot of reform measures were implemented, but as historian Iurii Aksiutin aptly noted, "Their goal was merely the improvement of the existing system, and not any core changes."[40] However, attempts to improve the system revealed dysfunctional core elements that were realistically impossible to ignore but politically unrealistic to correct. Adding to the political disincentives for reform were the progressive improvements in living standards: coupled with the "enthusiasm of people who believed in socialism, and that better times were ahead,"[41] they prevented deeper introspection and calls for more far-reaching efforts. Aksiutin maintains that the post-Stalin leaders had neither a personal nor political interest in shifting the government toward more accountability; hence they blamed everything on Stalin. They continued to be conceptually and politically invested in a system which had formed their thinking and their careers. They viewed their task as one of repairing a damaged but functional system rather than replacing a broken dys-functional system. Aksiutin concluded, "To the extent that the system was cre-ated under certain conditions, and called for a certain type of leader [*vozhd'*], it could not resume its former functioning in the changing circumstances; the attempts to modernize and transform it from totalitarian to authoritarian were inescapably leading to a tendency toward self-destruction, and that scared those on the top."[42] This fear of destabilizing the Party, its leadership, and perhaps the polity constrained the limits of reform, even as the official efforts for reform ex-posed the systemic failings of the government. New revelations led to new out-rage toward lower-level officials and deceased higher-level officials, but not to an effective call for accountability from officials still in power. Illustrative of both the effort to reform and the countervailing obstacles to reform is the experience of Ivan Aleksakhin.

Aleksakhin's credentials for appointment as a member of the traveling libera-tion commissions in 1956 were established by his having been in both the right and the wrong places. He had assisted Khrushchev in the Moscow Party Com-mittee in the thirties, but was arrested in 1937 and sentenced to eight years of Kolyma. After release, he was arrested again in 1949 and sent into perpetual exile in the Krasnoiarsk province until 1954. After rehabilitation and Party reinstate-ment, his appointment to membership in the traveling liberation commissions from April until September of 1956 was meant to signal the earnestness of post-Stalin reform.[43] But he was frustrated by both the meager resources allotted to the task and the lack of follow-through. In a letter to Shatunovskaia written in June of 1956 from Vorkuta,[44] Aleksakhin complained about his unmanageable case load and the limited scope of his mandate. He described uncovering cases that were so "concocted" that they stretched the human imagination, and wondered how thoroughly fifty such cases could be evaluated in a twelve-hour workday. But Aleksakhin was most troubled by his increasing awareness of how inconse-quential the efforts were of the commission to carry out reforms. He exclaimed: "Any sound-minded person has to ask when and who will instigate an indict-ment of these criminals who spent years destroying innocent Soviet citizens?" He persuasively presented an argument, later reinforced by Memorial founder Arse-nii Roginskii in 2008, that the commission addressed only the products of the crime—the victims—not the criminals who perpetrated it, much less the system that permitted it.[45] Aleksakhin asked: "Where is the Party-mindedness of our commissions if we only deal formally and bureaucratically with the products, that is, the victims, whom we liberate and rehabilitate, while shamefully being silent about those who carried out the crimes?"[46] As Aleksakhin knew, this challenge was central to the system that had permitted Stalinist rule; it tested the limits of de-Stalinization. Criminal proceedings against those responsible for criminal acts against millions of Soviet citizens were deemed too risky. Such accountability for misuse of power might undermine the legitimacy of many of those who were still in power, not least the Communist Party itself.

A test case, along with its failure, began hopefully for Aleksakhin when the Party Control Commission requested that he investigate the arbitrariness and abuses that took place in the notorious Dal'stroi in Kolyma. Aleksakhin enlisted two Party members who were also veterans of Kolyma, and together they chronicled the facts regarding the abuse of laborers in the mining of gold. N. M. Shvernik, head of the Commission, characterized their findings as "horrible hair-raising facts" and demanded that the report be sent to I. F. Nikishov, who had been in charge of the Dal'stroi from 1939 until 1948. "Let him explain this," ordered Shvernik.

A few days later, Aleksakhin received a phone call from Shvernik's assistant Kuznetsov, who had shown the report to Nikishov. In his response, Nikishov directed Shvernik's attention up the chain of command, adding, "Everything written here is just a drop in the bucket." He accounted for his behavior by blaming Beria, who had demanded that the quota set for the gold be fulfilled at any cost of expendable workers. "He told us, 'Don't fret about the prisoners. As long as the ships are still arriving, you can be assured of slave labor.'"[47] It seems that the pursuit of Aleksakhin's findings ended there, although Kuznetsov claimed that Nikishov provided a lengthy written explanation that he gave to the Party Control Commission. Whether or not he did, no judicial measures were taken against those who were implicated in abusing and persecuting their innocent fellow citizens—not then, and not later. In June of 1956 the Central Committee released a public decree on overcoming the cult of personality that slightly watered down—if not glossed over—the message of the Secret Speech. The liberation commissions were unceremoniously terminated in September of that year, without finishing their work. According to Shatunovskaia, there was no further official interest in their findings.[48]

The practice of acknowledging victims and crimes without acknowledging accountability and culpability has been critically challenged from time to time, but never successfully. Consider the case of Iosif Kernes, a Party member since 1932, who was captured by the Germans while heading an infantry division of the Red Army in 1942. After some time he managed to escape, but in January of 1943 he was arrested by the NKVD and charged with passing information to the Nazis. Kernes was interrogated in the Lubianka and then the Lefortovo. Despite continuous torture he refused to confess to being a German spy, and so he was sent to Vladimir prison. There, convinced that his sadistic interrogators were prepared to kill him, Kernes ultimately gave in to the pressure and told them that he was ready to confess to anything. In 1946, Kernes received a twenty-year prison term for "counterrevolutionary activities." That term included the time he had already served. Kernes persisted in sending appeals from Vladimir prison to the minister of defense, the minister of the interior, and the General Procuracy, all declaring his enduring loyalty to the Party. Even his lobbying efforts in April 1955 were to no avail. However, the September amnesty of that year reduced his term by half, and Kernes was released.[49]

Release, however, was not all that Kernes needed,[50] especially because his previous social support system had been depleted. His wife had remarried after being informed that he had died in 1942, and he was now a stigmatized ex-prisoner. Kernes wrote numerous letters pleading for his sentence to be revoked and for rehabilitation so that he could rejoin the Party and "start life again." These earnest efforts, demanding and begging for exoneration, continued right up until his death in 1969. It was not until twenty years later, in 1989, after review of Kernes's case, that the USSR Procuracy pronounced him innocent of the crimes for which he had been convicted.

Kernes's story was told in a 1993 work, *Henchmen and Victims*. It was written by military historians V. A. Bobrenev and V. B. Riazantsev, who had access at the time to KGB and Procuracy archives. As they tell it, the meaning of Kernes's life does not end with his death, because he was posthumously rehabilitated twenty years later. Nor, as the authors argue, does his posthumous rehabilitation really mean what it suggests. Correctly understood, posthumous pronouncements of innocence are an indictment of the system that victimized countless Kerneses. The authors wonder aloud: "How are we to qualify the activities of the members of the Special Commission [that had convicted Kernes], and all of those who influenced the fate of Iosif Kernes?"[51] How does this inform the national remembrance of Stalinism in a way that could prevent its reconstituted reemergence?

In a 2008 discussion on national memory, Memorial founder Arsenii Roginskii asserted that identifying victims was only one step in dealing with the repression. A further step would require identifying their oppressors, still mostly unnamed. Roginskii called attention to this proscribed subject:

> The memory of Stalinism in Russia is almost always the memory of victims. Victims, not crimes. . . . Unlike the Nazis . . . we mainly killed our own people, and our consciousness refused to accept this fact. In remembering the terror, we are incapable of assigning the main roles, incapable of putting the pronouns "we" and "they" in their places. This inability to assign evil is the main thing that prevents us from being able to embrace the memory of the terror properly.[52]

The Khrushchev era, which seemed to promise so much, could only begin to approach such issues, much less address their fuller implications. As with Kernes's story, delayed and posthumous rehabilitation and reinstatement were not the first steps but the only steps permitted by a Party that would only allow this much disclosure—and no accountability. Along with Roy Medvedev, many loyalists hoped that a completely different Party would emerge from the Twentieth Party Congress. He admitted, "I was very disappointed when it did not end up that way."[53] Disappointed, also, were the returnees whose sacrifice appeared to have resulted in no redeeming political changes, except a reluctant official admission of "mistakes." Even so, the core questions regarding the Stalinist repression became increasingly repressed. Some returnees accepted rehabilitation, but the experientially driven changes in their political views prevented them from requesting Party reinstatement.[54] It is not clear how large this group was.

A number of those who were outspoken in their demands for accountability later became dissidents, or left the Soviet Union. One such was M. Frenkin, who worked as a senior lecturer at the Historical Archive Institute in Moscow and who was arrested in 1932 and again in 1939. He spent a total of eighteen years in camps or exile until his rehabilitation in 1957. Frenkin was never a Party member, but contrary to the usual impediments imposed on returnees, he managed to resume his career, and even became a professor at his old institute. Despite his "new life" under Khrushchev, he found that he could not remain a historian in Russia, because he could not overcome his "disgust with the Soviet falsification of history." He left the Soviet Union in the Brezhnev wave of Jewish emigration. Writing from Jerusalem in 1983, Frenkin provided the kind of assessment that would have been impermissible from the Soviet Union:

> I view the problem of responsibility for the Stalinist–Soviet repression in
> the light of the culpability of the entire regime and its self-appointed lead-
> ers, starting with the seizure of power by the Bolsheviks, when terror, even
> as admitted by a number of Bolshevik leaders, was a necessary factor and the
> essence of the seizure of power. The whole system, starting with Lenin and
> continued by Stalin and their contemporary imitators, should be judged by
> the court of history, just as the Nazis were. The whole criminal apparatus
> has both political and criminal responsibility. . . . Kirov and many others
> bear full responsibility to the court of history for active participation in the
> creation of the Soviet terroristic system of government, and for millions of
> victims. . . ."[55]

Frenkin's views could not have been tolerated in the Soviet Union because he was unwilling to accede to the political expediency of distinguishing between the pre-Stalin era, the Stalin era, and the post-Stalin era. It was by proposing such a distinction that the Twentieth Party Congress narrative succeeded in acknowledging the history of the repression, while disowning its history in the repression.

The Institute of Marxism-Leninism (IML), a bastion of Communism, held tens of thousands of personal files on victims in its archives. It also housed all of the Party registration forms of excluded and/or deceased Communist Party members, their Party cards, working records, and other relevant documents. In addition, the institute had collected hundreds of memoirs of repressed Old Bolsheviks, which have been an invaluable resource for the current study. Elena Pavlovna Karagaeva, historian-archivist on staff there since 1957, detailed the institute's role in Party reinstatement. In the fifties, sixties, and seventies, the relatives of repressed Party members applied to the Party organs for posthumous reinstatement, and the Party organs turned to the IML for supportive documentation. In our 2008 interview, Karagaeva recalled, "people were practically screaming for reinstatement, and they wouldn't accept any interruption in their Party tenure."[56]

Elena herself was not privy to these personal dossiers until she worked with them in 1984, but others had earlier access. According to these staff members, their content with regard to betrayals and personal suffering was harrowing. Elena maintained, "I think the people who worked here had not really understood what happened [up until then] . . . and they were [suddenly] confronted with these 'hair-raising' documents and the denunciations. . . ." She told of how an old woman, whose name she did not recall, came to the Institute from the German Democratic Republic in the 1970s to assist in sorting out the Comintern archives. Her husband had been a victim of the repression. Karagaeva recalled her bewilderment at the woman's willingness to support this effort. She exclaimed, "And she sat here in this very room, helped me, made selections, we worked together to organize this archive. All the while, I thought, 'Why on earth would you want to come here?'"[57] Karagaeva dared not ask her, such were not the times, but it is possible the woman would not have considered it a relevant question—why not?

The 1970s ushered in a new wave of requests for rehabilitations and reinstatements of Trotskyites. To this end, the institute/archive sent thousands of Party registration forms to provincial committees throughout the Soviet Union. During this period, there was also an application for Bukharin's rehabilitation, but it was not successful. Also rejected were requests for reinstatement from the sons and daughters of executed Trotskyites.

As this decade progressed, fewer requests were processed, and the subject was less and less a topic of discussion at the institute. When I asked Karagaeva if this was because the issue was too sensitive, she responded, "We were raised to speak less. After my supervisor told me about how the stories made her hair stand on end, she never uttered another word about it again." The archive of memoirs did not become classified in the seventies, but unofficially, gaining access became increasingly difficult.[58]

If the Gulag experience was not enough to change the perceptions of some loyalists, the Brezhnev era provided an ideological tipping point. Many who had accepted the early repression of the Soviet system as a temporary expediency were suddenly confronted by Brezhnev with a measure of re-Stalinization, including the repression of discussions of the Gulag. As events associated with the Gulag were decreed "out of fashion," ex-prisoners, Party and non-Party members alike, were denied the right to process their own and their nation's history. This, coupled with other signs of burgeoning neo-Stalinism, impelled some loyalists to vent their disappointed expectations of the Party. Historian Juliane Fürst explains their Communist orthodoxy as follows: "True belief and deeper knowledge of socialist scriptures resulted both in a more highly developed moral and social conscience and in a better ability to express grievances in political terms."[59] Thus, in the sixties, seventies, and early eighties, efforts to democratize the Soviet Union originated not only from those opposed to the system, but from the system's loyal opposition. As Fürst observed, many of the "ideologically earnest . . . became the system's most outspoken critics."[60]

Philosophical Communists, including Pisarev and (for a long time) Kopelev, remained believers even after the camp; they did not want to leave the Party, but they did have a different vision of what the Party should be. However, the renewed repression, which now included incarceration in psychiatric hospitals, made it clear that the Party was hostile to their vision. Andrei Sakharov shifted from socialist to democrat—and dissident; but Roy Medvedev, also a dissident, continued to express his reverence for Lenin, and his conviction that Stalinism was an aberration of Leninism. Medvedev was convinced that reform should come "from above."[61]

But while Medvedev and some others maintained their loyal opposition in the post-Khrushchev era, many simply experienced an irreversible disillusionment because their earlier idealistic expectations had been shattered. The poems of ex-prisoner Vladimir Filin, written during that time but published only under Gorbachev, reflected this sentiment: "The epoch of [building Communism] can be construed as just another historical illusion that inevitably ha[d] to be let go."[62] But not all disillusionment was irreversible. Len (after Lenin) Karpinskii, Komsomol secretary and member of *Pravda's* editorial board, was the son of two Old

Bolsheviks who had not been incarcerated in the Gulag. Len grew up believing in the Party. He saw several relatives disappear in the thirties, but his parents told him that they had moved away. It was unclear to Len, and for that matter even to his father, why his immediate family did not get swept up in the terror. The Secret Speech, however, helped clarify his childhood questions on the terror, and he was pleased at the Party's acknowledgment of Stalin's responsibility for millions of deaths. He remained, however, concerned about Khrushchev's superficial treatment of the issue.[63]

In 1966 Karpinskii was fired from *Pravda* and sent to *Izvestiia* as a special correspondent. After a year and a half he complained that pro-Stalin articles were finding their way back into the paper. Within hours of that comment, the Central Committee ordered, "Don't let him write anything . . . give him a salary but don't give him a pen."[64] His career, or rather, his presence at *Izvestiia* ended altogether when he made some critical remarks on the 1968 Soviet invasion of Czechoslovakia. Karpinskii then began work in the department of scientific communism at Progress Publishers in 1973, but this too was terminated. In 1975 he was called in to the Party Control Commission and expelled for "antiparty activity." The charges apparently stemmed from a manuscript he had written in 1969 titled "Words Are Also Deeds," which he had given to Roy Medvedev to read. (In a 1989 interview with Stephen Cohen and Katrina Vanden Heuvel, Karpinskii explained that the political shift toward glasnost and perestroika realized the basic tenets he had presented in the 1969 article.)[65] This manuscript, along with several other papers, had been confiscated by the KGB in a 1970 search of Medvedev's apartment, but they waited five years to bring charges against Karpinskii. He was labeled as a dissident by those who had expelled him from the Party, but Karpinskii did not perceive himself as such. He recalled that he was more of a "half-dissident" at the time of the expulsion. As he explained, "Formally I was expelled from the party, but I remained a party member in my soul. . . . I didn't break with my Marxist-Leninist views or become an antisocialist like many dissidents. I was more like Roy Medvedev . . . who fought the deformations in our system but remained faithful to socialist ideals—who believed we had to start building socialism anew in the Soviet Union."[66] Karpinskii's appeal for Party reinstatement in 1987 was rejected. But as perestroika evolved Karpinskii found support among a number of like-minded allies, such as historian Iurii Afanasiev and playwright Mikhail Shatrov, who were fast gaining prominence. Karpinskii was finally readmitted to the Party in October of 1988. This was just around the time that such organizations as Memorial were picking up momentum.

For those who were still alive when Gorbachev assumed power, and particularly for those who lived to hear his 1987 address on the seventieth anniversary of the October Revolution, it was clear that real changes were planned. For the first time in almost three decades the Party chief himself raised the issue of the "thousands" of repressions, and gave the green light to pursue the facts. At a case-by-case level, such revelations did not appear to undermine faith in the Party and the system. But as the numbers of cases grew, so too did the possible threat to the Party's integrity. The risk that Khrushchev had foreseen was unfolding.

Gorbachev also recognized this risk, and in a 1988 Politburo session he expressed concern that the organization Memorial had aspirations of becoming more than just a "society."[67] He suspected that they did not merely want a monument to the victims of repression; they wanted to use the process of collecting material about the victims to raise public discussion of the repression. Gorbachev's concerns were heightened by talk of honoring victims of earlier terror—from the Revolution on. Such proposals were objected to by the ex-prisoner Party members who had attended these early discussions, but to no avail, according to Central Committee secretary Vadim Medvedev.[68]

After further deliberation, Gorbachev resolved that Memorial should be limited to the regional level, and kept under Party supervision. The organization would be permitted to function, but not as a public movement, and their mandate would be confined to the building of a monument.[69] The subsequent development of Memorial is beyond the scope of the present work, but it is clear that the Party leadership was apprehensive about the potential threat to its legitimacy that substantial investigation into the Stalinist past would pose.[70] (Also beyond the scope of the present work, but worth noting, is the role of revelations regarding the crimes of the Stalinist past in facilitating the collapse of the Soviet Union. They may not have been a major factor, since it resulted from many cumulative events,[71] but we might assess the importance of these historical revelations from the importance placed on constraining and controlling them by the policies of the previous and present ruling Party. The destabilizing, de-legitimizing potential of confronting an onerous past was recognized by Khrushchev and Brezhnev, later Gorbachev and Putin, and, sometimes Medvedev. They were concerned about the risk of a de-Stalinization that might emerge uncontrollably from below, and tried to contain it by curbing access to archives, limiting rehabilitation to victim compensation, and other similar measures. They may have been overestimating the importance of these historical revelations to the stability of the system, but our assessment might be calibrated in the light of theirs.)

Party Reinstatement: The Perestroika Period and Beyond

Thousands of applications for Party reinstatement followed in the wake of the Twentieth Party Congress, but a significant backlog developed in the post-Khrushchev era.[72] It was not until three decades later that tens of thousands more would apply. According to a 1990 memorandum by Boris Pugo, chairman of the Party Control Commission from 1988 to 1990, eighty thousand applications for Party rehabilitation (reinstatement) were honored during this time.[73] The motivations as well as the histories of the applicants varied. One ex-prisoner had been a Party member from 1964 until the dissolution of the Soviet Union in 1991, and his parents had been early Party members—his mother had joined in 1918, his father in 1924. Both were arrested in 1929, expelled from the Party as "unrepentant Trotskyites," and executed in Magadan in October of 1937. This applicant, born in a "political isolator" in the Urals in 1933, was transferred to an orphanage at age four after his parents' execution. In the Gorbachev era, he successfully petitioned for their posthumous reinstatement—his father's in 1989, and his mother's in 1991. He explained that their reinstatement had "great significance" for him.[74]

While the glasnost of the Gorbachev period confirmed the belief of some, it challenged it for others, because the reality of the past could no longer be denied or avoided. A few returnees, like the writer Lev Razgon, enthusiastically rejoined the Party under Khrushchev only to voluntarily leave it under Gorbachev. Some ex-prisoners both rejoined and left the ranks of the Party during the Gorbachev years. Razgon and others found that their views toward the system had undergone a "fundamental change" during this period.[75] And this change so distanced them from the Party that some candidates who were offered reinstatement outright refused it.[76]

However, accepting or rejecting the Party ideology was only one consideration regarding Party membership. Some who had developed a critical view of the system still sought Party membership because they felt some obligation to fulfill the hopes of their murdered parents. In addition, their social, vocational, and political life would be more difficult without Party reinstatement. One returnee, L. S. Iardovskaia, whose entire family was arrested in 1936–1937, emerged from the repression with no illusions about the Party: "I already understood everything in camp. I fully came to understand what kind of socialism we were building after the repression struck down my family."[77] After Iardovskaia's husband was executed, she was sentenced to eight years as the family member of an "enemy of the people"; her son was sent to an orphanage. Iardovskaia was not tortured, but her father, her husband, and their brothers were. None of them survived. Iardovskaia was rehabilitated in 1956. She applied for and was granted Party reinstatement in the Gorbachev era. When asked in 1995 about her motivation for seeking reinstatement, her reason was functional: "It would have been even more difficult to adapt without it."[78]

N. I. Zadorozhnaia was another returnee who lost faith in the system, but who had to find a way to live with it. As a child in the thirties she had witnessed the arrests of her mother, father, stepfather, grandfather, and brother. Zadorozhnaia's father and stepfather were executed, and her grandfather perished in the Gulag. Her mother was released from the camp in 1947 and re-arrested along with Zadorozhnaia in 1949. They were sentenced to perpetual exile but released under the 1953 amnesty that followed Stalin's death. Her brother survived and returned from Karlag in 1955. After release Zadorozhnaia became a history teacher, and she was fortunate enough to be given the opportunity to work. But this opportunity was contingent on her ability to be discreet about both *her* past and *the* past—a discretion that required constant self-censorship. It was a survival skill acquired from painful experience. She later revealed that quite early on she had developed "an understanding of this system, starting in 1937–38, and even earlier—after hearing the stories [her] nanny told [her] about collectivization in her village."[79] From these stories she had learned both how to fill in unspoken information and what information must remain unspoken.

Despite this knowledge and these feelings, Zadorozhnaia joined the Party in 1959. Years later, in the post-Soviet era, she accounted for that decision apologetically: "Joining the Party was partially because of the influence of my mother, who was an Old Bolshevik, but it was also out of a sense of self-preservation and the awareness that more persecution could still lie ahead."[80] She added her hope that such people as herself could change the balance of "decent and indecent" members of the Party—an expedient rationalization for resolving dissonant cognitions. Apparently, the negative associations she had about the Party could be safely deflected to individual members. Even if the group membership that the Party provided did not particularly offer her a sense of meaning or identity, it apparently did offer something Zadorozhnaia needed—a sense of security.

Exposing the Past

In the Gorbachev era there was no longer such a great disparity between what people were told and what they knew, and this closure of the knowledge gap generated a dialogue. The fact that rehabilitations were taking place on an increasingly large scale, and organizations like Memorial could influence the public discourse, challenged the ideological faith in the system with evidence about the operation of the system. One of the numberless examples of this evidence is epitomized by a 1989 letter from Dina Dmitrievna Buzanova in Odessa to Memorial. Her father had been a senior instructor at the Zhukov Military Aviation Academy when he fell victim to the terror. In her closing lines, she requests, "I very much want that my father, Buzanov Dmitrii Ivanovich, and uncle, Buzanov Vasilii Ivanovich, who gave their lives to the Soviet system and the Party and fell victim to repression, will not be forgotten. They have no graves. Memorial in Moscow will be a monument for them."[81] Buzanov had already been posthumously rehabilitated in 1956 and posthumously reinstated in the Party in 1957, but legal recognition and public remembrance are separate issues. Buzanova was emboldened by the transformation of the status of knowledge that Memorial was making possible. Transforming individual knowledge to mutually shared knowledge validates it, and could generate an impetus for political change.

The perestroika-era press was filled with contributions from readers about the terror. Not unlike the 1953 readers' letters to *Pravda,* even while describing the crimes of the past some praised the Party for allowing them to be revealed, and praised the returnees for preserving their belief in "our people," as represented by the Party. Just as it had after the 1953 amnesty and the Twentieth Party Congress, such press, sincerely or propagandistically, offered the public a cognitive way of relieving their dissonance by turning what might have been viewed as disconfirmation of Communism into confirmation. For example, an article written by a family member of victims of the terror thanks the Party for its commitment at the Nineteenth Party Conference to fill in the blank spots in history, and ends by affirming Party loyalty: "The people who were innocently condemned in those times deserve our respect. After all, those who managed to return from prisons and camps for the most part preserved their feeling of patriotism and belief in the Party and our people."[82] A bit more boldly, this author considered the restoration of forgotten pages of history to be a "Party and civic duty." As the pro-Party tenor of this and other articles suggests, officials, including Gorbachev, were trying to use these revelations to strengthen the Party. By portraying the Party as the "top-down" initiator of these revelations, they were trying to mitigate the political damage that Khrushchev so feared.[83] However, burgeoning "bottom-up" efforts to rediscover history, especially those by Memorial, pointed to a different reality. And judging from Gorbachev's efforts to constrain the mandate of Memorial, the Party recognized the politically destabilizing possibilities of these revelations.

During the Gorbachev era, the history of the Stalinist past was unveiled in feature and documentary films, on television, in literature, and on stage, raising hitherto publicly forbidden questions. The officially sanctioned approach to the past had familiar limitations—the experience of the victims was the focus. Very occasionally, however, the perpetrators were discussed. In what light were they to be seen? Were they malevolent, or were they "actively defending" the interests of the Party and the state? The documentary film "Letters from Alzhir" addressed this question.[84] Apparently some of the women incarcerated in this camp for the wives and widows of "enemies of the people" recalled two "good supervisors" who had allowed packages and were not heavy-handed in their treatment of the prisoners. One perestroika-era reviewer noted that these men had "served the Party since the 1920s," and wondered whether their obedience was out of fear or out of conviction. She concluded that under a totalitarian regime, it was difficult if not impossible to be the "master of one's own fate,"[85] so the distinction may be moot. From this perspective, the perpetrators were victims too.

While an accurate estimate of the numbers of victims was difficult, this was the most accessible segment of the history of the repression. Less accessible was information about the perpetrators, and least accessible was information about the government's responsibility for permitting them to operate with impunity. The role and function of the perpetrators and the issue of culpability were not permissible topics for public discourse in the Gorbachev era, nor in the first two decades of the post-Soviet era, even though resolving such issues is generally recognized as part and parcel of any move toward democracy. This recognition may have informed the Party's policy to thwart such public discourse. In the Gorbachev era, great attempts were made to preserve the Party's image, so while the stories that emerged may have been, in courtroom terminology, "nothing but the truth," they were not "the whole truth." This trend could continue to date, because, as Arsenii Roginskii explained, "Popular consciousness has nothing to hold onto from a legal point of view. The state has produced no legal document that recognizes state terror as a crime."[86]

Paradoxically, it may have been more difficult for loyalists to reconcile with failure because they had come so close to succeeding. To loyalist returnees and the families of non-survivors, it seemed that the Twentieth Party Congress and the Khrushchev reforms were proceeding toward the fulfillment of the prophecy that had sustained them through the camp experience and post-camp repression. Their faith in Communism was further reinforced by rehabilitation and reinstatement, and access to the history of the Gulag. The ensuing re-Stalinization and renewed repression of even the history of the repression required a reassessment. Had the prophecy failed, or just been delayed? Had Stalinism failed Communism, as the Party claimed, or had the Party failed Communism, as some dissidents claimed? Was the question even relevant to the nation, so long as the Party maintained control, especially if dissidents were powerless to effect any change? The responses to these issues varied with the political history of our informants and often intertwined with a family history shaped by a repression that rendered some orphaned and displaced.

In this chapter we examined the narratives of those whose belief in the Party endured and survived the personal and political perturbations of the Gulag, Khrushchev's de-Stalinization, and Brezhnev's re-Stalinization. We also recorded the explanations of those who had stopped believing in the Party. Under Gorbachev, many loyalist returnees believed that their faith was being affirmed and the prophecy of a humane socialism was finally moving toward realization. Those who died during this period had lived into the "bright future" foretold by this vision. The more prescient, however, recognized a resurgence of censorship in the Party's efforts to insulate itself from responsibility for the terror by limiting the scope of inquiry.

When the Soviet Union and the CPSU collapsed in 1991, Communist loyalists were confronted with the most unsettling challenge to their ideology since Khrushchev's Secret Speech. Now, loyalist Gulag survivors had to live with the fact that the Party and the Soviet system, which gave them "meaning," in which they believed and for which they had sacrificed, no longer existed in the real world. But it continued to exist as an unresolved issue in the minds of the survivors and the lives of their children. More voices of those children will be heard in the following chapter, as they describe their struggle to adjust to a post-Soviet world, now bereft of their parents' dreams. Some filled this space with positive attitudes toward the now defunct CPSU and Soviet system. Such positive attitudes could hardly have been based on an accurate assessment of how the Soviet regime had repressed their parents. Rather, it may reflect the absence of a "normal" childhood, the absence of public discussions of the repression, the usurpation of familial loyalty by the Party, and the influence of national narratives that valorize the Communist past.

CHAPTER 5

The Legacies of the Repression

The dissolution of the Soviet Union and the demise of the Party had not been foreseen by either Communists or non-Communists. But the Communist faithful were particularly ill-prepared to make sense of the disappearance of an empire, much less the political institution that had successfully conflated itself with "the people" and patriotism. Where, now, was meaning to be found, especially for those raised in Soviet orphanages, where the policy was to indoctrinate them to believe that their parents' incarceration was justified by a now defunct Party? Their narratives describe an amalgam of idealism and alienation, as well as an intermingling of open and clandestine rejections of Communism. But the narrators are often so guarded that it is difficult to distinguish between their accommodation *to* the immutable and their assimilation *of* the immutable—probably even for them.

As the orphaned and displaced "heirs of the Gulag," the children of executed or imprisoned Communist loyalists bore unique political and psychological burdens. But all the "heirs of Stalin" had to find a way of adapting to Stalin's immediate and long-term influence. Some were infected by the repression and became carriers of the repression; others became resisters of repression and tried to spread resistance. In this final chapter, we will explore some of the questions that confronted the second generation (the children of repressed loyalists), and look at the short- and long-term legacies of decades of repression. In conclusion we will consider what, if anything, might be learned from a repression that had succeeded and a system that failed.

When the Soviet Union collapsed, so also did the meaning it had created for its citizens. The first generation of Party loyalists had to salvage meaning from the failure of their dedicated efforts. The children of repressed Communists bore their own set of issues, different from the first generation, but equally complex. They had to salvage meaning from their own and their country's past, and from the sacrifices of their parents.[1]

The enormity and the suddenness of the collapse made it seem incredible, especially to the Party loyalists. Following the dissolution of the Soviet Union, the conflict of old and new politics was displayed on the first day of the 1992 hearing on the constitutionality of banning the Communist Party. The arguments of the Party's defenders were acidly described in *Izvestiia* by Iurii Feofanov. For example, one defender challenged the justification of banning the most "massive Party in the country," the very Party that had "rallied many millions of countrymen and served their interests" and led them to victory in the "Great Patriotic War, for which three million Communists sacrificed their lives."[2] Such claims reminded Feofanov of the bombast that had always characterized Party Congresses. "In light of everything we know about our Party," he asserted the speech was "pathetic," and sounded like the "honking of a goose."[3] In 1992, it was safe to write such things.

Also on display was the personal and political legacy bequeathed by the first generation of Communists to their children. Feofanov was bewildered by the impassioned defense of the Party delivered by People's Deputy D. Stepanov, a man whose father had been arrested in 1940 and died in the camps. He marvels: "Here was this son defending with sincere pathos that same Party that had killed his father. It's some phenomenon, this Communist conviction in the righteousness of a cause so soaked in bitterness, tears, and blood."[4] Feofanov's bewilderment reflected the viewpoint of many skeptics, but it also revealed an inability to comprehend the emotional appeal of the Communist Party. Feofanov had no difficulty understanding the allegiance of ordinary Party functionaries who were at risk of losing the perks and power they had accumulated; these were material and practical losses. But he gave insufficient weight to the immaterial, emotional component of Party membership—the intrinsic satisfaction of union with an ideologically inspired community that this study has investigated. Such satisfactions may have been counterintuitive to nonbelievers, but were powerfully compelling to adherents like People's Deputy Stepanov. He was grateful to the Party that had permitted him to overcome an unpromising beginning. Despite his family's political history, he had worked his way up to a political position of some standing and this rise was abetted by an attitude consistent with what was expected of a Party member in his position.

Early in their lives, Stepanov and many others in his generation lost their parents to the terror and grew up in orphanages that stigmatized their "criminal" parents, while indoctrinating them in the socially redeeming legitimacy of the terror. They responded with a wide range of adaptations. Some, following their parents' example, became active, dedicated Party members.[5] Others (in fact, according to historian Roy Medvedev, the majority of his peers), were apolitical or felt antipathy toward the Party that had persecuted their parents. As "children of enemies of the people," moreover, most had few opportunities for Party careers, or for that matter any careers. They were often denied access to higher education, government-run institutes, and merited advancement.

Medvedev himself did not seek a Party career because he was certain the blemish of his father's tragic fate would have barred his acceptance.[6] Instead he became a respected pedagogue and a scholar. In 1971, he published *Let History Judge* abroad; this was a pioneering work that was instrumental in exposing the crimes of the Stalinist apparatus. It supported the Leninist line, deplored Stalinism, and denounced Stalin and other Party officials, but it shielded the system by attributing culpability to individual miscreants.

While the political sentiments of a group are predictable, the sentiments of any single member are not. Stepanov, Medvedev, and a host of dissidents, such as Petr Yakir, emerged from the personal, familial, and political trauma of losing a parent with different attitudes toward the Party. We will listen to how they account for this.

Nadezhda Ioffe

If the parents did survive, they were often able to exert influence on their children's perceptions of the Gulag experience, or the Soviet system. Some parents, such as Nadezhda Ioffe, daughter of Adolf Ioffe (see the introduction), withheld their negative views of the Party from their children. In a 1997 interview, Nadezhda confessed her deep regret on one of the occasions when she was being sent back to the Gulag that she had not told her daughter, Natasha, the things she had experienced in the Gulag, and the things she knew about the terror: "Why didn't I tell her why they shot her father? Why didn't I tell her the truth about collectivization and industrialization? That the country was being destroyed. That the peasantry was being physically wiped out. . . ."[7] She accounted for this concealment by saying she had wanted Natasha to be able to retain the support offered by the ideology of Communism. Natasha was an active Komsomol member, head of her organization, and "she believed in all of it—in socialism, in Communism, that the Soviet regime was the best in the world. That we were an example to the world's proletariat."[8] However, protecting her daughter from the psychological stress of cognitive dissonance and the political risks of disclosure could also have justified withholding this information from Natasha. It was during Stalin's time that Nadezhda's three imprisonments (1929, 1936, and 1949) took place, and children were encouraged to place Party loyalty over family loyalty.[9]

Nataliia Rappaport

There were also survivors' children, like Nataliia Rappaport, who rejected the Party that their formerly repressed parents continued to support. Nataliia's father, Iakov Rappaport, had been a Party member since World War II and was a prominent physician when he was swept up in 1953 by the Doctors Plot, Stalin's last wave of terror. At the time of his arrest on false charges of plotting to kill the Kremlin leadership, Nataliia was fourteen years old. She and her sister were both members of the Komsomol. Nataliia recalled how terrified she was during the anti-Semitic campaign prior to her father's arrest, when she overheard her schoolmates debating whether the executions of these "killer doctors" would be public.

When her father was taken to the Lefortovo prison, her mother was required to leave their home in order to witness a search of their dacha. Upon her return the next morning, she found Nataliia huddled in the corner where she had fearfully spent the night. Nataliia had despaired of ever seeing her mother again. As for Iakov Rappaport, he was initially subjected to "conveyor-belt" interrogations of sleep deprivation for days on end, then unexpectedly released in April of 1953. His life had been saved by Stalin's death. He waited twenty years before recording his experiences in the 1970s, but did not publish the memoirs until 1988, at age ninety.

The doctors were the first to be rehabilitated, and Rappaport was reinstated in the Party.[10] He claimed to have had his doubts about the Party but hoped that "someday common sense would triumph."[11] When he heard Gorbachev's reference to the Doctors Plot in his November 1987 speech, he was gratified that he had lived to see that day. However, Nataliia had been stigmatized as an outcast as a result of her father's arrest, and she spent decades resenting the Party that had mistreated her family. Yet, she revealed in a 1988 interview that if she had been asked to join anew, now in the Gorbachev era, she probably would have done so.[12] Nataliia, like her father, was receptive to returning to the hope that originally imbued their past with the new beginning promised by Gorbachev.

Evgeniia Vladimirovna Smirnova

Evgeniia Vladimirovna Smirnova's story describes a gradual, informed departure from the beliefs of her parents, all the while recognizing that what worked for them did not work for her. Both parents were veteran Party members. Her father, Vladimir Solomonovich Markovich, a Party member since 1920, was an engineer who directed an institute on rail modernization of the People's Commissariat of Transportation. He was expelled from the Party and the institute in 1936, arrested in 1937 as a Trotskyite and German spy, and executed in June of 1939. Her mother, Evgeniia Aleksandrovna Shtern, had joined the Party in 1919 and worked as a censor in a Moscow publishing house. She was arrested for "counterrevolutionary activities" in 1937 and sentenced to five years in prison. She spent the first two years of her incarceration in the notorious Iaroslavl political isolator and was then transferred to Kolyma. She was released in 1944 but rearrested in 1949 and sentenced to perpetual exile in Kolyma.[13] At that time, Evgeniia, the daughter, had managed to get a job in Moscow, no small feat for a child of repressed parents. However, her superiors cautioned her to avoid contact with her mother, and she did.[14]

However, Evgeniia's mother sent letters to her from Kolyma. She wrote with seeming pride, "We are working in Kolyma, trying to fulfill the norms, we almost always succeed."[15] Evgeniia's mother sometimes even overfulfilled the norms. She was a tough and driven woman who, already at age sixteen, had served on the front in the Civil War. Yet, Evgeniia thought about her mother's petite stature and shuddered at what a strain such heavy labor might impose on her health.

Even as a child, Evgeniia's mother had been an ardent Communist, deeply influenced by an older sister, who envisioned a fulfilling struggle toward a "bright future." Her mother embraced the reforms of the Twentieth Party Congress as evidence that the Party was returning to its right path. Her values affirmed, the mother returned to active Party work. In the seventies she worked hard to promote Communism, even gathering materials for a museum on the history of the Komsomol.

Evgeniia, however, had a different reaction to the unfolding course of events in the country and in her family. She had been raised as a Leninist, a Pioneer and Komsomol member, and with such an idealistic view of Communism that at the beginning of the war with the Nazis she could not understand how the proletariat of one country would fight another: "From my youth, I always considered that the proletariat of all countries should unite."[16] But even though many of her values had been "internalized," as she described them, she "parted with her illusions" in response to the realities of the repression. Unlike her mother, Evgeniia did not want to become a Party member. Although she stopped short of actively joining the human rights movement of the sixties, she "did what she could" by providing a hiding place for samizdat manuscripts (*Khronika Tekushchykh Sobytii*, a key underground journal of human rights activities) in her apartment—a location considered above suspicion. Of course, she never told her mother. In this act she was taking a legal risk, justified by a political shift, based on an earlier ideological shift. In our interview, I asked if this was a big step for her. She explained that it was already clear by then that this was the right thing to do. She had been raised to do the "right thing," but, in contrast to her mother, she had lost faith in the Party's rectitude.

When asked what she thought of Khrushchev, Evgeniia expressed mixed feelings. On the one hand, the fact that he allowed people to "come back to life eclipsed everything else . . . of course he was also behind mass shootings. . . . He also made it possible for masses of people to get apartments." Khrushchev in fact did all of those things, but which should be selected to judge him? Evgeniia's selection of this range of events highlighted her struggle to reconcile her early ideological indoctrination into the promise of Communism with her later reassessment of its failures.

Evgeniia's mother died in 1987, but she lived to witness the beginning of perestroika, which they both hailed as an "improvement of the Party" rather than a move against it. Two years after her mother's death, Evgeniia joined Memorial. With their help, she was able to uncover the true story of her father's victimization, since the information on his death certificate had been falsified. She learned that he was imprisoned for two years, in Sverdlovsk and then in Moscow. It was claimed that he had confessed, but there was also a petition he had sent to the court in which he denied his confession—the type of legal catch-22 that could take rehabilitation commissions decades to decipher. This is how it read: "I understand that under the current circumstances the Party cannot believe anyone's words and should carefully check every individual. But they checked me, and did not find anything criminal. And now I request that my case be closed and that I be given the opportunity to work as a Soviet engineer, and contribute my efforts and knowledge to benefit the Motherland."[17] Evgeniia participated with Memorial in publicizing the plight of victims of the terror. She began her efforts by delivering a speech in her father's former institute, at an event held in honor of her father. She worked with Memorial, going to returnees' houses with questionnaires that were used to establish an accessible archive of the victims of the terror. In so doing, Evgeniia met the victims—most of them ordinary citizens, non-Party members—who had been subjected to extraordinary terror. Unlike her mother, Evgeniia found no redeeming value in the repression. This is her account of one interview:

One of the people I went to see had been incarcerated in Svobodny [camp in the Far East]. He had a lovely wife, when I went to him we talked for two days. His children were already grown. He told me that he had a wonderful family, but that I was the first person to whom he had told this story of his camp history. He has since died. He said at that time that if he had not been in camp, he would have gladly volunteered to be at the front. He said that he knew he would have died there but that it would have been better than what happened to him.[18]

Other victims, even in 1989, would not talk to her at all about their camp experience. As Evgeniia gathered stories of victims, she struggled to understand how her ideologically principled mother and her similarly principled comrades in arms could have remained devoted to a system that had victimized them, along with millions of others. She recognized that her mother's devotion to Communism provided her life with an enduring sense of meaning, such that even the labor camp could be a satisfying labor of love, but Evgeniia found it painful to think about how different and devoid of meaning the incarceration must have been for the majority of the victims. She lamented, "Look at who is listed in [Memorial's publication] *Rasstrel'nye spiski* (Execution Lists).[19] People with a low education, accused of anti-Soviet agitation. It's just horrible. . . . These poor souls did nothing, they had no relationship to the system whatsoever . . . they didn't bother anyone."[20] Evgeniia wondered why her mother and her mother's peers had retained their ideological beliefs during and after the Gulag, when the political outcome seemed so different from what they had originally expected. She contrasted this with her own outcome-dependent assessment of the Communist Party—and that of others: "There are people who, when faced with new circumstances, change their opinion." She attributed her mother's changeless convictions to her "internal constitution." In context, this could be interpreted as a combination of rigidity and a steadfast commitment to a more far-reaching ideological vision. Evgeniia also recognized that her mother and many of her dedicated comrades in arms had framed the Gulag experience as a meaningful, redeeming ideological journey destined to achieve the goals of Communism. So viewed, her mother's steadfast dedication was a rational, outcome-dependent assessment. Retaining their beliefs may have helped loyalists survive the camp and post-camp experiences, and so their enduring allegiance was, at the very least, a matter of self-preservation.[21]

Mariia Ilinichna Kuznetsova

Like Evgeniia, Mariia Ilinichna Kuznetsova was a daughter of Communist parents who had been repressed, but she retained a much more positive view of the Party and the system. Mariia's view endured her father's execution and her mother's incarceration because it was guided by her mother's enduring belief. But there was a downside. While Mariia's positive attitude toward Communism had facilitated her adaptation to the repression, it hindered her adaptation to the Gorbachev-era disclosures about the repression.

Mariia's father, Ilia Lvovich Ilin, had been a prominent Communist Party official who served as the secretary of the Kiev Provincial Party Committee and then as the secretary of the Astrakhan City Party Committee. He was arrested in July of 1937, executed in November of that year in Moscow, then buried in the notorious Donskoi Cemetery. Her mother, Mariia Markovna Ilina, was the director of a silk combine in Kiev when she was arrested in 1937 as the "family member of an enemy of the people." She was incarcerated in the Potma camp and then sent on to a Gulag location in the Komi Autonomous Republic until her release in 1948. Camp records show that she was an *udarnik* (shock worker; i.e., she excelled) in the camp. After liberation she lived in Cherkassy until her rehabilitation in 1956.

Upon their parents' arrest, Mariia and her two brothers, Feliks and Vladimir, were sent to orphanages.[22] Vladimir had turned sixteen shortly after his arrival at the children's home, so he was soon dispatched to a camp in the Far East. Mariia's mother had managed to keep track of her children's whereabouts even from camp; she begged the authorities to take her son out of the Gulag and send him to the front so that he could die an honorable death. But the authorities paid little heed to the requests of families of "enemies of the people." Her plea was not granted, and Vladimir died in the camp.[23]

Despite all the hardships her family had experienced, Mariia's attitude toward life was that "the world is not without good people." With opportunity, such an attitude is likely to generate positive responses from others, and it did for Mariia. A campmate of Mariia's mother had a sister who was a doctor in the orphanage. That doctor became Mariia's guardian angel. For example, Mariia recalled, when her leg became so badly infected that they were planning to amputate it, this doctor treated her and saved the leg. This was a rare (reported) instance of compassion in a system that often brought out the worst in people. After eleven years Mariia was able to reunite with her mother, and in 1948, after her mother was liberated, she took Mariia out of the orphanage and put her into a school. There she excelled, and the teachers treated her well. They even added her name to a list of children of war victims so that she would not suffer the discrimination so regularly heaped on a child whose father had been an "enemy of the people." Unimpeded by such customary obstructions to social advancement, Mariia became a Pioneer and a Komsomol member and even served as secretary of her Komsomol organization.

In spite of her mother's encouragement, Mariia chose not to join the Party—but not because of any ideological objections. By the time she had reached the age when she could join, Mariia was already married to a Party member who wanted her to stay home and take care of the family. For him, "one Communist in the family was enough," so she deferred to his wishes. We do not know how his family's history of repression might have influenced this request. His father had survived a Nazi camp only to be incarcerated as a "traitor" in a Soviet camp until after Stalin's death.

Mariia and her husband each viewed Party membership differently. Mariia was an idealist who was inspired by the Party. He was a pragmatist who had joined the Party to advance his career. Mariia and her mother maintained an idealized vision of the Party even after their experience of repression. As Mariia explained, her mother found a way to look past what had happened to her own family, and focus, instead, on the goal: "She knew there were enemies. She believed in the progress of the socialist system. . . . She believed in the victory of the Revolution. She just figured there were mistakes, and there were chips. You know the expression 'When you cut wood, chips fly,' she was a chip. . . . [She resolutely expected that] a just, wonderful Communist society would be built."[24] Although many wives of "enemies of the people" maintained that their own husbands had been unjustifiably arrested, they justified the expediency of such measures because "there were enemies."[25] At least, according to Mariia, this is "what they said." She recognized that they might have thought otherwise but were voicing explanations provided and permitted by the Party. However she had little doubt regarding her mother's attitude toward such challenging issues. Nor did her mother; when in doubt she would simply pick up a Soviet-speak instruction manual titled "One Hundred Questions, One Hundred Answers"[26] and that settled the issue by dictating the politically correct response. Mariia sometimes wondered if her mother was so positive for Mariia's sake, in order to spare the conflict of growing up with discordant beliefs, but she concluded that her mother's sentiments had to have been genuine.[27]

Shortly after the Twentieth Party Congress, Mariia's mother was reinstated, and she immediately resumed her Party work. This entailed bolstering the Party's image, by, for example, speaking about the victories of the Party at Pioneer gatherings. The subject of the camps was not on the agenda at these meetings. She seemed to take it personally when Mariia chose not to join the Party. Disappointed, her mother scoffed: "If you don't need the Party, the Party doesn't need you." But Mariia had a more nuanced response. She did not need to be a card-carrying Party member to be a devoted Communist. She proudly raised her two children as Pioneers and Komsomols, with the ideals that had informed her upbringing—the conviction that the cause of Communism was just and would triumph. Even so, there was a generational shift. Mariia's daughter wanted little to do with this cause.

In 2008, as Mariia reflected on her mother's life, she tried to understand how her mother had dealt with the personal and material losses of the repression. In brief, she concluded that those losses were bearable because they were not what her mother most valued in life. "My mother was very bright, she found happiness not in material things, but in spiritual things. Spiritual was not God, but the Party—you give your life in service and sacrifice."[28] Having found this spiritual connectedness to the Communist ideology in the same way that others find it in religious faith, Mariia's mother could sustain her loyalty to Communism, despite disappointments in the behavior of some Communists. According to Viktor Frankl, if suffering can be recast as sacrifice, it ceases to be perceived as suffering.[29]

Many Communists, including Mariia's mother, could have no ideological quarrel with the Party because they relied on the Party as the authority that provided the correct interpretation of Communism. Mariia's mother's faith in Communism was not challenged for her as it would later be for Mariia. Her mother died in 1964, still believing that the repression was a harsh, but high-minded, necessity for creating a just Communist society. Unlike Mariia, she did not have her faith challenged by the post-Khrushchev fluctuations in the Party's approach to the past, including the Brezhnev-era re-Stalinization and the Gorbachev-era disclosures on repression under Lenin. Mariia said that she and her husband did not support the dissident movement, but they felt generally positive about it. The Party had changed, and the dissidents, according to Mariia, were against the Party at that time, not the old Party. Mariia concurred in the dissidents' disapproval of how the Party functioned under Brezhnev but affirmed her enduring belief in the ideals represented by the Party.

Regarding the Gorbachev era, Mariia experienced it as unsettling. She liked him, but questioned his priorities—she thought it was a mistake to have opened the archives. She asserted: "Instead of working on the economic situation, he was working on the Party system. People were saying, 'Until everything that happened becomes revealed, we can't be involved in economics.' My reaction was to point out that China didn't raise the issue of archives, it focused on economics."[30] Early on, Mariia's response to the revelations about the Stalinist past emphasized their damaging effects on the public image of the Soviet Union. She objected that these disclosures had gone too far because they seemed to nullify everything that the Soviet Union had achieved. She explained, "We became disheartened by what we heard." Moreover, though Mariia approved of modernization, change, and improvement, she maintained that a basis of socialism could still have been retained.

However, the increasing public attention to the repression was having an unanticipated influence on Mariia. By a process that was confusing even to her, Mariia found it harder to maintain her belief in Communism after the information from the archives became public. This challenge to her faith in Communism was confusing because the archives should not have revealed much more than she already knew from personal experience. What was different now was an audience that brought a different interpretive frame. A new meaning to old events was now reflected back to Mariia through the response of a different audience. Until Gorbachev lifted the censorship on public discussions of the terror and exposed it to the scrutiny of public discourse, Mariia had been able to maintain a limited view of the chronology and scope of the repression. Now she was forced to revisit and critically assess the old, mutually validating interpretations of the repression that she had learned from her mother and her cohorts. Now she was forced to realize that the use of physical coercion to promote the Communist ideology was also practiced under Lenin. She admitted: "I was the last of everyone I knew to really understand that so much of the system of repression started with Lenin, we always wrote everything off to Stalin."[31] Mariia would have preferred to remain oblivious to this because it undermined so much that was foundational to her understanding of her family and her country. Confronted with dissonant facts, Mariia had to change her cognitions and search anew for meaning. She explained, "It was very hard, you lose the ground beneath your feet because you don't understand what the truth is."[32] She might more aptly have said that she now recognizes other "truths." From this, she wondered if, perhaps, her father had died in vain and her mother had labored in vain. In activating these latent issues, seemingly settled, but still unsettling, she reluctantly acknowledged, "I guess what they did wasn't right, but they were fighting for the good of the people, sincerely fighting. It was not for themselves."[33] As we talked, it became clear that the part that "wasn't right" presumably referred to her father's work in Kiev.

Mariia acknowledged being "very upset" by the fact that her father had occupied a high position—secretary of the Provincial Committee in Kiev—at the time of the 1932–1933 famine in Ukraine. She could not understand how he could have overseen the Party's murderous policies of confiscating grain from starving peasants. She claimed that her mother was unaware of this, though they had all been living there at the time. I asked Mariia if, perhaps, her mother knew what was happening but had considered it too risky to discuss the famine with Mariia, unless she could buttress the mass starvation with an ideological justification.[34] This risk would have been at two levels: for one, it might have diminished the Party's standing in Mariia's eyes; for another, any balanced discussion of Party policy could have been interpreted as an expression of anti-Soviet sentiments. Mariia conceded that these would be plausible grounds for her mother's censorship.

Fortuitously, the very archives that Mariia had dreaded to read provided her with a potentially positive view of her father. This is a rich example of the catch-22 legal/ethical conundrum that still stymies the rehabilitation process. When Mariia was finally able to read his case file, she discovered that he had been accused of disagreeing with the Party's policies in the villages. If this was really true, rather than fabricated charges trumped up to justify executing him for other reasons, then she could valorize her father as a "hero." However, the materials necessary to corroborate her speculation were not accessible. And though she was aware that most of the charges in these files were fabricated, she was comforted by the hope that her father was nobly guilty as charged.

Nearly two decades after the collapse of the Soviet Union, Mariia felt some ambivalence about the Party, but her feelings were primarily favorable. Like her mother, Mariia was able to look past negative events to find support for such positive feelings. She claimed to have an unfavorable attitude toward the "KGB-FSB . . . it started with the opening of the archives. When I understood their role [in the country's history of repression], I understood that they were capable of anything." She was shocked at the election of an FSBer (i.e., Putin). And though she had revered Lenin—and perhaps still did—she wanted to see his body removed from the mausoleum and buried. She proffered an apolitical reason: "We are not an Eastern country. . . . His relatives and he himself would not have wanted this."[35] For decades Mariia believed that those who made the Revolution had "mostly clean hearts and hands." She needed to. But when contradictory facts entered the public discourse, she reluctantly conceded that even Lenin did "horrible things" and was "cruel." Even so, her overall favorable assessment of the Party testifies to the triumph of what she would prefer to feel over what she knows.

Gertruda (Gerta) Evgenevna Chuprun

The parents of Gertruda Evgenevna Chuprun were Party devotees who, like many others, gave their daughter a Party name: *geroinia truda* (heroine of labor), or Gertruda for short. Her father, Evgenii Borisovich Ioelson-Grodzianskii, was a professor at the Bauman (Technical) Institute and Director at the Institute of the Refrigeration Industry. In the late twenties he worked in Hamburg, arranging for refrigerators and parts to be sent to the Soviet Union. An acknowledged expert on refrigeration, he was consulted about problems with cooling by the builders of the

Lenin Mausoleum. His privileged life was to spiral downward in 1937. One day he came home and told his wife that he had been expelled from the Party because they claimed that he had married her to cover up his nonproletarian roots. Evgenii's father was a doctor, and his mother an artist, but his wife was a worker at the Serp i Molot factory. Shortly thereafter, the authorities found a graver charge to pin on him. In December of 1937 Evgenii was arrested as a "German spy," and a month later, reportedly executed and disposed of in the Kommunarka mass grave on the outskirts of Moscow.

Gerta's mother, Dina (Evdokiia) Sidorovna Ioelson-Grodzianskaia, had been a factory worker, advanced to become a deputy in the Moscow Soviet from 1931 to 1934, and then went on to study medicine. In 1937 she was expelled from the Party for being married to a "traitor to the motherland." On the day of her husband's execution, she was arrested and sentenced to eight years in Karaganda. Their two children, Aleksandr and Gerta, were put in the Children's Detention Center on the grounds of the Danilov Monastery in Moscow. Gerta was five at the time.

Under the circumstances, Gerta had the relatively good fortune to be taken in by her father's cousin, a Moscow State University mathematics professor, who had a different surname. According to Gerta, he was "terrified his whole life" as a result of this humane act of allowing the daughter of an executed German spy to live in his house. At some point, Gerta moved in with the cousin's mother. Gerta's foster family were not Party people, but Gerta nevertheless enthusiastically joined the Komsomol at age thirteen. In 1948, without a passport but with a Komsomol card in hand, Gerta went to inquire about her father's fate. She had heard rumors that someone saw him in Kolyma, so she still had some hope. The authorities confirmed that he was indeed still alive, and she and her mother held on to that hope until 1956. As for Dina, she had been freed two years earlier but was not yet allowed to return to Moscow because of passport restrictions. According to Gerta, her mother returned from the Gulag the same "sacred believer" in Communism that she had been when she entered.

Gerta recalled how strange her first meeting was with her mother. Here was a Gulag returnee who had just detrained from Kazakhstan reuniting with a fourteen-year-old daughter whom she had not seen for almost ten years and who had grown up in a (non-Party) professor's urban family. Gerta visited her mother in the communal apartment beyond the one-hundred-first kilometer from Moscow[36] where she first stayed, but she had little in common with the people who lived there, including her mother. After Stalin's death, the political restrictions relaxed sufficiently for Gerta's mother to move to the sovkhoz of the Serp i Molot factory, a location much nearer to Moscow. Though they were not close, Gerta would spend the summers there with her.

Up until the Twentieth Party Congress in 1956, Dina as well as many others maintained that Stalin probably did not know about the repressions, and that Yezhov and Beria were the real malefactors. Consequently, Khrushchev's revelations of Stalin's complicity came as a political and psychological shock. Gerta recalled that the Chinese students at her institute were no longer allowed to talk to the Soviet students, because the Chinese were "not permitted to have doubts about the holiness of Stalin and the Communist idea."[37]

That same year, Gerta also had to abandon the illusion that her father had somehow survived. She received a death certificate stating that he had died of pneumonia during an epidemic in 1939. Later, apparently during perestroika, she was issued a second death certificate. The new document gave the cause of death as "execution" and the year as 1938. Gerta's father was posthumously rehabilitated, and her mother immediately applied for and received rehabilitation, Party reinstatement, and a personal pension with privileges. Dina claimed that she had applied for these benefits to restore family honor and in the interest of justice—and not financial compensation. She did, however, avail herself of the privileges attendant to Party veterans. For example, she was offered a separate apartment, which was an unprecedented luxury after her years of communal living.

As for Gerta, she too benefited by receiving a coveted rehabilitation certificate, but she was quick to point out the irony of Soviet life. With her characteristic sense of humor, she declared, "I did not suffer political repression, but you need this paper. We live in a country of fools. We need a paper for everything. I am rehabilitated, but I had never been judged."[38] Gerta's situation was much better than that of many of her peers, who, as children of the repressed, fought hard for their status as "victims"—both for recognition and for privileges. Gerta was contemptuous of the compensation: "They [the state] paid 20,000 rubles—two months salary—for the dead body of my father." Her mother bought furniture with the money. Gerta mocked the political calculations that had determined that widows whose husbands were of lesser status receive less money.

Gerta became an engineer, but she never joined the Party. She subscribed to the tenets of Communism but did not feel the need for Party membership. Looking back on her disinclination to join the Party, Gerta explained that it was not that she did not believe in "the bright future" promised by the Party. "It was just," she laughingly added, "that many of the people who joined believed in their own personal bright futures."[39]

Gerta's mother did not belong to this category; the Party took priority over everything else. Dina's emotional dependence on the Party was so central to her experience of life that she held no opinions contrary to the Party line. She was grateful to Khrushchev for liberating her, and she never conceded that she was guilty of the crimes for which she was imprisoned but did not blame those who had imprisoned her. The Party took priority above all else. Gerta recalled a vivid illustration of how powerfully her mother was motivated by the Party. Dina was addicted to nicotine and smoked incessantly, in spite of frequent admonitions from everyone. Dina would respond by saying: "If I am reinstated in the Party, I will stop smoking, but now I need it for my nerves." Without intending to propose that the same neurobiological reward mechanisms that are stimulated by addiction are also stimulated by her passionate connection to the Party, Dina had intuitively grasped this truth.[40] The same might also be said of Marx, although his was a derisive observation: "Religion is the opium of the people." After reinstatement, Dina became actively reengaged in Party and community work.

In the meantime, Gerta got married and had a child, but her mother, now also a grandmother, placed her responsibilities to the Party above those to her family. She would not commit to baby-sitting because she worried that "there might be a Party meeting." All during Brezhnev's period of stagnation, Dina proudly donned her Party Veteran medal and never uttered one negative comment about the Party. It was Gerta's belief that this absence of criticism was the result of Dina's purposive self-control and self-censorship—she did not "allow herself to" find fault with the Party.

Then shortly after perestroika/glasnost was introduced, Dina became ill and was hospitalized in a clinic for Old Bolsheviks—Hospital No. 60. From her sickbed, Dina experienced a more personal glasnost. She confessed to Gerta that she had had some doubts about Brezhnev and the direction the Party had taken. Gerta came to believe that these doubts had been building for a while but that Dina was afraid to admit them, even to herself, because she did not want to live without the "bright idea"—the ideology and promise of Communism that gave meaning to her life. In addition to Dina's psychological reasons, Gerta believed that her mother also had practical reasons to shield herself from doubting. Dina was afraid of the very same political repression that had intimidated everyone. No matter what their fate had been or where they stood in the hierarchy, Gerta claimed, "the entire country was in deep fear of speaking ill of the Party"—perhaps of thinking ill of the Party. The fear notwithstanding, when Dina died in 1987, she was still a devoted Party member. She had occasionally doubted, but never dissented.

Recent discussions of the Soviet self and subjectivity have raised the pivotal question of whether "faith in the revolutionary utopia and socialist mores" could coexist with "disbelief, irony, and even resistance to certain aspects of the system."[41] The narratives in this study confirm that this is possible and that faith can also coexist with doubt. While Gerta did not compare her mother's devotion to Communism with Mother Teresa's devotion to Catholicism, such a comparison may be apt. In her diaries, Mother Teresa confessed to both frequent doubts and steadfast faith. On Dina's white marble tombstone, engraved in gold letters, Gerta memorialized so much that was central to her mother's life with the inscription "Veteran of the CPSU."

In 2008, as Gerta looked back on the trajectory of Communism and the end of the Soviet experience, she voiced some regrets, her own and perhaps those of her parents who had left their families nearly a century earlier to join the Revolution. Their dream was never realized, a political derailment she blamed on Gorbachev and perestroika: "I think we made a terrible mistake. Gorbachev, Iakovlev and other perestroika figures could have chosen a more Chinese variant. . . . People believed in the equality of nations and ideals. Gorbachev is responsible for ruining everything."[42] Like Mariia, Gerta too would have preferred to see a version of modernization and reform that retained the socialist basis and ideals in which she had believed (even if this were not quite the "Chinese way").

The View from within

The issues attendant to the second generation—many of whom were not the "builders of socialism," or card-carrying Party members—venture slightly beyond the scope of this study. However, even such a limited sample of children of repressed Party loyalists, who do not speak for their entire cohort, permits us to draw some conclusions. Their reflections direct us to larger relevant questions. With varying degrees of emphasis on one or another need, these stories describe the struggle of the children of repressed parents to satisfy three basic needs: for safety, community, and meaning. In the absence of a protective family and an institutionalized religion, the Communist Party was often the only organization that could provide for these needs. Regarding safety, the route to safety was, paradoxically, proffered by repression. As illustrated by the Stockholm syndrome, coercion provided a draconian route to safety—conformity to the Party in word and deed, a task that would be easier if conformity extended to thoughts. Regarding community, children separated physically and psychologically from stigmatized parents were impelled to find community by sometimes striving to fit in with Communist peer groups. Regarding meaning, people deprived of the coherent meaning that religion characteristically confers on otherwise insignificant existence could find value and purpose by embracing the ideology of the Party, including the idealization of Lenin, or bonding with the charismatic movement of Communism.

After People's Deputy Stepanov lost his father and his political security to the repression, he was able to repair his political security by adapting to the Party that he was now defending in the Duma (Russian Parliament). Roy Medvedev, a dissident historian whose father fell victim to the terror, was able to find community in the dissident movement, and he had the courage to risk his safety by criticizing Stalin at a time when the Party was trying to partially rehabilitate him. They found enduring meaning in what the Party had meant for their fathers. Natasha Ioffe's mother, Nadezhda, shielded her from the knowledge that Natasha's father had been executed as an "enemy of the people." Nor did Nadezhda reveal the criminal behavior she had witnessed in the Gulag in order to help Natasha to live more comfortably in a world controlled by the Communist Party. Nataliia Rappaport could find no such comfort in the Communist Party because, after her father's arrest in 1953 for the Doctors Plot, she was alienated by and from the rampant state-sponsored anti-Semitism. As an adult, she would conceivably have been open to joining the Party in the Gorbachev era (though she had emigrated and made a good career in the West).

Neither Evgeniia Smirnova, nor Mariia Kuznetsova, nor Gerta Chuprun reported any sense of indignation or even surprise at their mothers' enduring loyalty to the Party, even after losing their husbands and being incarcerated in the Gulag. The loyalty that had survived in the returnee parents had also to some extent survived them—in their children. Two decades after the end of the Soviet Union, even in hindsight, these daughters of repressed parents had questions, but they did not condemn the Party; in fact they praised the sincerity of the efforts that had been made to build Communism. These efforts were ultimately unsuccessful, but the system that had been built, encouraged, and at times brutally enforced in the course of decades remained for some a source of safety, community, and meaning. The ambivalence in these narratives attests to the difficulty of assessing the past on an individual level. On a national level such a task is even more complicated.

THE SHADOW OF STALIN

In 1962, Yevgeny Yevtushenko's acclaimed poem "The Heirs to Stalin" celebrated the removal of Stalin's body from the Lenin Mausoleum, but asked how Stalin was to be removed from Stalin's heirs. This was a prescient question. In a 2005 survey conducted by the Levada Center, 1,600 Russians were asked their opinion of Stalin and his role in the country's history. Their response was quite positive. Stalin's leadership was credited with the victorious outcome of the Great Patriotic War, and 32 percent of the respondents believed this overshadowed whatever defects he might have had and any mistakes he may have made.[43] By 2008, another survey found that respondents viewed Stalin as one of the three "most eminent figures of all times."[44] Still, opinions on Stalin remain decidedly mixed. For example, while 58 percent of the respondents in a 2010 poll found that "the sacrifices made by the Soviet people in the Stalin era could never be justified by any lofty goals" and 47 percent of those polled associated the death of Stalin with the cessation of terror and mass repression and the liberation from the camps of millions of innocent victims, 50 percent of that same group of respondents did not think that Stalin should be declared a "state criminal." When asked about their attitude toward Stalin, 23 percent of this group "on the whole respected" him, while only 5 percent expressed "revulsion or hate."[45]

Based on what he knew about Stalin, Anatolii Sivakov, of the Ryazan Memorial, could not account for Stalin's favorable ratings. He reckoned that these respondents were either unaware of Stalin's criminal activities or underestimated their importance, or perhaps they were responding to a different part of Stalin's and the country's history. Sivakov knew firsthand of the contrast between facts on the ground and propaganda in the air. In the village of his youth, he lived through the postwar experience of poverty, hunger, and repression while reading in the textbooks about how amply Stalin and Lenin had provided for children. He remembers Pioneer meetings closing with the chant: "Thank you, dear comrade Stalin, for our happy childhood."[46] Even so, he observed a lack of enthusiasm among many of the chanters, and he also observed their prudent silence when opportunities for criticism presented themselves. Not so with his imprudent aunt, who lived in a neighboring village. Once, while visiting her, Sivakov began preaching the standard Pioneer gospel he had been taught. "Don't talk to me about them!" she raged, "They were the ones who came up with these damned kolkhozes!"

Clearly his aunt was not a beneficiary of Stalin's largesse, but Sivakov recalled others who were. In an attempt to analyze who could be so nostalgic for Stalin, and what they would be so nostalgic about, Sivakov recalled that the children of the elite in his village had good clothes, did not go hungry, graduated from institutes, and found good positions. "Today they are senior citizens and cannot say anything bad about Stalin. They had normal lives by Soviet standards." Under that system, their pensions were more secure and they enjoyed a sense of stability.[47] It was Sivakov's conjecture that those who were apparently more equal than others may be those who longed for the Stalin era, and for the things that came packaged with the repression.

Different people had different pasts and different backgrounds. A more fundamental reason why this discussion—and "Stalin's ghost," as Yevtushenko put it—could rise again and again is because all of the official attempts to reckon with the Stalinist past were inconsistent. They were borne of ambivalence—an ambivalence that resonated both from the "top down," and from the "bottom up," as attested by many of the narratives we have considered. A popular adage circulating in Russia in 1990 went, "It's easy to talk about the future and the present, but the past keeps changing every day."[48] At that time, a veritable revolution of revelations was taking place, and their content challenged the foundations of belief in the Party and the system. This was a conscious, albeit failed, political strategy. Then and now, what we choose to remember about the past is always a selection of events, regularly informed (if not determined) by and tailored to present needs.

NATIONAL MEMORY

The triumph of expedient national history over actual national history is demonstrated by the sanitized version of the Stalinist past, currently approved for history teaching in Russian high schools. Putin, who described the collapse of the Soviet Union as "the greatest geopolitical catastrophe of the 20th century"[49] in a nationally broadcast address in 2005, was an influential advocate of this narrative. Two years later, in a June 2007 televised meeting with social studies teachers, he argued that Russia should not be made to feel guilty about the Great Purge of 1937, because "in other countries, even worse things happened."[50] He admitted that there were some "problematic pages" in their history, but asked in the same breath what state had not had these.[51] This stance is part consequence and part symptom of the fact that Russia made no substantial attempts to come to terms with the legacy of Soviet Communism.

The June meeting was partially to promote a new teachers' manual, titled *The Modern History of Russia, 1945–2006,* commissioned by the presidential administration.[52] The contents smacked of Soviet-era textbooks. The administration had issued the following guidelines to the textbook's authors on how to present various leaders: "Stalin—good (strengthened vertical power but no private property); Brezhnev—good (for the same reasons as Stalin); Gorbachev and Yeltsin—bad (destroyed the country, but under Yeltsin there was private property); Putin—the best rule (strengthened vertical power and private property)."[53] Shortly after the conference, the Duma introduced and quickly passed a new law authorizing the Ministry of Education to recommend which textbooks should be published and used in schools.[54]

In consequence, educational materials were hewn to reflect which way the political winds were blowing. In 2008, in an effort to promote patriotism among younger people, another new teachers' manual, titled "The History of Russia 1900–

1945," was officially approved for use in schools. Achieving such a goal through the use of history required considerable whitewashing. In the manual, teachers were instructed on how to address the period of Stalinist repressions. They were told to explain that "Stalin acted in a concrete historical situation, as a leader he acted entirely rationally—as the guardian of the system." The text also acclaims his consistent efforts to reshape the country into an industrialized state. Since the scope of the repression does not quite fit into the concept of "rational governance," the manual suggests working the numbers a bit. For example, it recommends that "a formula could be used wherein only those who received death sentences and those who were executed would be counted."[55] These figures are significantly lower than the additional millions who languished and then died from disease and forced labor in the Gulag. A subtext of this history lesson is that the political ethos is not yet ready to change.[56]

AFTERMATH

In closed societies, many of whose constraints on individual rights persist in Russia, political systems are rarely subjected to critical public scrutiny, nor are they accountable to their citizens. Rather, the burden is on the citizens to accommodate to the system or assimilate it in order to survive. To this end the political system shapes its citizens' cognitive appraisals by supplying versions of events that justify its methods of governance. Since Stalin's death, the view of the Stalinist past has been adjusted to fit individual and the nation's needs. The power of a system to control the individual's appraisal of events is attested to by the convictions the loyalists incorporated into their personal experience narratives.

While recognizing the arbitrary hardships imposed on them, few loyalists blamed the Party or the system. To the extent that we respect the sincerity of our narrators, we recognize that they are the arbiters of their needs, and their appraisal of events may be assumed to fit their needs. A critical reappraisal of what had happened to them and their Party could be wrenching and potentially destabilizing because it would risk devaluing the meaning of their suffering in the camps, their redemptive martyrdom, and the triumph of survival. Moreover, some loyalists were inspired by faith-based beliefs whose validity was not contingent on such outcome measures as material gains or human rights, and hardship was recast as sacrifice. Other overlapping determinants that shielded the Party from blame included an unconditional acceptance of the official Party line, cognitive dissonance, the enduring effects of a traumatic bond, and the order and simplicity provided under the old system, all buttressed by the horizontal and vertical supports controlled by the Party.

Efforts by organizations such as Memorial to bring the repression—its scope and consequences—into the arena of public discourse often were, and are, not officially encouraged. In the Soviet era there was a fairly consistent recognition that a fuller history of the repression could undermine the legitimacy of the regime, and in the post-Soviet era the past was promoted as a rallying point for patriotism and national pride, among many things. Consequently, the Party and many loyalist survivors defended *their* history of the repression as *the* history of the repression by claiming authority over the "facts" as well as the interpretation of the facts.

When repressive regimes fall, it is incumbent upon the successor government(s) to assess past crimes, condemn past practices and perpetrators, properly compensate, acknowledge, and memorialize victims, conduct trials or set up truth commissions, and set the historical record straight in textbooks for the new generation. However, aside from symbolic reparations, the post-Soviet governments have done none of the above. The consequence is that the significance of the past and the past itself remain open to negotiation, both in the individual's psyche and in the public domain.

There was no "happy ending" to the story of Soviet Communism. The system represented by the Party ended up murdering millions of its own citizens, including those who supported and built it. For several reasons, it also ended up collapsing,[57] leaving most citizens with conflicting memories of the Soviet experience. Instead of constructively gleaning lessons from its failure—an exercise that could perhaps achieve a politically different "happy ending"—there has been a conscious effort to turn the defeat into victory through a careful selection of what should be remembered and which elements of the past should not be attended to. This selection becomes reflected in the personal and political narratives that emerge.

Two decades after the end of the Soviet Union, with no established transitional justice mechanisms in place, Russia crafted an approach to its Stalinist history that would burnish its national image: its citizens were encouraged not to focus on the crimes that had taken place under the Soviet regime, but rather to look to the "bright past" of national achievements. For many individuals, and for the nation, this formula, or mythical depiction, offered a ready solution to the age-old dilemma of finding meaning and maintaining identity when faced with the fact that the "bright future"—forged at such a heavy human price—never arrived.

The "Bright Past," or Whose (Hi)Story?

Those who have witnessed the collapse of a regime, presided over an unsuccessful civil war, or mourned the demise of a political party could respond by undertaking a painful reappraisal of what went wrong. Instead, they often divert attention from the failed present to a "golden past" / "bright past," now retrofitted with a glory it had never originally possessed. "Why shouldn't we be proud of our past," a Serbian aphorism claims, "when each new day is worse than the previous one?"[1] The aphorism wittily and perhaps unwittingly addresses one of the critical impediments to the often wrenching national process of coming to terms with an onerous past. Both for individuals and for nations, ontological events are imparted with different meanings, which constitute different truths. The aphorism's subversive disjunction of time frames illustrates that the construction of history need not adhere to chronology or facts; the purposes of the present can change the meaning of the past without changing the facts. The meaning of these facts can seem self-evident if they are put into a persuasive story, whether a personal or national narrative, that meets the current needs of the audience. The longer-term needs of the audience would be better served by a narrative that acknowledges failure and invites audience participation in seeking a remedy. However, this was not the story promulgated by Russia, Serbia, and other formerly repressive regimes.

In Russia, two decades after the collapse of the Soviet Union, Stalin's popularity resurged in nationwide polls, reflecting the longing of many for the country's former prestige and their previous sense of security.[2] Likewise, many Serbs, who formed the largest group in former Yugoslavia, look back with nostalgia to a time of greater national pride and material comfort—for themselves.[3] By contrast, the dominated ethnic populations were frustrated in their striving to share a similar national pride. Each polity has a story fashioned by selected and connected events that promotes its national interests. Consequently, instead of the individual or national memory affecting the narrative that emerges, the process is the other way around.

Efforts to employ institutionally sanctioned approaches to arrive at a just resolution in the aftermath of mass atrocities—trials, truth commissions, vetting, or their various combinations—regularly fall short of fundamentally reconciling contradictory versions of past events. In effect, they are exercises in "the art of the possible."[4] Legal proceedings, for example, may fail in arriving at "the truth" regarding ethnic clashes because this requires considering many competing "truths" based on different perceptions, as well as different interpretations. Contending parties often enter and leave the court with "their own truths."[5] This is not to say that all valid truth claims have equal standing; courts must make judgments that weight evidence. However, even when their verdicts or legal interpretations are final, their reading of events is not, because ultimately the account produced is the "tacit narrative of the user [i.e., the prosecution or defense]."[6]

The International Criminal Tribunal for the Former Yugoslavia (ICTY) attempted to set the record straight, overcome ambiguity, and "police a violent past"[7] by adjudicating claims and counter-claims, all supported by irreconcilable narratives. For example, while the central Serb narrative tends to characterize the catastrophic war in former Yugoslavia as an internal conflict, a civil war in which Serbs were also victims,[8] the central Bosniak narrative frames these same harrowing events as unbridled external Serb aggression.[9] Thus, years after the physical battle in former Yugoslavia has ended, the divisiveness remains and is perpetuated by competing narratives of what happened and why.

As in Russia, the content of school history books and curricula provides useful indicators of how the state prefers the narrative of the past to be shaped.[10] In the former Yugoslavia, the teaching of history remains a "thorny issue." In Bosnia, the three peoples generally do not even share the same view of how the war started.[11] These views are reinforced by selective attention, omissions, and emphasis. And in Serbia, while the gruesome facts of Srebrenica were aired on Serbian television in June of 2005 in a video that graphically depicted the brutal murder of six Muslim men by the Scorpions (a Serbian paramilitary unit), "there remained public amnesia about the killings."[12] This amnesia is institutionally perpetuated by the school system. The history of Srebrenica is not covered in school history books,[13] where it could provide a forum for discussion and conflict resolution. Instead, the divisiveness continues to roil in the popular culture as competing narratives that slip past each other or collide, but hardly engage in a dialogue.

Negotiating a mutually acceptable narrative of the past is a complex task in a post-repressive society and state, but it is necessary in order to create a common ground for the political negotiation of problems.

Public expressions of ongoing anti-Muslim sentiments and Srebrenica denial among Serbs and Bosnian Serbs were displayed at an October 2005 World Cup qualifying soccer match between Bosnia-Herzegovina and Serbia-Montenegro in Belgrade. There, one enormous banner read, "Knife, Wire, Srebrenica." Another stated, "Thank you Ratko." The Serb authorities did nothing to curb these actions.[14] Despite the ICTY verdicts, there is relative consensus that Serbia is reluctant to accept political responsibility for the crimes committed by its military and paramilitary forces.[15] In this climate of impunity, Mladic remained at large for 15 years, and an indignant crowd of thousands rallied in Belgrade's streets in July of 2008 to protest the extradition of Radovan Karadzic to The Hague to stand trial.[16] For his part, Karadzic, starting with his initial nonappearance in court, may be following Milosevic's lead (and Mladic, Karadzic's lead), using destructive behaviors purposed to have a delegitimizing effect on public opinion of the ICTY. Moreover, Karadzic's defense commenced with a vehement denial of genocide and revisionism.

Even two decades after the collapse of the Soviet Union, not one henchman had been tried, nor is there a national, state-sponsored memorial or museum center dedicated to the memory of victims of political repression.[17] According to Grigorii Iavlinskii, longtime leader of the liberal opposition party, the inconsistent and ambiguous attempts to confront the Stalinist past have resulted in the emergence of a "post-modern Stalinism," only superficially evidenced by Stalin's renewed popularity. More profoundly, this popularity represents an "invisible Stalinism" without the Gulag, a resurgence of the principle that achieving political ends justifies the deprivation of individual rights.[18] Iavlinskii maintained that "the official policy of vagueness, half-heartedness, and hypocrisy regarding Bolshevism and Stalinism" caused a "deep crisis of self-identity" for Russians.[19] This was especially so for the victims of repression who found little official validation of their experience.[20]

Perhaps unrelated to the state's officious ambiguity with regard to the Stalinist past, on the eve of the first international Approaches to Stalinism conference in Moscow in December of 2008, the Memorial office in St. Petersburg was raided by masked federal security agents, who proceeded to confiscate the organization's computer hard drive and numerous archival dossiers.[21] The pretext was the St. Petersburg Memorial's alleged association with an extremist article in the newspaper *Novyi Peterburg.* Among other transgressions, the authorities carried away Memorial's belongings without leaving an inventory.

Irina Flige, chairman of the St. Petersburg Memorial, asserted that the state glossed over the state-sponsored crimes of the terror, emphasizing instead its great accomplishments in modernization and its victory over the Nazis. This omission in the historical record led Memorial to draft an international appeal in 2008, wherein they lamented that "instead of a serious nationwide discussion about its Soviet past, the Soviet State patriotic myth with small changes is reviving. This myth views Russian history as a string of glorious and heroic achievements."[22]

The voluminous materials that Memorial holds on the scope and nature of the terror provide an unwelcome addition to this image. Memorial had reason to believe that the St. Petersburg raid, and similar such actions, are part of a concerted effort by the authorities to brand Memorial as a dissident/extremist group and marginalize the importance of its revelations.[23] If so, this would represent a politically retrogressive trend; the pursuit and dissemination of information on Soviet repression has not been considered a "marginal" activity since the Brezhnev era.[24] But it may be unofficial policy; archival documents on the terror are now less accessible than they were in the 1990s.[25] In January of 2011 the Supreme Court of the Russian Federation dismissed a lawsuit filed by Memorial to gain access to documents on the repression. Many of these materials are subject to a seventy-five-year period of inaccessibility from the day the case closed due to "violations of privacy."[26] Apparently, an accurate account of the victimizations under seven decades of Soviet rule cannot yet be integrated into Soviet history. Until it can be, this part of the past will continue to challenge the credibility of Russia's present version of history.[27]

In support of this assessment, Ian Rachinskii, Moscow Memorial chairman, pointed out that the historical record contains many descriptors that were more compliant than correct. Such formulations as "honest Communist" and "devoted Party son," so often found in Gulag memoirs, "sound strange in light of what we now know about the Party."[28] Rachinskii believed that these sentiments, coupled with the narrators' claims that they built socialism not "out of fear" but "out of conscience," were facilitated (if not aided and abetted) by the "absence of a judicial condemnation of Bolshevism."[29] The Memorial activist argued that the Soviet era engendered an "almost unconscious ambiguity whereby people sometimes hid their opinions even from themselves." This problem was so deep-rooted that Rachinskii does not expect it to change. He concludes that if Russians could not "overcome this ambiguity, cease judging people by their degree of loyalty to the authorities or state ideology, and learn the tragic lessons [of the past], we will remain in the past, and will remain a population, instead of becoming a nation."[30] His prescription for developing a national unity and authentic identity was to fully confront and integrate the past. Such a fuller history would seek disclosures instead of seeking to avoid them.

In 2009, the state undertook the management of the historical narrative with the establishment by presidential decree of a Commission to Counter Attempts to Falsify History to the Detriment of Russian Federation Interests. This decree was further evidence of the increasing politicization—if not censorship—of history in Russia. The commission was made up of state and public officials and historians, who were charged with looking at past events for misrepresented or manipulated facts that cast Russia in a negative light. Memorial chairman Arsenii Roginskii expressed concern about the "struggle against the falsification of history" becoming an "affair of the state," because, he cautioned, the state cannot be the arbiter of the "truth." He reasoned: "Truth is achieved not by the resolution of a state commission, even the highest created by decree of the president, but is defined in free discussion among professionals or simply among people, among societies and peoples in various countries if this involves the definition of one and the same event."[31]

In a positive sign, the current administration is considering establishing a commission on the "Perpetuation of the Memory of the Victims of the Totalitarian Regime and National Reconciliation."[32] However, while integrating the story of the terror into the mainstream discourse of Russia seems like a relatively simple undertaking at the level of historical scholarship, at the political level, at the present time, it may be insurmountable. It would require a fundamental shift from a system of governance that devalues human rights toward a democratic ethos that prioritizes them. Russia has no historical democratic traditions for balancing individual rights with collective responsibilities. For now, there are at least two competing narratives. Both address different issues, and endorse different priorities, means, and ends. If these narratives can shift from dueling to dialoguing, Russia will begin to come to terms with the Soviet past.

Such a dialogue would expose the systemic problems attendant to the claim that unjust laws should be opposed, and would consider what forms of opposition would be—or would later be adjudicated to be—acceptable. For example, the Rehabilitation Commission struggled with how to judge the status of those Gulag prisoners who violated Soviet law by rebelling in the camps. Ultimately, these returnees were simply exonerated, as were most other Gulag returnees, but the commission wondered whether they, instead, should have been honored as heroes because of their anti-Soviet activity.[33]

A similar predicament was the subject of a "searing debate" in the Czech Republic. How should the Czechs label people who had escaped from a repressive Iron Curtain regime by using such unlawful methods as hijacking cars, stealing guns, and drugging and killing adversaries? The controversy pivoted on the question of whether they were to be considered terrorists or heroes.[34] This highlights the issue of comparing the unlawfulness of an oppositional behavior with the justness of the opposed law, an issue regularly confronted by societies in transition from the repression of, to the protection of, human rights. It also highlights the question of what means are acceptable for which ends.

The further question of how far down a repressive regime's chain of command culpability should be assigned remained open in Iraq after the overthrow of Saddam Hussein. His party, the Arab Socialist Renaissance Party, or Ba'ath Party, ruled from 1968 to 2003. De-Ba'athification policies, introduced shortly after the fall of the regime, created an "epic struggle" between the regime's opponents and supporters, and with regard to what principles of justice should be applied to the lower-level functionaries.[35] Some saw their wholesale dismissal as a form of "collective punishment," while others resented the fact that hundreds of thousands of lower-level Ba'athists, who may have been guilty of abuses, were permitted to remain in civil service positions.[36] How to maintain the operation of civil functions without these functionaries was also a pragmatic consideration. In 2008 reforms were instituted, but they were criticized for still relying too heavily on membership categories rather than individual deeds as a criterion for dismissal. As with the lower levels of Nazi Party membership under Hitler and Communist Party membership in Russia, Ba'ath Party membership may primarily have reflected fear and careerism. Also, apparently many Ba'ath Party members were obliged by their government jobs to join.[37]

Still, these determinants can lead from accommodation to repression to the assimilation of and allegiance to a repressive ideology. This mechanism explains how it is possible for people to continue to maintain feelings of loyalty when faced with the facts of the human toll associated with the repressive regime (Saddam's Iraq, Stalin's Russia and the CPSU, Milosevic's Serbia, or country and political party X).

Those who had adapted to a repressive regime by acquiescence and accommodation could likewise adapt to a nonrepressive regime. But those who had adapted by the assimilation of the repressive ideology would probably be resistant to change in at least two ways. First, any evidence that might conflict with their assimilated ideology could be reinterpreted as irrelevant or confirmatory. For example, human rights violations would be overshadowed by the demands of patriotism, and false imprisonment would be cast as a necessary personal sacrifice for the greater good. Second, the meaningful experience of feeling connected to a revered leader, a cohesive group, and a visionary ideology can be so emotionally satisfying that it needs no more confirmatory evidence than does religious faith.

While the "bright future" envisioned by Communist ideology was expected to be realized in this life, on this earth, the fact that it has endured the contradictions of the repression, the refutation of the disclosures, and endless delays suggests that it occupies a psychosocial niche similar to that inhabited by "heaven" or "paradise" in theology.

Given that the "bright future" of Communism now belongs to the "bright past" of the Soviet empire, what changes can be made in the present to improve the future? This question is also relevant to Serbia, Iraq, or any number of states struggling to come to terms with an onerous past. Since many look back with pride at the accomplishments under the former regime, it is not clear whether and how a confrontation with the "facts" of what happened can change such perceptions. Nor is it clear how much ability or willingness there is in a given group/nation/individual to undergo the wrenching process of judgment.[38] On the other hand, both the opening of archives and the proper placement of those records that have been accessed for political trials could potentially contribute to the creation of a "common past," a "shared narrative,"[39] or at least a "shared custody"[40] of the past. That past may necessarily become less "bright" for some, but a national process of reckoning could facilitate sufficient consensus to prevent new opportunities for old sentiments to surface. Moreover, there may be a tipping point—as in South Africa—when the cumulative impact of public disclosures shifts the balance and expands the validating audience. This might then be aphoristically expressed as: "Why shouldn't we expect a bright future when, every day, more people make constructive use of our terrible past."

NOTES

Preface

1. Nanci Adler, *Trudnoe vozvrashchenie: Sud'by sovetskikh politzakliuchennykh v 1950–1990-e gody* [The difficult return: The fates of Soviet political prisoners from the 1950s–1990s] (Moscow: Zven'ia, 2005).

2. Zoria Leonidovna Serebriakova, interview, Nikolina Gora, April 19, 2006.

Introduction

Some parts of this chapter have appeared in Nanci Adler, "Enduring Repression: Narratives of Loyalty to the Party Before, During and After the Gulag," *Europe-Asia Studies* 62, 2 (March 2010): 211–234 (www.informaworld.com). I gratefully acknowledge *Europe-Asia Studies* for their permission to reproduce these sections.

1. Among the published memoirs that deal with this theme are: Iulii Daniel', *Pis'ma iz zakliucheniia: Stikhi* [Letters from imprisonment: Poems] (Moscow: Obshchestvo "Memorial," Zven'ia, 2000); Anna Mikhailovna Larina, *This I Cannot Forget: The Memoirs of Nikolai Bukharin's Widow* (London: Hutchinson, 1993); Richard Lourie, *Sakharov: A Biography* (Waltham, MA: Brandeis University Press, 2002); Raisa Orlova and Lev Kopelev, *My zhili v Moskve* [We lived in Moscow] (Ann Arbor, MI: Ardis, 1988); Petr Ionovich Yakir, *A Childhood in Prison* (London: Macmillan, 1972).

2. See, for example, Steven Greene, "Understanding Party Identification: A Social Identity Approach," *Journal of the International Society of Political Psychology* 20, 2 (1999): 393–403; Agnes Horvath, "Tricking into the Position of the Outcast: A Case Study in the Emergence and Effects of Communist Power," *Journal of the International Society of Political Psychology* 19, 2 (1998): 331–347; see also Stephane Courtois, Nicolas Werth, et al., *The*

Black Book of Communism: Crimes, Terror, Repression (Cambridge, MA: Harvard University Press, 1999).

3. Roy Medvedev, interview at his Moscow dacha, June 19, 2005.

4. Nina Gagen-Torn, "O verakh," in Semen Vilenskii, ed., *Dodnes' tiagoteet* [Till my tale is told], vol. 2 (Moscow: Vozvrashchenie, 2004), 22. The first volume of this brilliant collection of memoirs has been published in English: Simeon Vilensky, ed., *Till My Tale is Told: Women's Memoirs of the Gulag*, trans. John Crowfoot (Bloomington: Indiana University Press, 1999).

5. During our interview she could not recall which year she had entered camp. In my 1995 questionnaire to her, she recorded that she had been sentenced to eight years. She probably spent a total of fifteen to seventeen years in camp or exile.

6. Nataliia Alekseevna Rykova, interview, Moscow, October 18, 2005.

7. V. A. Kozlov and S. V. Mironenko, eds., *Kramola: Inakomyslie v SSSR pri Khrushcheve i Brezhneve 1952–1982* [Uprising: Dissidence in the USSR under Khrushchev and Brezhnev 1952–1982] (Moscow: Materik, 2005), 170.

8. See interview in "Obeliat' Stalina bessmyslenno [It is senseless to vindicate Stalin]," *30 oktiabria* 84 (2008): 4–5.

9. See Oleg V. Khlevniuk, *The History of the Gulag: From Collectivization to the Great Terror* (New Haven, CT: Yale University Press, 2004), 78.

10. For a review and apt analysis of the various estimates, see Michael Ellman, "Soviet Repression Statistics: Some Comments," *Europe-Asia Studies* 54, 7 (2002): 1151–1172. In 2000, Russian criminologists Vladimir Kudriavtsev and A. I. Trusov introduced the figure of 6.1 million sentenced on political articles between 1918 and 1958; by 1991 this number had increased by 5,000. They estimated that up to 1,165,000 of these arrestees were executed. In sum, they calculated 13 million victims of political repression in all, including the victims of collectivization and mass deportation. They cautioned, however, that some of these victims may have been actual offenders. Still, they concluded that "even inconclusive data . . . indicate an incomparable scope of mass repression" (V. N. Kudriavtsev and A. I. Trusov, *Politicheskaia iustitsiia v SSSR* [Political justice in the USSR] (Moscow, 2000), 312–318.

See also J. A. Getty, G. T. Rittersporn, and V. N. Zemskov, "Victims of the Soviet Penal System in the Pre-war Years: A First Approach on the Basis of Archival Material," *American Historical Review* 4 (1993): 1017–1049; Steven Rosefielde, "Stalinism in Post-Communist Perspective: New Evidence on Killings, Forced Labour and Economic Growth in the 1930s," *Europe-Asia Studies* 48, 6 (1996): 959–987; Stephen Wheatcroft, "The Scale and Nature of German and Soviet Repression and Mass Killings, 1930–45," *Europe-Asia Studies* 48, 8 (1996): 1319–1353.

In his speech at the opening plenary session of the international conference Itogi Stalinizma (Moscow, December 5, 2008), Oleg Khlevniuk argued that the 20 million arrests frequently quoted in statistics are just the "tip of the iceberg." Yoram Gorlizki reported the following rough repression statistics from the sessions titled "Politics: The Institutions" and "Methods of Stalin's Dictatorship": 6 million were sentenced on political charges; 1.2 million were executed; 6 million were deported; 5–6 million died in famines; and millions of others were arrested for infractions that would not have constituted crimes in other countries (Summary report, Moscow, December 7, 2008).

11. One of the few assessments has been made by Russian historian V. N. Zemskov in "Massovoe osvobozhdenie spetsposelentsev i ssylnykh (1954–1960 gg.) [Mass liberation of special settlers and exiles (1954–1960)]," *Sotsiologicheskie issledovaniia* 1 (1991). His focus is on special population groups and exiles. Some rehabilitation facts can be found in A. N. Iakovlev et al., eds., *Reabilitatsiia: Kak eto bylo, mart 1953–fevral' 1956, Dokumenty prezidiuma TsK KPSS i drugie materialy* [Rehabilitation: As it happened, March 1953–February 1956, Documents of the Presidium of the CC of the CPSU and other materials], T. 1 (Moscow: Mezhdunarondnyi Fond Demokratsiia, 2000); see also Ellman, *Europe-Asia Studies.*

12. Nanci Adler, *The Gulag Survivor: Beyond the Soviet System* (New Brunswick, NJ: Transaction Publishers, 2004), 30–34, 168–171.

13. RGANI, f. 6, op. 6, d. 1077, ll. 4–5.

14. Ibid., d. 1165, l. 2.

15. The political history of the prisoner's family was relevant because oppositional family sentiments sometimes resulted in successive generations of Gulag prisoners. Prominent examples of intergenerational Party membership, dissidence, and incarceration include the Bogoraz-Daniel family and the Iakirs.

16. See Nicolas Werth, "Stalinist State Violence: A Reappraisal Twenty Years after the Archival Revolution," anniversary lecture, Center for Holocaust and Genocide Studies, Amsterdam, September 23, 2010.

17. For a discussion of this problem, see Hiroaki Kuromiya, *The Voices of the Dead: Stalin's Great Terror in the 1930s* (New Haven, CT: Yale University Press, 2007).

18. Lev Razgon, response to questionnaire for project on the return from the Gulag, 8 December 1994.

19. Ol'ga Konstantinovna Shireeva, questionnaire, December 12, 1995.

20. Louis O. Mink, "History and Fiction as Modes of Comprehension," *New Literary History* 1 (1969): 557–558.

21. Thomas D. Albright, Eric R. Kandel, and Michael I. Posner, "Cognitive Neuroscience," *Current Opinion in Neurobiology* 10, 5 (2000): 612–624.

22. Marc D. Feldman and Jacqueline M. Feldman, with Roxanne Smith, *Stranger Than Fiction: When Our Minds Betray Us* (Washington, DC: American Psychiatric Press, 1998).

23. J. O. Beahrs, "Memory as Power: Who Is to Decide?" *Journal of the American Academy of Psychiatry and the Law* 27, 3 (1999): 462–470; Jerome Bruner, "Life as Narrative," *Social Research* 71, 3 (Fall 2004): 11–32.

24. Jerome Bruner, "The Narrative Construction of Reality," *Critical Inquiry* 18, 1 (1991): 1–21.

25. See Jolande Withuis's discussion on memory, internal negotiation, and revision of historical interpretation in *De jurk van de kosmonaute: Over politiek, cultuur, en psyche*

[The cosmonaut's dress: On politics, culture, and the psyche] (Amsterdam: Boom, 1995), 32–59.

26. Albright, Kandel, and Posner, "Cognitive Neuroscience."

27. Hannah Arendt, "On Violence," in *Crises of the Republic* (New York: Harcourt Brace Jovanovich, 1969), 164.

28. See Erving Goffman, *Asylums: Essays on the Social Situation of Mental Patients and Other Inmates* (New York: Anchor Books, 1961).

29. Richard Crossman, ed., *The God That Failed* (New York: Columbia University Press, 2001), 6.

30. Ibid.

31. See Erik van Ree, "Stalin as Writer and Thinker," *Kritika: Explorations in Russian and Eurasian History* 3, 4: 702–703; and *The Political Thought of Joseph Stalin* (London: RoutledgeCurzon, 2002), chapters 9–12.

32. "Segodnia [Today]," NTV, October 18, 2005.

33. See, for example, Rene Fülop-Miller, *The Mind and Face of Bolshevism* (London: G. P. Putnam's Sons, 1926); Mikhail Vaiskopf, *Pisatel' Stalin* [Stalin the writer] (Moscow: Novoe literaturnoe obozrenie, 2002); Oleg Kharkhordin, *The Collective and the Individual in Russia: A Study of Practices* (Berkeley: University of California Press, 1999); Isaac Deutscher, *Stalin: A Political Biography* (London: Oxford University Press, 1967); see also notes 45 and 46.

34. "A Battle to Ensure Russia's Future Doesn't Resemble Its Past," *The National*, CBC, January 14, 2003.

35. Karl Marx, "Introduction," *Marx's Critique of Hegel's Philosophy of Right (1843)* (Cambridge: Cambridge University Press, 1970).

36. Thomas R. Insel, "Is Social Attachment an Addictive Disorder?" *Physiology & Behavior* 79, 3 (2003): 351–357; Marc Galanter, "Alcohol and Drug Abuse: Healing through Social and Spiritual Affiliation," *Psychiatric Services* 53, 9 (2002): 1072–1074.

37. Viktor Frankl, *Man's Search for Meaning: An Introduction to Logotherapy* (London: Hodder and Stoughton, 1959), 99.

38. Catherine Merridale, *Night of Stone: Death and Memory in Russia* (London: Granta Books, 2000), 214, 418; Anne Applebaum has asserted in *GULAG: A History* (New York: Doubleday, 2003) that this question needs further exploration.

39. In this context, it is relevant to note that the word "religion" is associated with the Latin *religare,* shares a root with "ligature," and means "binding together."

40. Aleksandr Solzhenitsyn, *The Gulag Archipelago,* abridged ed. (London: The Harvill Press, 1999), 242–246.

41. Boris Diakov, *Povest' o perezhitom* [The story of what we (I) went through] (Moscow: Sovetskaia Rossiia, 1966). See Leona Toker's insightful discussion on Diakov's role and work in *Return from the Archipelago: Narratives of Gulag Survivors* (Bloomington: Indiana University Press, 2000), 48–52.

42. Crossman, *The God That Failed,* 166.

43. Frankl, *Man's Search for Meaning,* 115.

44. My thanks to Erik van Ree for drawing my attention to this determinant. For more on Weber's conception of the "charismatic community," see Max Weber, *Wirtschaft und Gesellschaft, Grundriss der Verstehende Soziologie* [Economy and society, sketch of comprehensive sociology], 5th ed. (Tübingen: J.C.B. Mohr, 1985).

45. Stephen Kotkin, *Magnetic Mountain: Stalinism as a Civilization* (Berkeley: University of California Press, 1995), 153.

46. Igal Halfin, *Terror in My Soul: Communist Autobiographies on Trial* (Cambridge, MA: Harvard University Press, 2003), 250–251.

47. Robert Conquest, *The Great Terror: A Reassessment* (London: Pimlico, 1992), 113.

48. Ibid, 275. For a full English-language version of the letter, see Nadezhda A. Joffe, *Back in Time: My Life, My Fate, My Epoch,* trans. Frederick S. Choate (Oak Park, MI: Labor Publications, 1995), 55–63.

49. Alexander Etkind, *Eros of the Impossible: The History of Psychoanalysis in Russia* (Boulder, CO: Westview, 1997).

50. For an explanation of the possible meanings of z/k, see Toker, *Return from the Archipelago,* 256.

51. Lev Gavrilov, "Zapasnoi kommunist [Reserve communist]," in Vilenskii, *Dodnes' tiagoteet* 2:225–234.

52. Mikhail Timofeevich Adeev, "Beda i bol'shevistskaia sovest' [Misfortune and Bolshevik conscience]," Memorial, f. 2, op. 1, d. 2, l. 0001 2909 0067, 0068, 0070.

53. Ibid., l. 0001 2909 0105.

54. Ibid., l. 0112.

55. Golfo Alexolopolus, *Stalin's Outcasts: Aliens, Citizens, and the Soviet State, 1926–1936* (Ithaca, NY: Cornell University Press, 2003), 102, 140.

56. Kotkin, *Magnetic Mountain,* 220, 199–237.

57. On the issue of the omnipresence of ideology in Soviet life, see Martin Malia's essay "Soviet Studies after the Soviet Union: The Archives of Evil," in *The New Republic* 29 (November 2004). See also Joseph Berger, *Shipwreck of a Generation: The Memoirs of Joseph Berger* (London: Harvill, 1971); Lev Kopelev, *Khranit' vechno* [To be preserved forever] (Ann Arbor, MI: Ardis, 1975).

58. Jochen Hellbeck, "Fashioning the Stalinist Soul: The Diary of Stepan Podlubnyi, 1931–9," in Sheila Fitzpatrick, ed., *Stalinism: New Directions* (London: Routledge, 2000), 77–116; Jochen Hellbeck, *Revolution on My Mind: Writing a Diary under Stalin* (Cambridge, MA: Harvard University Press, 2006). See also Jochen Hellbeck, "Everyday Ideology: Life during Stalinism," *Eurozine,* February 22, 2010.

59. GARF, f. 7523, op. 85s, d. 255, l. 20.

60. Ibid.

61. "Ukaz prezidiuma Verkhovnogo Soveta SSSR 'Ob amnistii sovetskikh grazhdan sotrudnichavshchykh s okkupantamy v period velikoi otechestvennoi voini 1941–1945' [Decree of the presidium of the Supreme Soviet of the USSR 'On the amnesty of Soviet citizens who collaborated with the occupiers in the period of the Great Patriotic War 1941–1945']," 17 September 1955, GARF, f. 7523, op. 72, d. 522, ll. 110–112.

62. Veniamin Borisovich Epshtein, Memorial, f. 1, op. 1, d. 5479, l. 0036 1502 0054.

63. Ibid.

64. Robert Jay Lifton, *Thought Reform and the Psychology of Totalism: A Study of "Brainwashing" in China* (New York: W. W. Norton, 1963), 66.

65. Anna Freud, *The Ego and the Mechanisms of Defense* (London: Hogarth Press, 1937).

66. Leon A. Festinger, *A Theory of Cognitive Dissonance* (Stanford, CA: Stanford University Press, 1957). See also Eddie Harmon-Jones and Judson Mills, *Cognitive Dissonance: Progress on a Pivotal Theory in Social Psychology* (Washington, DC: American Psychological Association, 1997), chapter 1.

67. For further discussion of the "belief-disconfirmation paradigm," see Christopher T. Burris, Eddie Harmon-Jones, and W. Ryan Tarpley, "'By Faith Alone': Religious Agitation and Cognitive Dissonance," *Basic and Applied Social Psychology* 19 (1997): 17–31. This process was characterized by the members' efforts to persuade others of their beliefs in order to make their cognitions consonant. Another theory to spin off of the Cognitive Dissonance concept was called the "effort-justification paradigm." It looked at difficult and easy initiation processes into a group that did not ultimately turn out to be all that interesting. Those who had endured more to gain entrance judged the group more favorably than those who had gone through mild initiation rituals. On the dynamics of group systems, see Herbert M. Adler and Van Buren O. Hammett, "Crisis, Conversion, and Cult Formation: An Examination of a Common Psychosocial Sequence," *American Journal of Psychiatry* 130, 8 (August 1973): 861–864.

68. Corroborating neuroscientific evidence for the adaptive function of reducing cognitive dissonance is provided by a recent brain imaging study demonstrating both that cognitive dissonance activates brain regions correlated with distress and that an attitudinal change that increases consonance reduces this activation. See Vincent van Veen, Marie K. Krug, Jonathan Schooler, Cameron S. Carter, "Neural Activity Predicts Attitude Change in Cognitive Dissonance," *Nature Neuroscience* 12 (2009): 1465–1475.

Another neuroscience study has demonstrated that after a difficult decision is made between two similarly valued choices, the physiological activity in the brain is altered to increase the positive emotions accompanying the chosen object and the negative emotions accompanying the alternative choice. See Tali Sharot, Benedetto De Martino, and Raymond J. Dolan, "How Choice Reveals and Shapes Expected Hedonic Outcome," *The Journal of Neuroscience* 29 (2009): 3760–3765.

69. "Svodka pisem po povodu Ukaza Prezidiuma Verkhovnogo Soveta SSSR ob amnistii [Summary of letters regarding the decree of the Presidium of the Supreme Soviet of the USSR on amnesty]," GARF, f. 7523, op. 85s., d. 235, l. 6.

70. See Adler, *Gulag Survivor,* chapter 3, and Miriam Dobson, *Khrushchev's Cold Summer: Gulag Returnees, Crime, and the Fate of Reform after Stalin* (Ithaca, NY: Cornell University Press, 2009), 40–42, 112–113.

71. Aleksandr I. Solzhenitsyn, *The Gulag Archipelago: 1918–1956: An Experiment in Literary Investigation,* vol. 3, trans. Harry Willetts (New York: HarperPerennial, 1992), 489–490.

72. See Adler, *Gulag Survivor*, chapter 5.

73. Kotkin, *Magnetic Mountain*, 220.

74. Alex Inkeles and Raymond Bauer, *The Soviet Citizen: Daily Life in a Totalitarian Society* (Cambridge, MA: Harvard University Press, 1961).

75. Roy Medvedev, interview at his Moscow dacha, June 19, 2005.

76. L. Iaronts, response to questionnaire, December 12, 1995.

77. N. I. Zadorozhnaia, response to questionnaire, December 12 1995.

78. Sandi Mann, "'People-work': Emotion Management, Stress, and Coping," *British Journal of Guidance and Counselling* 32, 2 (2004): 205–221; Hillel M. Finestone and David B. Conter, "Acting in Medical Practice," *The Lancet* 344, 8925 (1994): 801–802.

79. Jeffry A. Simpson and W. Steven Rholes, "Stress and Secure Base Relationships in Adulthood," *Advances in Personal Relationships* 5 (1994): 181–204.

80. Louis Jolyon West and Paul R. Martin, "Pseudo-identity and the Treatment of Personality Change in Victims of Captivity and Cults," *Cultic Studies Journal* 13, 2 (1996): 125–152; Irka Kuleshnyk, "The Stockholm Syndrome: Toward an Understanding," *Social Action and Law* 10, 2 (1984): 37–42; Harvey W. Kushner, *Encyclopedia of Terrorism* (Thousand Oaks, CA: Sage Publications, 2003).

81. See Goffman, "On the Characteristics of Total Institutions," 1–124, in *Asylums*, particularly 89.

82. Eric Kandel and L. Squire, "Neuroscience: Breaking Down Scientific Barriers to the Study of Brain and Mind," *Science* 290, 5494 (2000): 1113–1120.

83. Kerstin Uvnäs-Moberg, "Physiological and Endocrine Effects of Social Contact," *Annals of the New York Academy of Science* 807 (1997): 146–163; C. Sue Carter, "Neuroendocrine Perspectives on Social Attachment and Love," *Psychoneuroendocrinology* 23, 8 (1998): 779–818.

84. Herbert M. Adler, psychiatrist, M.D., Fellow of the American College of Psychiatrists, interviews, New York, December 2005.

85. GARF, f. 7523, op. 107, d. 235, ll. 7–8.

86. See Richard D. Alexander, *The Biology of Moral Systems* (Hawthorne, NY: DeGruyter, 1987); Robert L. Trivers, *Social Evolution* (Menlo Park, CA: Benjamin/Cummins, 1985); J. O. Beahrs, "Memory as Power: Who Is to Decide?"

87. This trend is manifested in, among other things, official unwillingness to exhume newly discovered mass graves and the steady restoration of Soviet- or Stalin-era symbols. See Nanci Adler, "The Future of the Soviet Past Remains Unpredictable: The Resurrection of Stalinist Symbols amidst the Exhumation of Mass Graves," *Europe-Asia Studies* 57, 8 (2005): 1093–1119.

88. My thanks to Amir Weiner for his critical reflections on this research, and particularly for his insightful reference to the war as "the elephant in the living room." The war cultivated allegiance even in Gulag prisoners, many of whom tried to be released in order to serve the motherland. (Those who were released were often sent right to the front. Political prisoners were generally considered too suspect to defend their country.) Fighting Nazism gave Communism a better name, and victory was the triumph of good over evil.

War veterans and Gulag survivors competed for decades for privileged status. For more on veterans' views, see Catherine Merridale, *Ivan's War: Life and Death in the Red Army, 1939–1945* (New York: Metropolitan Books, 2006).

89. George Gerbner, "Cultural Indicators: The Third Voice," in George Gerbner, Larry P. Gross, and William H. Melody, eds., *Communications Technology and Public Policy* (New York: John Wiley and Sons, 1973), 555–573.

90. Such questions could be settled by the reinterpretive process of cognitive dissonance. A different psychosocial process might be employed by those whose "conversion" (Adler and Hammett, "Crisis, Conversion, and Cult Formation") to the regime's form of Communism was rewarded. Such rewards included the promise of social, political, vocational, and material benefits. Survival was enhanced by authentically embracing the ideology.

1. The Gulag Prisoner and the Bolshevik Soul

1. "Vospominaniia—ocherki Slavianinoi O. A. [Memoirs—essays of O. A. Slavianina]," RGASPI, f. 560, op. 1, d. 36, ll. 4–6.

2. Ibid., l. 72.

3. Ibid., l. 5.

4. Ibid., ll. 2, 73.

5. Ibid., l. 6.

6. More specifically, a report by Shvernik on the work of the Party Control Commission (KPK) from February 1956 to June 1961 states that 30,954 Communists received Party rehabilitation, many posthumously (RGANI, f. 6, op. 6, d. 1165, l. 2). Elsewhere this report states that 24,038 appeals from former POWs were sent to the Twentieth and Twenty-first Party Congresses, and 12,498 other applicants appealed to the KPK for restoration of Party membership. Approximately 55 percent of the appeals to the Twentieth Party Congress and 40.6 percent of those to the Twenty-first Party Congress were honored. (A. N. Iakovlev et al., eds., *Reabilitatsiia: Kak eto bylo, fevral' 1956–nachalo 80-x godov* [Rehabilitation: As it happened, February 1956–early 1980s], T. 2 (Moscow: Mezhdunarodnyi Fond Demokratsiia, 2003, 363; see also 252). A 1957 report attributes the high percentage of reinstatements to the fact that "among the applicants were many rehabilitated [persons], who were excluded from the Party for political reasons" (RGANI, f. 6, op. 6, d. 1077, l. 2). Tens of thousands more were to apply only a few decades later. This backlog was handled during Gorbachev's de-Stalinization. According to a memorandum by Boris Pugo, chairman of the Party Control Commission from 1988 to 1990, 80,000 applications for Party membership were honored. Iaklovev et al., *Reabilitatsiia: Kak eto bylo, seredina 80-kh godov–1991* [Rehabilitation: As it happened, mid-1980s–1991], T. 3 (Moscow: Materik, 2004), 520.

7. Igal Halfin was one of the first historians to explore this phenomenon in *Terror in My Soul*.

8. Merridale, *Ivan's War,* 383–384.

9. Alexander Etkind, "Whirling with the Other," *The Russian Review* 62 (2003): 565–588.

10. *Merriam Webster's Collegiate Dictionary,* 10th ed. (Springfield, MA: Merriam-Webster, 1993), 1123.

11. Goffman, *Asylums.*

12. Richard Dawkins, *The God Delusion* (New York: Bantam Books, 2006).

13. My thanks to Professor Hans Ulrich Gumbrecht (fellow participant in Eyewitness Narratives, conference at Hebrew University, November 25–27, 2007) for bringing my attention to this work, and particularly to this parable.

14. Louis Sebastien Mercier, *Het jaar twee duizend vier honderd en veertig: een droom,* eerste deel [Dutch translation of *L'An 2440*; The year 2440: a dream], part 1 (Haarlem: F. Bohn en A. Loosjes, 1787), 105.

15. Ibid., 106–107.

16. Ibid., 106.

17. Ibid., 111.

18. Herbert M. Adler and Freda Adler, "A Group-System Hypothesis as an Explanation of Sociologic Phenomena," *Social Psychiatry* 10 (1975): 72, 75.

19. Adler and Hammett, "Crisis, Conversion, and Cult Formation."

20. For a current discussion on the aftermath of being compelled to comply, see Choe Sang-Hun, "Brutally Shaped by a North Korean Gulag," *International Herald Tribune,* July 10, 2007.

21. See Ludmilla Alexeeva, *Soviet Dissent: Contemporary Movements for National, Religious, and Human Rights,* trans. Carol Pearce and John Glad (Middletown, CT: Wesleyan University Press, 1985), 284–287; Philip Boobbyer, *Conscience, Dissent and Reform in Soviet Russia* (London: Routledge, 2005).

22. Aleksandr Rekemchik, *Skudnyi materik* [Poor continent] (Moscow: Sovetskii pisatel', 1974), 427, 429.

23. Ibid., 430.

24. Festinger, *A Theory of Cognitive Dissonance.*

25. See Adler, *Gulag Survivor.* See also Stephen F. Cohen, *The Victims Return: Survivors of the Gulag after Stalin* (Exeter, NH: Publishing Works, 2010).

26. Frankl, *Man's Search for Meaning,* 115.

27. Kotkin, *Magnetic Mountain,* 295–296.

28. For an overview of related literature, see Erik van Ree, "Stalin as Writer and Thinker," *Kritika: Explorations in Russian and Eurasian History* 3, 4 (Fall 2002): 699–714. See also Arthur Jay Klinghoffer, *Red Apocalypse: The Religious Evolution of Soviet Communism* (Lanham, MD: University Press of America), 1996.

29. See this discussion in Erik van Ree, "Stalin as Writer and Thinker," 704.

30. Reneé Fülop-Miller, *The Mind and Face of Bolshevism,* xiv.

31. Michael Burleigh, *Earthly Powers: The Clash of Religion and Politics in Europe from the French Revolution to the Great War* (New York: Harper Collins, 2005), 81. Burleigh credits the utopian Campanella for the first use of the term "political religion," in his de-

scription of the political use of religious belief. See also Philippe Burrin, "Political Religion: The Relevance of a Concept," *History and Memory* 9, 1 (Spring/Summer 1997): 322.

32. Fülop-Miller, *The Mind and Face of Bolshevism,* 71.

33. Robert C. Tucker, ed., "Two Tactics of Social Democracy in the Democratic Revolution," *The Lenin Anthology* (New York: W. W. Norton, 1975), 142–143.

34. George Gerbner, "Cultural Indicators: The Third Voice," 555–573, in Gerbner et al., *Communications Technology and Public Policy.*

35. Jochen Hellbeck, "Fashioning the Stalinist Soul," in Fitzpatrick, *Stalinism,* 96.

36. Hellbeck, *Revolution on My Mind,* 297.

37. Ibid., 305.

38. Ibid., 327.

39. Ibid., 335, 337.

40. Ibid., 312.

41. Halfin, *Terror in My Soul,* 59.

42. Hellbeck, *Revolution on My Mind,* 312–313.

43. Burrin, *Political Religion,* 324–325.

44. Emile Durkheim, *Selected Writings* (Cambridge: Cambridge University Press, 1972), 228–232.

45. See Jan Plamper, "Introduction: Modern Personality Cults," in Klaus Heller and Jan Plamper, eds., *Personality Cults in Stalinism* (Gottingen: V & R unipress GmbH, 2004), 39.

46. Cited in Oleg Kharkhordin, *The Collective and the Individual in Russia,* 80.

47. Anatolii Lunacharskii, *Religiia i sotsializm* [Religion and socialism], 2 vols. (St. Petersburg: Shipovnik, 1908–1910), 2: 363, cited in Kharkhordin, 80.

48. Lunacharskii, *Religiia i sotsializm.*

49. My thanks to Leona Toker for drawing my attention to this aspect of Russian Orthodoxy through Nikolai Losskii's 1957 work *Kharakter russkogo naroda* (in *Usloviia absoliutnogo dobra*) [Character of the Russian people, in Conditions of absolute good] (Moscow: Politicheskaia literatura, 1991).

50. Cited in Halfin, *Terror in My Soul,* 282.

51. Irina Paperno, "Intimacy with Power: Soviet Memoirists Remember Stalin," in Heller and Plamper, *Personality Cults in Stalinism,* 361.

52. Hellbeck, *Revolution on My Mind,* 342.

53. Halfin, *Terror in My Soul,* 283.

54. My thanks to Alexander Etkind for raising this point.

55. Dzhana Kut'ina, Andrei Broido, and Anton Kut'in, *Ob ushedshem veke: Rasskazyvaet Ol'ga Shatunovskaia* [On a century passed: Ol'ga Shatunovskaia speaks] (La Jolla, CA: DAA Books, 2001), 333.

56. Mikhail Davidovich Baital'skii, "Tetradi dlia vnukov [Notebooks for the grandchildren]," Memorial, f. 2, op. 1, d. 8, l. 0698.

57. Ibid., l. 0704.

58. Ibid., l. 0701.

59. Ibid.

60. See Iurii Druzhnikov, *Informer 001: The Myth of Pavlik Morozov* (New Brunswick, NJ: Transaction Publishers, 1997).

61. Alexolopolus, *Stalin's Outcasts,* 144.

62. Cited in Hellbeck, "Fashioning the Stalinist Soul," 109.

63. "Vospominaniia Kuznetsova N. S. [The memoirs of N. S. Kuznetsov]," RGASPI, f. 560, op. 1, d. 21, l. 18.

64. Ibid., l. 87.

65. Ibid.

66. Ibid., l. 97.

67. Ibid., l. 99.

68. Ibid., l. 102.

69. Ibid.

70. Ibid., l. 103.

71. See Adler, *Gulag Survivor,* chapter 3, and Dobson, *Khrushchev's Cold Summer,* 40–42, 112–113.

72. "Nezabyvaemoe," Vospominaniia Ol'berta L. A. [Unforgettable, the memoirs of L.A. Ol'bert], RGASPI, f. 560, op. 1, d. 29, l. 72.

73. Ibid., l. 69.

74. Primo Levi, *If This Is a Man* (London: Sphere Books, 1987), 135–136.

75. For a discussion of the "blind discipline" of believing in the ultimate wisdom of Stalin, see L. A. Man'kovskii, "K voprosu o psikhologii kul'ta Stalina [On the question of the psychology of the Stalin cult]," *Voprosy filosofii* 1 (1989): 162–166.

76. See Irka Kuleshnyk, "The Stockholm Syndrome: Toward an Understanding," *Social Action and Law* 10, 2 (1984): 37–42.

77. See Anne Applebaum, *GULAG: A History,* 244, 306; see also Solzhenitsyn, "The Soul and Barbed Wire" (Harvill Press edition), 299–327.

78. Ol'bert, RGAPSI, f. 560, op. 1, d. 29, l. 39.

79. "Avtobiografiia N. M. Busareva i ego vospominaniia [The autobiography of N. M. Busarev and his memoirs]," RGASPI, f. 560, op. 1, d. 4, l. 58.

80. Ibid. l. 135.

81. Ol'bert, l. 40.

82. Rozaliia Isaakovna Veisman, "Oktiabrem okrylennye [October wings]," Memorial, f. 2, op. 1, d. 32, l. 0001 2909 0915.

83. Ibid., l. 0001 2909 0969.

84. For more on its meaning in Russia, see Merridale, *Night of Stone.*

85. Aleksandr Galich, *Pokolenie obrechennykh* [Generation of the doomed] (Frankfurt/Main: Posev, 1972), 71–72.

86. Gene Sosin, "Alexander Galich: Russian Poet of Dissent," *Midstream* 20, 4 (1974): 32.

87. Ol'bert, l. 70.

88. Cited in Dariusz Tolczyk, *See No Evil: Literary Cover-Ups and Discoveries of the Soviet Camp Experience* (New Haven, CT: Yale University Press, 1999), 234–235.

89. Mariia Moiseevna Gol'dberg, "Rasskaz o tom, chto bylo i chto ne povtoritsia [The story of what happened and what will not be repeated]," Memorial, f. 2, op. 1, d. 47, ll. 1993 0511 0110-0111.

90. Ibid., l. 1993 0511 0113.

91. Ibid.

92. Sheila Fitzpatrick and Alf L. Lüdtke, "Energizing the Everyday: On the Breaking and Making of Social Bonds in Nazism and Stalinism," in Michael Geyer and Sheila Fitzpatrick, eds., *Beyond Totalitarianism: Stalinism and Nazism Compared* (Cambridge: Cambridge University Press, 2009), 300. See also Jochen Hellbeck, "Everyday Ideology: Life during Stalinism," www.eurozine.com.

93. See Harmon-Jones and Mills, *Cognitive Dissonance,* chapter 1.

94. Alexander Solzhenitsyn, *One Day in the Life of Ivan Denisovich,* trans. Max Hayward and Ronald Hingley (New York: Bantam Dell, 1963), 88–89.

95. See Tolczyk's discussion of Ivan's motivation in *See No Evil,* 294–295.

96. Applebaum, *Gulag,* 227.

97. Lesia Padun-Luk'ianova, "Ekaterina Olitskaia," in Semen Vilenskii, ed., *Dodnes' tiagoteet* 2:44–45.

98. Applebaum, *GULAG,* 347. Also in English translation, Semeon Vilensky, *Till My Tale is Told,* trans. John Crowfoot (Bloomington: Indiana University Press, 1999).

99. Ekaterina Olitskaia, "Na Kolyme [At Kolyma]," in *Dodnes' tiagoteet* 2:46. Ekaterina Olitskaia, *Moi vospominaniia* [My memoirs] (Frankfurt: Posev, 1971).

100. From 1990 to 2004, editor S. Vilenskii writes in a footnote, over 1.5 million books of remembrance were published in the Soviet Union and successor states (judging by the number, this category would include brochures and essays); *Dodnes' tiagoteet* 2:65.

101. Olitskaia, "Na Kolyme," 65.

102. Varlam Shalamov, "Inzhener Kiselev," in *Sobranie sochinenii v chetyrekh tomakh* [Engineer Kiselev, in Collected stories in four volumes], vol. 1 (Moscow: Khudozhestvennaia literatura, Vagrius, 1998), 422–431.

103. Vasily Grossman, *Forever Flowing,* trans. Thomas P. Whitney (New York: Harper & Row, 1972), 105.

104. Ibid.

105. Pis'mo Marii Ksenofontovny Malyshevoi [Letter of Mariia Ksenofontovna Malysheva], Memorial, f. 1, op. 3, d. 3063.

2. Reconciling the Self with the System

1. Lev Mendelevich Gurvich, *Imet' silu pomnit'* [Have the strength to remember] (Moscow: Moskovskii rabochii, 1991), 3.

2. My thanks to Arsenii Roginskii for an impassioned discussion on how deeply embedded these questions are in the Soviet consciousness. Interview, Amsterdam, March 14, 2007.

3. RGASPI, f. 560, op., 1, d. 4, N. M. Busarev, "Avtobiografiia N. M. Busareva i ego vospominaniia [Autobiography of N. M. Busarev and his memoirs]," l. 57.

4. Mikhail Trofimovich Adeev, "Beda i bol'shevistskaia sovest [Misfortune and Bolshevik conscience]," Memorial, f. 2, op. 1, d. 2, ll. 0001 2909 0049, 0064, 0067.

5. Ibid., ll. 0069–70. Few ventured beyond the interpretation imposed from above, though events like the 1968 Soviet invasion of Prague under Brezhnev forced some returnees, such as Iosif Bogoraz, to reevaluate their stance. He turned in his Party card.

6. Alexander Daniel, unpublished report on state memory vs. social memory, March 6, 1994, 7.

7. Cited in Orlando Figes, *The Whisperers: Private Life in Stalin's Russia* (London: Penguin Books, 2007), 274.

8. Arthur Koestler, *Darkness at Noon* (London: Vintage Books, 2005), 27–28.

9. "Ob amnistii: Ukaz Prezidiuma Verkhovnogo Soveta SSSR ot 27 Marta 1953 [On amnesty: decree of the Presidium of the Supreme Soviet of the USSR of 27 March 1953]," *Pravda,* March 28, 1953, 1.

10. Between 1948 and 1953, by order of the MGB, 37,951 individuals were sent into unlimited exile; an additional 20,267 ex-prisoners were dispatched to far places by decision of the Special Conference between 1949 and 1953 (RGANI, f. 89, op. 18, d. 26, l. 2.)

11. GARF, f. 7523, op. 107, d. 255, l. 68.

12. Ibid., l. 70.

13. See discussion on the group system in chapter 1.

14. For a concise discussion on the ends (the welfare of the Soviet Union and the classless society it was creating) justifying the means (ruthless repression), see Erik van Ree, *Bloed broeders: Stalin, Hitler en hun Pact* [Blood brothers: Stalin, Hitler and their pact] (Amsterdam: Jan Mets, 1989), 159–161.

15. Koestler, 137.

16. Ibid., 141.

17. See Weber, *Wirtschaft und Gesellschaft* [Economy and society], 327–329, 658, 660–663; see also Ken Jowitt, *New World Disorder: The Leninist Extinction* (Berkeley: University of California Press, 1992), 1, 7. My thanks to Erik van Ree for drawing my attention to these discussions.

18. See Koestler's insightful passages on the dilemma of the revolutionary, 51–52, 187–188, 206.

19. G. L. Man'kovskaia and I. L. Man'kovskaia, "Pamiati Otsa [Memories of father]," and L. A. Man'kovskii, "K voprosy o psikhologii kul'ta Stalina [On the question of the psychology of the Stalin cult]," *Voprosy filosofii* 1 (1989): 161–163.

20. Nataliia Sats, who directed the Children's Theater in Moscow, was arrested in 1937 along with her husband. In her memoirs, she recalls that while she was imprisoned, many people helped her to the extent that their position and circumstances allowed. That made her wonder why these good Soviet people could not see that she was not guilty. The answer may lie in an incident she relates between a soldier-guard and another female prisoner, who was weeping and swearing that neither she nor her husband was guilty. His re-

sponse characterized the way both sides were supposed to think at the time. He straight-forwardly pointed out that if she was educated, she herself should have realized that her husband was an enemy. Nataliia Sats, *Novelly moei zhizni* [Sketches from my life] (Moscow: Gosizdat, 1984). The message was thus that those who did not expose an enemy that was so close must be implicated themselves. And so the concentric circle of victims grew.

21. See Andreas Kalyvas, *Democracy and the Politics of the Extraordinary: Max Weber, Karl Schmitt, and Hannah Arendt* (Cambridge: Cambridge University Press, 2008), 1–64.

22. Solomon Pavlovich Shur, "Pod kolesom istorii (Khronika nezabyvaemykh dnei) [Under the wheel of history, chronicle of unforgettable days]," part 2, Memorial, f. 2, op. 1, d. 139, l. 0008 3111 0795.

23. See Toker's discussion of Dombrovskii's fictional writings on the breakout of the "closed system" and deconversion, in *Return from the Archipelago,* 219–220.

24. Semen Vilenskii, ed., *Soprotivlenie v Gulage* [Resistance in the Gulag] (Moscow: Vozvrashchenie, 1992).

25. Shur, l. 0008 3111 0795.

26. V. Litvinov, materials from Roy Medvedev, letter to Stephen Cohen, November 17, 1983.

27. Lennart Samuelson, "Sharashki: Stalinist Repression of Scientists and Engineers," discussion paper for the History and Legacy of the Gulag conference at Davis Center, Harvard University, November 2–5, 2006, 4.

28. J. S. Atherton (2005), Learning and Teaching: Assimilation and Accommodation (UK), http://www.learningandteaching.info/learning/assimacc.htm.

29. Busarev, RGASPI, f. 560, op. 1, d. 4, l. 57.

30. Ibid., l. 133.

31. Kolchak's forces fought against the Red Army in the Civil War.

32. Vladimir L'vovich Timoshin, "Obrashcheniia i zaiavleniia grazhdan po voprosam reabilitatsii zhertv politicheskikh repressii kak istoricheskii istochnik po izucheniiu mental-iteta rossiiskogo obshchestva [Citizens' appeals and applications on questions of rehabilitat-ing victims of political repression as a historical source to study the mentality of Russian society]," diplomnaia rabota, RGGU (istoriko-arkhivnyi institut), Moscow, 1997, 72–74.

33. Joseph Berger, *Shipwreck,* 246–247; see also Shatunovskaia, chapter 1.

34. Ibid., 64.

35. Ibid.

36. Czeslaw Milosz, *The Captive Mind* (New York: Limited Editions Club, 1983).

37. Berger, *Shipwreck,* 26.

38. Anatolii Brat, "Glazami raznykh pokolenii [Through the eyes of different genera-tions]," Memorial, f. 2, op. 1, d. 28, l. 0001 2909 0393.

39. Kuromiya, *Voices of the Dead,* 10.

40. Igal Halfin, "Stalinist Confessions in an Age of Terror," paper, international sym-posium Eyewitness Narratives, Hebrew University, Jerusalem, November 27, 2007. See also Renata Jambresic Kirin's discussion on the "cross-investigations" and "cross punish-ment by internees" on Goli otok, Tito's concentration camp for Communists: Renata Jam-

bresic Kirin, "The Retraumatization of the 1948 Communist Purges in Yugoslav Literary Culture," in Marcel Cornis-Pope and John Neubauer, eds., *History of the Literary Cultures of East-Central Europe; Junctures and Disjunctures in the 19th and 20th Centuries,* vol. 1 (Amsterdam: John Benjamins, 2007), 124–132.

41. Halfin, *Terror in My Soul.*

42. Halfin, "Stalinist Confessions." See also Barry McLoughlin and Kevin McDermott, eds., *Stalin's Terror: High Politics and Mass Repression in the Soviet Union* (Houndsmills: Palgrave Macmillan, 2004), 190–191; Wendy Z. Goldman, *Terror and Democracy in the Age of Stalin: The Social Dynamics of Repression* (New York: Cambridge University Press, 2007), 252–254.

43. Halfin, "The NKVD and the Extraction of Confessions," 70–71, unpublished lengthier version of chapter 2 in Halfin, *Stalinist Confessions: Messianism and Terror at the Leningrad Communist University* (Pittsburgh: University of Pittsburgh Press, 2009). I acknowledge my gratitude to Professor Halfin for sharing this prepublication manuscript. Elsewhere, Halfin examines a 1928 Tomsk verification commission that investigated student oppositional activities, terming the tribunal a "court of conscience." He asserts that the interrogators "ultimately sought insight into the defenders' subjective state, not their outward behavior" (Igal Halfin, "Looking into the Oppositionists' Souls," *The Russian Review* 60 (July 2001): 324. He goes on to assert that the interrogator's task was "more complicated" than exposing the truth; he had to find out whether the defendant was "unaware of what his spiritual condition was." Ibid., 328.

44. Ibid., "The NKVD and Extractions," 23.

45. Ibid., 24.

46. Ibid., 67.

47. Ibid.

48. Ibid., 77.

49. Ibid., 139–140.

50. Ibid., 16. See Evgeniia Ginzburg's description in *Krutoi marshrut* [Into the whirlwind], vol. 1 (New York: Posev, 1985), 63–67.

51. Ibid., 39. For a survey of the various approaches to the Soviet self, see Choi Chatterjee and Karen Petrone, "Models of Selfhood and Subjectivity: The Soviet Case in Historical Perspective," *Slavic Review* 67, 4 (Winter 2008): 967–986.

52. Veisman, "Oktiabrem okrylennye," Memorial, f. 2, op. 1, d. 32, l. 0001 2909 0835.

53. Nadezhda Mikhailovna Dabudek, "'Donoschik,' materialy semeinogo arkhiva [Informer, materials of the family archive]," Memorial, f. 2, op. 1, d. 51, l. 1993 0511 0626.

54. Ibid., l. 0627.

55. Petr Osipovich Sagoian, "1937 god v moei zhizni [The year 1937 in my life]," Memorial, f. 2, op. 1, d. 104, l. 1993 1510 1633.

56. Brat, l. 0001 2909 0405.

57. Memorial, f. 1, op. 1, d. 989, ll. 0013 0612 1099–1100, 1109–1111, 1145–1146.

58. Ekaterina Olitskaia, "Na Kolyme," in Vilenskii, *Dodnes' tiagoteet* 2:46; also in English, *Till My Tale is Told.*

59. Ibid.

60. Brat, l. 0001 2909 0403. This manuscript was rejected for publication in the Gorbachev years because the period of repression it dealt with—before and after the Stalin years—was too broad.

61. Goffman, "On the Characteristics," 1–124. This is the mechanism of cognitive dissonance as well.

62. Leonid Furman, response to Stephen Cohen's questionnaire, May 30, 1982. A fellow non-Party returnee insisted that no one, with the exception of "maniacs," maintained their faith in the Party. Nadezhda Markovna Ulanovskaia, Cohen questionnaire, Jerusalem, July 17, 1980.

63. Evgenii Eduardovich Gagen, "Vospominaniia [Memoirs]," vol. 1, Memorial, f. 2, op. 1, d. 42, ll. 0001 2909 1863–1864.

64. Peter H. Solomon, Jr., *Soviet Criminal Justice under Stalin* (Cambridge: Cambridge University Press, 1996), 402–403.

65. Gagen, vol. 4, Memorial, f. 2, op. 1, d. 45, l. 1993 0510 1075.

66. Ibid., ll. 1993 0510 1097–1098.

67. Ibid., ll. 1123–1124.

68. So he writes in his memoirs. Once judicially rehabilitated, the actual procedure was for an applicant to petition the Party Control Commission for reinstatement; appeals for reinstatement had to go to a Party office within the Central Committee apparatus. Nevertheless, according to many of the documents I came across, the Presidium of the Supreme Soviet received and fielded many appeals, and generally forwarded such correspondence to the appropriate agency.

69. Gagen, vol. 4, Memorial, f. 2, op. 1, d. 45, l. 1142.

70. Galina Mikhailovna Paushkina, "Tragediia nevinovnykh [Tragedy of innocents]," Memorial, f. 2, op. 1, d. 92, l. 1993 1510 0630.

71. Ibid., l. 0631.

72. Ibid., l. 0634.

73. Ibid., l. 0635.

74. "Goriachii kartser diktatury [Intense punishment cell of the dictatorship]," *Vecherniaia Moskva*, October 28, 1995, 2.

75. Evgenii Gnedin, *Katastrofa: Vtoroe rozhdenie, memuarnye zapiski* [Catastrophe, second birth, memoir notes] (Amsterdam: Alexander Herzen Foundation, 1977), 259, 263, 265–266, 319.

76. GARF, f. 9474, op. 16, d. 478, l. 54. The report may date from 1954.

77. Ibid. They, of course, may have been arrested themselves.

78. See Vilenskii, *Dodnes' tiagoteet* 1:309–325.

79. Zoia Dmitrievna Marchenko, interview held in her Moscow home, April 6, 1995.

80. Nikita S. Khrushchev, "The Crimes of the Stalin Era: Special Report to the 20th Congress of the Communist Party of the Soviet Union," in *The New Leader,* section two, July 16, 1956, S7.

81. Ibid., S8.

82. Ibid., S20–21.

83. Ibid., S32.

84. Ibid., S17.

85. N. A. Barsukov, "XX S'ezd v retrospektive Khrushcheva [Twentieth Party Congress in Khrushchev's retrospective]," *Otechestvennaia Istoriia* 6 (1996): 172–173; see also V. N. Naumov, "N. S. Khrushchev i reabilitatsiia zhertv massovykh politicheskikh repressii [N. S. Khrushchev and the rehabilitation of victims of mass political repression]," *Voprosy istorii* 4 (1997): 20, 22.

86. William Taubman, *Khrushchev: The Man and His Era* (New York: W. W. Norton, 2004), 74.

87. Ibid.

88. I. Ia. Vozzhaev, "Vospominaniia Vozzhaeva [Memoirs of Vozzhaev]," RGASPI, f. 560, op. 1, d. 7, ll. 15–16.

89. The gradual release of political prisoners was made possible by a May 19 decree of the General Procurator, the Minister of Justice, the Minister of Internal Affairs, and the Chairman of the Committee of State Security; see GARF, f. 8131, op. 32, d. 3284, ll. 40 ob., 41, ob.

90. See, among others, Andrea Graziosi, "The Great Strikes of 1953 in Soviet Labor Camps in the Accounts of their Participants: A Review," *Cahiers du monde russe et soviétique* 33, 4 (October–December 1992): 419–446; Marta Craveri, "The Strikes of Norilsk and Vorkuta Camps and Their Role in the Breakdown of the Stalinist Forced Labor System," unpublished paper, 1994; see also Petr Mitsner, "Ia byl ministrom sviazi v Kengirskom lagere . . . [I was the minister of communications in the Kengir camp]," *Novaia Pol'sha* 1 (2001).

91. Solzhenitsyn, *The Gulag Archipelago 1918–1956: An Experiment in Literary Investigation,* vol. 3, parts V–VII, trans. Harry Willets (New York: HarperPerennial, 1992), part 5, chapter 12.

92. Steven A. Barnes, "'In a Manner Befitting Soviet Citizens': An Uprising in the Post-Stalin Gulag," *Slavic Review* 64, 4 (Winter 2005): 824.

93. Solzhenitsyn, *Gulag Archipelago 1918–1956,* 311.

94. Barnes, "'In a Manner Befitting,'" 843.

95. Solzhenitsyn, cited in Barnes, "'In a Manner Befitting,'" 841.

96. Barnes, "'In a Manner Befitting,'" 826.

97. Roy Medvedev, interview in his Moscow dacha, June 19, 2005.

98. Vilenskii, interview, Moscow, June 21, 2005.

99. Beria himself had advocated certain liberal reforms; see Adler, *Gulag Survivor,* 78–81.

100. See Adler, *Gulag Survivor,* chapter 3.

101. Citing N. A. Formozov, Craveri notes that there had been approximately sixty strikes, revolts, and armed escapes in the thirties; Craveri, "Strikes of Norilsk and Vorkuta Camps," 4. There were also isolated armed insurrections and escapes in the forties and early fifties in Vorkuta, Arzamas, Kolyma, Ekibastuz, Ozerlag, and other points of the Gulag

(Craveri, "Krizis Gulaga: Kengirskoe vosstanie 1954 goda v dokumentakh MVD [Crisis of the Gulag: The Kengir uprising of 1954 in documents of the MVD]," 322). See also Semen Badash, "Soprotivlenie, iz vospominanii uchastnika zabastovki zakliuchennykh v Ekiba-stuze i vosstaniia v Noril'ske [Resistance, from the memoirs of a participant of the prisoner strike in Ekibastuz and the uprising in Norilsk]," *30 oktiabria* 58: 7; 59: 7.

102. Barnes, "'In a Manner Befitting,'" 825–826.

103. See Adler, *Gulag Survivor.*

104. Barnes, "'In a Manner Befitting,'" 842.

105. Ibid., 849.

106. Ibid., 848.

107. See the discussion on the rehabilitation of the 1921 Kronstadt rebellion partici-pants in Adler, "Future of the Soviet Past," 1093–1119.

108. Vilenskii, interview, Moscow, November 16, 2003. See Grigorii Klimovich, "O nereablitirovannykh [On the unrehabilitated]," *Volia* 2–3 (1994): 204–205; Galina Ves-novskaia, "Rabota po reabilitatsii [The work on rehabilitation]," *Volia* 2–3 (1994): 207–209.

109. Marlen Korallov, interview, Moscow, June 22, 2005; Marlen Korallov, "Vozvra-shchenie i proshchanie [Return and farewell]," *Pamiat'* 24, 197 (June 16–22, 2004); *30 oktriabria* 21 (2004), 55 (2005).

110. Korallov, ". . . i tomik Pasternaka [. . . and the Pasternak volume]," *Shakhmatnoe obozrenie* 19 (1990), 64.

111. Korallov, "Vozvrashchenie i proshchanie."

112. Korallov, interview.

113. See Jerome Bruner, *Actual Minds, Possible Worlds* (Cambridge, MA: Harvard Uni-versity Press, 1986).

114. Ibid.

115. George Gerbner, "Cultural Indicators: The Third Voice," in George Gerbner, Larry P. Gross, William Harry Melody, eds., *Communications Technology and Social Policy* (New York: John Wiley and Sons, 1973), 555–573. For more on the factors of selection, see the introduction to the present work.

116. On the purpose of the normative personal experience narrative, see Kenneth J. Gergen and Mary G. Gergen, "Narratives of the Self," in Theodore R. Sarbin and Karl E. Scheibe, eds., *Studies in Social Identity* (New York: Praeger, 1983), 254–273.

3. Beyond Belief

1. "Vospominaniia Taninoi T. L. 'V te gody' [The memoirs of T. L. Tanina 'In those years']," vol. 1, RGASPI, f. 560, op. 1, d. 36, l. 25.

2. For more on this women's camp, see Arsenii Roginskii and Aleksandr Daniel', "Arestu podlezhat zheny [Women subject to arrest]," in A. I. Daniel', L. S. Eremina, et al., eds., *Uznitsy 'Alzhira'* [Prisoners of Alzhir] (Moscow: Zven'ia, 2003), 6–30.

3. "Vospominaniia Taninoi," l. 302.

4. Susan Folkman, "The Case for Positive Emotions in the Stress Process," *Anxiety, Stress, Coping* 21 (2008): 3–14; Glenn Affleck and Howard Tennen, "Construing Benefits from Adversity: Adaptational Significance and Dispositional Underpinnings," *Journal of Personality and Social Psychology* 64 (1996): 899–922.

5. Ira J. Roseman and Andreas Evdokas, "Appraisals Cause Experienced Emotions: Experimental Evidence," *Cognitive Emotions* 18 (2004): 1–28; Martin E. P. Seligman and Mihaly Csikszentmihalyi, "Positive Psychology: An Introduction," *American Psychologist* 55 (2000): 5–14.

6. Jolande Withuis points out that this mental world may have some similarities with the term "culture," but mentality constitutes more than the accepting or rejecting of norms and values. One of the prime examples Withuis offers is the movement's conviction in the righteousness of the decision of Julius and Ethel Rosenberg, who refused to buy their lives with a confession. The movement did not consider the price they paid too high. Jolande Withuis, *Opoffering en Heroik: De mentale wereld van een communistische vrouwenorganisatie in naoorlogs Nederland, 1946–1976* [Sacrifice and heroism: The mental world of a Communist women's organization in postwar Holland, 1946–1976] (Amsterdam: Boom Meppel, 1990), 135–162.

7. "Vospominaniia Taninoi," l. 295. For more on the sense of gratitude toward the Party among returnees, see Diakov, *Povest' o perezhitom*. In this "made-to-social-order narrative," which "disinfected" the camp theme (Toker, *Return from the Archipelago*, 50–51), the author, a rehabilitated returnee, tells various stories of inmates. He also provides brief sketches of returnees, who had never lost hope that the day would come when they would be liberated. They were grateful to the Party for having undone that which was wrong, and they are happy to be back in the mainstream of Soviet life.

8. Jeffrey B. Brookings and Andrew J. Serratelli, "Positive Illusions: Positively Correlated with Subjective Well-being, Negatively Correlated with a Measure of Personal Growth," *Psychological Reports* 98 (April 2006): 407–413.

9. Jerry Lopper, "The Power of Positive Attitude: Benefits of Positive Thinking, Positive Mental Attitude and Optimism," February 3, 2007, http://changing-personal-habits.suite101.com.

10. *Merriam-Webster's Collegiate Dictionary, Tenth Edition* (Springfield, MA: Merriam-Webster, 1993), 575.

11. Raymond A. Bauer, "The Development of Attitudes Towards the Soviet Regime: Selected Case Histories," Project on the Soviet Social System [AF no. 33 (038)-12909], March 31, 1952.

12. "Public Response to a Passage in a Khrushchev Talk," *The Current Digest of the Soviet Press*, August 5, 1959, 21–22.

13. See the discussion in Sergy Yekelchyk, "The Civic Duty to Hate: Stalinist Citizenship as Political Practice and Civic Emotion (Kiev, 1943–1953)," *Kritika: Explorations in Russian and Eurasian History* 7, 3 (Summer 2006): 529–531.

14. Isaak Solomonovich Shur, "Na povorote: drama v trekh deistviiakh [At the turning point: Drama in three acts]," Memorial, f. 2, op. 1, d. 134, l. 0008 3111 0091.

15. Iakovlev et al., *Reabilitatsiia* 2:22.

16. Ibid., 23.

17. "O rassmotrenii del iskliuchennykh iz KPSS za antipartiinoe povedenie [On the consideration of cases of those excluded from the CPSU for anti-Party conduct]," RGANI, f. 6, op. 6, d. 1077, ll. 3–4.

18. Iakovlev et al., *Reabilitatsiia* 2:140–141.

19. Ibid.

20. Karl E. Loewenstein, "Ideology and Ritual: How Stalinist Rituals Shaped *The Thaw* in the USSR, 1953–4," *Totalitarian Movements and Political Religions* 8, 1 (March 2007): 99.

21. "Avtobiografiia N. I. Busareva i ego vospominaniia [Autobiography of N. I. Busarev and his memoirs]," RGASPI, f. 560, op. 1, d. 4, ll. 140–141.

22. "Karpov on Glorification of Stalin, Brezhnev," *National Affairs,* October 23, 1987.

23. Iakovlev et al., *Reabilitatsiia* 2:534, 530–535.

24. "Vospominaniia ocherki Slavianinoi O. A. [Memoirs essays of O.A. Slavianina]," RGAPSI, f. 560, op. 1, d. 36, ll. 499.

25. Ibid., ll. 244, 258.

26. See chapter 1, note 6. The figures are at best inconclusive because appeals to the Twentieth Party Congress could also come from petitioners excluded for other reasons. However, a December 1956 list of appeals, letters, and requests to the Party Control Committee states that 19,545 personal Party cases were submitted in the months between March and December of 1956 (RGANI, f. 6, op. 6, d. 1091, l. 213). This constituted a significant increase from the previous year. For a breakdown of the number of appeals addressed to regional, provincial, and republic Party Control Committees, see "Otchet o rassmotrenii apelliatsii, postupivshikh k XX S'ezdu KPSS [Report on consideration of appeals to the Twentieth Party Congress of the CPSU]," RGANI, f. 6, op. 6, d. 1075, ll. 1–5. It is also difficult to calculate the number of repressed Communists because Party cards were often confiscated prior to arrest, in which case the arrestee was categorized as "*bezpartinyi*" [non-Party]; see V. Rogovin, *Partiia rasstreliannykh* [Party of the executed] (Moscow: V. Z. Rogovin, 1997), 486–489.

27. Iakovlev et al., *Reabilitatsiia* 2:119–120.

28. Memorial, f. 1, op. 1, d. 3500, ll. 0026 1901 0136.

29. Grigorii Ivanovich Chebanov, "Vremena i liudi [Time and people]," RGASPI, f. 560, op. 1, d. 41b, ll. 70–78.

30. Ibid., l. 4.

31. Memorial, f. 1, op. 1, d. 5224, l. 0034 1002 1593.

32. Ibid., ll. 1993 1510 1587–1595.

33. Mariia Moiseevna Gol'dberg, "Rasskaz o tom, chto bylo i chto ne povtoritsia [The story of what happened and what will not be repeated]," Memorial, f. 2, op. 1, d. 47, l. 1993 0511 0051.

34. Veisman, "Oktiabrem okrylennye," Memorial, f. 2, op. 1, d. 32, l. 0001 2909 0835.

35. Gol'dberg, Memorial, f. 2, op. 1, d. 47, l. 1993 0511 0057.

36. Ibid., l. 1993 0511 0095.

70. Roy Medvedev, *Let History Judge: The Origins and Consequences of Stalinism* (New York: Columbia University Press, 1989), 495.

71. Ibid., 31.

72. Ibid., 106.

73. Ibid., 389.

74. Ibid., 391–400.

75. "Perepiska s Prokuraturoi SSSR i KGB pri SM SSSR po zaiavleniam grazhdan i rodstvennikov osuzhdennykh lits po voprosam o peresmotre sudebnykh del i reabilitatsii etikh lits [Correspondence with the Procuracy of the USSR and KGB of the Council of Ministers of the USSR on the applications of citizens and the relatives of convicted persons on the question of review of judicial cases and the rehabilitation of these individuals]," GARF, f. 7523, op. 107, d. 138, ll. 4–5.

76. Ibid., l. 9.

77. Ibid., l. 7.

78. Ibid., l. 12.

79. "Zametki [Notes]," Anonymous, RGASPI, f. 560, op. 1, d. 44, l. 2.

80. Ibid.

81. Raisa Orlova and Lev Kopelev, *My zhili v Moskve*, 33.

82. Lev Kopelev, *The Education of a True Believer,* trans. Gary Kern (New York: Harper & Row, 1980), 249. Kopelev was the prototype for Rubin in Solzhenitsyn's *The First Circle,* and he was also author of the memoir dealing with his and Solzhenitsyn's sharashka—*Ease My Sorrows.*

83. *The New York Times,* June 20, 1997.

84. Kopelev, *Education,* 267.

85. Lev Kopelev, *Khranit' vechno,* 47, 522, 541, 583.

86. Orlova and Kopelev, *My zhili v Moskve,* 77.

87. Lifton, *Thought Reform,* 66. Lifton's research was conducted in the 1960s. Fifty years later, "reeducation through labor" was still common practice in China. See Erik Eckholm, "China Hones Old Tool: 'Re-educating' Unruly," *The New York Times,* February 28, 2008.

88. Lifton, *Thought Reform,* 286.

89. "Nathan Hale," *Encyclopedia Britannica,* www.britannica.com/EBchecked/topic/52301/Nathan-Hale.

90. A. A. Baev, "Moia biografiia [My biography]," *Vestnik Rossiiskoi Akademii Nauk* , 4 (1994): 358. See also "Shtrikhi k portretu A. A. Baeva [Strokes in the portrait of A. A. ev]," *Vestnik Rossiskoi Akademii Nauk* 65, 12 (1995): 1074–1093.

91. Galina Serebriakova, *Smerch* [Whirlwind] (Moscow: Pashkov Dom, 2005), 14.

92. "Nashe Vremia [Our time]," *Gazeta Organizatsiia ROSDP,* December 1, 2000.

93. Iakovlev et al., *Reabilitatsiia* 2:889, 892.

94. Serebriakova, *Smerch,* 33–34.

95. Ibid., 35.

96. Ibid., 36.

37. Ibid., l. 1993 0511 0118.

38. Mariia Karlovna Sandratskaia, "Vospominaniia [Memoirs]," Memorial, f. 2, op. d. 105, l. 1993 1510 1718.

39. Ibid.

40. Ibid., l. 1993 1510 1717.

41. Ibid., l. 1993 1510 1718.

42. Ibid., l. 1719.

43. Nina Dmitrievna Zlenko, "Vospominaniia o bylom [Memories of the past]," morial, f. 2, op. 1, d. 65, ll. 1993 0710 0823–24.

44. Ignazio Silone in Crossman, *The God That Failed*, 102.

45. Ibid., 113.

46. Aleksandr Mil'chakov, *Molodost' svetlaia i tragicheskaia* [Bright and tragic (Moscow: Moskovskii rabochyi, 1988), 102–103.

47. Ibid., 7, 88–89. Zaveniagin allegedly helped to save many specialists.

48. Eugenia Ginzburg, *Within the Whirlwind* (San Diego, CA: Harcourt Br novich, 1979), 390.

49. Adler, *Gulag Survivor*, 77–108.

50. Mil'chakov, *Molodost' svetlaia*, 39.

51. Ibid., 57.

52. Ibid., 58.

53. Ibid., 94.

54. Ibid., 94–95.

55. See Adler, *Gulag Survivor*, 169–172; see also Solzhenitsyn, *The Gul* 3:489–490.

56. Mil'chakov, *Molodost' svetlaia*, 97.

57. See Adler, *Gulag Survivor*, 169–172, 174, 178–184.

58. Mil'chakov, *Molodost' svetlaia*, 99.

59. Ibid., 100.

60. Ibid., 101.

61. "Vospominaniia Lazareva V. N. [Memoirs of V. N. Lazarev]," RC 1, d. 22, l. 89.

62. Ibid., ll. 15–16.

63. Ibid., l. 33.

64. Ibid., l. 43.

65. Ibid., l. 64.

66. Adler, *Gulag Survivor*, 152–155.

67. "Vospominaniia Lazareva V. N.," l. 89.

68. Ibid., ll. 89–90. Lazarev cited a conversation on this topic l and Lenin, as described in her memoirs.

69. Suren Gazarian, *Eto ne dolzhno povtorit'sia* [This should not manuscript, 22. I am grateful to Stephen Cohen for sharing this wo published in *Zvezda* 1 (January 1988).

97. Ibid., 38.

98. Ibid., 41.

99. Ibid., 55.

100. Ibid., 104–105.

101. See, for example, 126–129.

102. Ibid., 135.

103. *Pravda,* December 27, 1961.

104. See Raymond H. Anderson, "Soviet Writer Protests Book Publication Abroad," *The New York Times,* December 28, 1967.

105. See Adler, *Gulag Survivor,* 184–186.

106. Zoria Leonidovna Serebriakova, interview, Nikolina gora, November 29, 1996.

107. Zoria Serebriakova, report of a conversation with the delegate in question, April 19, 2006.

108. Zoria Serebriakova, interview, Nikolina gora, April 19, 2006.

109. Iakovlev et al., *Reabilitatsiia* 3:663, 665.

110. Ibid.

111. Galina Serebriakova, 174.

112. See my discussion on this theme in "Future of the Soviet Past," 1093–1119.

113. For the history of the dacha, see "Reider Vyshinskii, ili Podmoskovnaia dacha pokazanii [Raider Vyshinskii, or suburban dacha of evidence]," *Novaia gazeta* 48, July 7, 2008; Adler, *Gulag Survivor,* 185–186.

114. Both generations were incarcerated in the Gulag and/or age-specific institutions such as orphanages. But while that experience led some to strengthen their identity with the Party, it led others to first question and then to openly reject it. See "The Death of Pyotr Yakir," *Radio Free Europe–Radio Liberty* 485/82, December 3, 1982; Iulii Daniel', *Pis'ma iz zakliucheniia;* "Petr Iakir i dvizhenie za grazhdanskie prava [Petr Iakir and the movement for civil rights]," *Novoe russkoe slovo,* March 5, March 6, and March 7, 1973. In *The Whisperers* Orlando Figes argues that children of "enemies of the people" often became Soviet activists as a survival strategy, 353.

115. "Pis'mo N. A. Rykovoi-Perli N. S. Khrushchevu [Letter of N. A. Rykova-Perla to N. S. Khrushchev]," Iakovlev et al., *Reabilitatsiia* 2:351.

116. A. B. Roginskii and L. S. Eremina, eds., *Rasstrel'nye spiski Moskva 1937–1941, "Kommunarka" Butovo* [Execution Lists Moscow 1937–1941, "Kommunarka" Butovo] (Moscow: Zven' ia, 2000), 356.

117. For more on these years, see Nataliia Rykova, interview by Miklos Kun relating to the Soviet Union, in "Oral History Interviews with Communist Party Officials, Their Relatives and Dissidents," HU OSA F. 314, series 2, d. 4, 1996–1997.

118. "Pis'mo N. A. Rykovoi-Perli v presidium XXII S'ezda KPSS [Letter of N. A. Rykova-Perla to the presidium of the Twenty-second Congress of the CPSU]," Iakovlev et al., *Reabilitatsiia* 2:366.

119. Nataliia Alekseevna Rykova, interview, Moscow, October 19, 2005.

120. Ibid.

121. While recording Rykova's oral history, Radio Liberty Interviewer Miklos Kun was shown some photos of her family. He observed that her father is no longer seen smiling after 1930.

122. Iakovlev et al., *Reabilitatsiia* 2:366.

123. "Kommunist on Question of Expelling Party Members," *Current Digest of the Soviet Press* 9, 31 (September 11, 1957): 7.

124. Iakovlev et al., *Reabilitatsiia* 2:351.

125. Ibid., 351.

126. Ibid., 814.

127. Ibid., 366.

128. Anna Larina, *This I Cannot Forget,* 348–349.

129. Rykova, answer to author's questionnaire, December 12, 1995.

130. Ibid., interview, October 19, 2005.

131. Mikhail Baital'skii, "Tetradi dlia vnukov," Memorial, f. 2, op. 1, dd. 8 and 9; and Mikhail Baitalsky, *Notebooks for the Grandchildren: Recollections of a Trotskyist Who Survived the Stalin Terror* (Atlantic Highlands, NJ: Humanities Press, 1995).

132. Adler, *Gulag Survivor,* 109–150.

133. GARF, f. R-7523sch, op. 85s, d. 255, ll. 30–34; see also ibid., ll. 47–53, GARF, f. 9474, op. 16, d. 434, ll. 28–31, 33, 34.

134. Khava Volovich, "Povest' bez nazvaniia [Story without a name]," Memorial, f. 2, op. 1, d. 36, ll. 0001 2909 1274–1276. Her memoir has subsequently been published in Vilenskii, ed., *Dodnes' tiagoteet* 1 and *Till My Tale is Told.*

135. Zakhar Isaakovich Ravdel', "Kaplia okeana [A drop in the ocean]" Memorial, f. 2, op. 1, d. 100, l. 1993 1510 1232.

136. Ibid.

137. Ibid., l. 1993 1510 1293.

138. Ibid.

139. Evgeniia Martynovna Bor'ian, Memorial, f. 1, op. 1, d. 556, l. 0011 0113 0913. In most of the memoirs of those who still tried to reconcile their belief with their reality, such formulations could be found: "I believed that it was a misunderstanding that was bound to be cleared up soon. Everything that I knew about my husband confirmed my conviction" (Zinaida Davidovna Usova, "ChSIR [Acronym for family member of a traitor to the motherland]," Memorial, f. 2, op. 1, d. 118, l. 0007 3111 0964).

140. Petr Grigorenko, "V podpol'e mozhno vsretit' tol'ko krys [You only meet rats underground]," manuscript (New York, 1979), 1034–1036. Petro Grigorenko, *Memoirs: Pietro G. Grigorenko* (New York: W. W. Norton, 1984).

141. Tamara Deutscher, "Intellectual Opposition in the USSR," *New Left Review* 96 (March–April 1976): 105.

142. D. Tarskii/Glikshtein, letter to Stephen Cohen, September 9, 1983.

143. Grigorenko, "V podpol'e," 1031–1033. See also Sidney Bloch and Peter Reddaway, *Soviet Psychiatric Abuse: The Shadow over World Psychiatry* (London: Victor Gollancz, 1984), 18–19.

144. Merridale, *Ivan's War,* 306.

145. Ibid., 300.

146. There were, however, also peasant conscripts whose memory of collectivization bred a defiant attitude. As one exclaimed, "I'm not going to defend Soviet power. If it comes to it I will desert. My father was a fool to die in the civil war, but I'm not a fool. The Communist Party and the Soviet power robbed me" (Merridale, *Ivan's War,* 54–55).

147. Kopelev, *Education,* 197.

148. Viktor Iakovlevich Shaskov and Sergei Sergeevich Kozlov, "Spetspereselentsy na zashchite Otechestva [Special settlers in defense of the fatherland]," *Voprosy istorii* 5 (2005): 161.

149. David Moiseevich Rakhlin, "Griaznaia istoriia [Dirty history]," Memorial, f. 2, op. 1, d. 101, l. 1993 1510 1246.

150. Georgii Shelest, "Kolymskie zapiski [Kolyma notes]," *Znamia* 9 (1964): 179, as cited in Rachel Platonov's excellent unpublished paper, "The Intelligentsia Sings Criminal Songs: The Musical Legacy of the Gulag," note 16, History and Legacy of the Gulag conference, Harvard University, November 2–5, 2006.

151. Rakhlin, "Griaznaia istoriia," l. 1993 1510 1247.

152. Valentin Pron'ko and Andre Baidzhii, "Taina doklada Berii: Vyigral by SSSR voinu protiv Germanii, esli by v nem ne bylo GULAGa [Beria's secret report: Would the USSR have won the war against Germany if it had not had the GULAG?]," *Nezavisimaia gazeta,* December 23, 1993.

153. Lev Gavrilovich Gavrilov, "Zolotoi most [Golden bridge]," Memorial, f. 2, op. 1, d. 41, l. 0001 2909 1516.

154. Ibid., l. 0001 2909 1525.

155. "Polkovodtsy [Military leaders]," *Pravda,* April 26, 1995, 4.

156. Ibid. See also "Voina i mir Vladimira Karpova [The war and peace of Vladimir Karpov]," *Literaturnaia gazeta,* August 1–7, 2007; "Karpov on Glorification of Stalin, Brezhnev," *National Affairs,* October 23, 1987.

157. Merridale, *Ivan's War,* 134.

158. Annick Shaw, Stephen Joseph, and P. Alex Linley, "Religion, Spirituality, and Post-traumatic Growth: A Systematic Review," *Mental Health, Religion and Culture* 8, 1 (2005): 1–11.

159. Merridale, *Ivan's War,* 192.

160. Ibid., 155.

161. Figes, *The Whisperers,* 618.

162. Grigorii Grigorievich Budagov, "Zapiski . . . [Notes]," Memorial, f. 2, op. 1, d. 30, l. 0001 2909 0514.

163. See Adler, "The Future of the Soviet Past," 1099, 1114.

164. Harvard Project on the Soviet Social System. Schedule A, Vol. 35, Case 355, p. 53.

165. Elena Petrovna Smaglenko, "Vospominaniia [Memoirs]," Memorial, f. 1, op. 1, d. 111, l. 0007 3111 0145.

166. "Russia Marks Battle of Stalingrad," *BBC News World Edition,* February 2, 2003; "U poslednei cherty: Strana vstrechaet ocherednoi den' rozhdeniia tovarishcha Stalina [The country marks another birthday of comrade Stalin]," *Izvestiia,* December 21, 2002; see also Adler, "The Future of the Soviet Past," 1099. Merridale, *Ivan's War,* 179.

167. Merridale, *Ivan's War,* 387. She also makes the distinction between the type of *partiinost'* (party spirit) on the frontline and elsewhere. According to Merridale, "front-line ideology" was very strong and very different from that of the "civilian elite" (229–230).

168. Merridale, *Ivan's War,* 285.

169. A term coined by Ilia Ehrenburg, *The Thaw,* trans. Manya Harari (London: Harvill), 1955.

170. Vadim Kozhevnikov, "Den' letiashchii [Flying day]," *Znamia* 10 (October 1962): 115–120.

171. The higher power could be the greater whole of the extraordinary historic, political, or social mission of which charismatic movements make their followers (feel) a part.

172. My special thanks go to Tania Langerova for bringing this memoir to my attention.

173. Jo Langer, *Convictions: Memories of a Life Shared with a Good Communist* (London: Andre Deutsch, 1979), 170. (A new edition of this work was published by Granta Books in 2011, titled *Convictions: My Life with a Good Communist.*)

174. Ibid., 10, 21.

175. Ibid., 35.

176. Ibid.

177. Ibid., 43.

178. Ibid., 55–56.

179. Conversation with Tania Langerova, Uppsala, Sweden, October 22, 2008.

180. Tania Langerova, personal communication, January 11, 2011.

181. Langer, *Convictions,* 103.

182. Ibid., 141.

183. Ibid., 199–200.

184. For a discussion on the complexity of denial, see Stanley Cohen, *States of Denial: Knowing about Atrocities and Suffering* (Cambridge: Polity Press, 2001).

185. Vospominaniia Taninoi, l. 534.

186. Vospominaniia M. N. Kuznetsova [The memoirs of M. N. Kuznetsov], RGASPI, f. 560, op. 1, d. 46, ll. 5, 9, 286.

187. Semen Vilenskii, interview, Moscow, June 6, 2007.

4. Striving for a "Happy Ending"

1. For more on Shatunovskaia, Snegov, and Pikina, see Cohen, *Victims Return,* chapter 4. Iurii Gastev, letter to Stephen Cohen, May 4, 1985.

2. Cohen, *Victims Return,* 92–93.

3. S. A. Mikoian, "Aleksei Snegov v bor'be za 'destalinizatsiiu' [Aleksei Snegov in the battle for de-Stalinization]," *Voprosy istorii* 4 (2006): 70.

4. See Kathleen Smith, "Gulag Survivors and Thaw Policies," unpublished paper for the History and Legacy of the Gulag conference, Harvard University, November 2–5, 2006, 10.

5. "Listki iz bloknota: Trudnye voprosy vremeni [Sheets from a writing pad: Difficult questions of our time]," *Novoe russkoe slovo,* March 17, 1977.

6. Roy Medvedev, transcript of interview with Stephen F. Cohen, early eighties, p. 8. For other comments on Snegov's role, see Stephen F. Cohen, "Gulag Survivors after Stalin," in Paul Hollander, ed., *Political Violence: Belief, Behavior, and Legitimation* (New York: Palgrave Macmillan, 2009).

7. Smith, "Gulag Survivors," 13.

8. Mikoian, "Aleksei Snegov," 69. The original Russian text reads: "pobedil svoikh 'pytochnykh del masterov.'"

9. Ibid.

10. Frankl, *Man's Search for Meaning,* 99, 115.

11. Mikoian, "Aleksei Snegov," 71.

12. Ibid.

13. Ibid., 77. See also Sergo Mikoian, oral history, OSE, F. 314, series 2, d. 32.

14. Mikoian, "Aleksei Snegov," 78.

15. Ibid., 74. In his interview with Stephen Cohen in the eighties, Roy Medvedev claimed that Snegov was placed in this position already in 1954.

16. Smith, "Gulag Survivors," 11.

17. Mikoian, "Aleksei Snegov," 84.

18. Kut'ina, Broido, and Kut'in, *Ob ushedshem veke,* 281.

19. Ibid.

20. Ol'ga Shatunovskaia, transcript of oral history interview with N. I. Starkov, 1989.

21. Grigorii Pomerants, "Pamiati odinokoi teni [Memories of a solitary shadow]," *Znamia* (July 2006): 165.

22. Roy Medvedev, Cohen interview transcript.

23. Kut'ina, Broido, and Kut'in, *Ob ushedshem veke,* 287–288.

24. "Rehabilitation," materials sent from Antonov-Ovseenko to Stephen Cohen, with the explicit instruction that this document not be published during her lifetime, 1980s.

25. Kut'ina, Broido, and Kut'in, *Ob ushedshem veke,* 291.

26. Iakovlev et al., *Reabilitatsiia* 3:222.

27. A. V. Korotkov, S. A. Melchin, and A. S. Stepanov, compilers, *Kremlevskii samosud: Sekretnie dokumenty Politbiuro o pisatele A. Solzhenitsyne* [Kremlin lynching party: Secret politburo documents on the writer A. Solzhenitsyn] (Moscow: Rodina, 1994), 361.

28. Antonov-Ovseenko documents.

29. Oleg Khlevniuk uses the term "extermination camps" and even "provisional death camps" in a discussion of the consequences of decree 00447; he asserts that their "exterminatory" character had been emerging since 1933 (Khlevniuk, Itogi Stalinizma [Approaches to Stalinism] conference, and Khlevniuk, 170–172, 178).

30. Iakovlev et al., *Reabilitatsiia* 3:121–122.

31. Pomerants, "Pamiati," 72.

32. Iakovlev et al., *Reabilitatsiia* 3:122.

33. Ibid., 222–223.

34. Ibid., 459–507.

35. Ibid., 596–597.

36. Iurii Gastev, letter to Stephen Cohen, 1985.

37. Adler, *Gulag Survivor,* 167.

38. Gastev, letter to Stephen Cohen.

39. In her memoir, Evgeniia Ginzburg asserted that Mil'chakov had securely knotted together the ends of '37 and '54, 390.

40. Iurii Aksiutin, *Khrushchevskaia 'ottepel'' i obshchestvennye nastroeniia v SSSR v 1953–1964gg.* [Khrushchev's "thaw" and the public mood in the USSR from 1953–1964] (Moscow: ROSSPEN, 2004), 484.

41. Ibid.

42. Ibid., 485.

43. On these commissions, see Vilenskii, ed., *Dodnes' tiagoteet* 2:478. Also see Marc Elie, "Khrushchev's Gulag: Camps, Colonies and Prisons in the USSR, 1953–1964," conference paper, Berkeley, California, April 2005, 11–16; Adler, *Gulag Survivor,* 168–172.

44. In accordance with the decree of the Supreme Soviet of the USSR that ordered the commissions, former prisoner-members were not sent to the camp from which they had most recently returned. Vilenskii, ed., *Dodnes' tiagoteet* 2:489.

45. Arsenii Roginskii, plenary speech, Itogi Stalinizma [Approaches to Stalinism] conference, Moscow, December 5, 2008.

46. Kut'ina, Broido, and Kut'in, *Ob ushedshem veke,* 276.

47. Vilenskii, ed., *Dodnes' tiagoteet* 2:490.

48. Kut'ina, Broido, and Kut'in, *Ob ushedshem veke,* 289. See also Smith, "Gulag Survivors," 20–22.

49. V. A. Bobrenev and V. B. Riazantsev, *Palachi i zhertvy* [Henchmen and victims] (Moscow: Voennoe izdatel'stvo, 1993), 3, 352–360.

50. This sentiment can be found in many memoirs and in correspondence. Even while in camp, prisoners understood how their ex-criminal status would affect their life on the outside. As one prisoner, Petr Alekseev, wrote to his wife, "I don't want freedom without rehabilitation" ("Pjotr—brieven uit de Goelag [Petr—letters from the Gulag]," film, Jan Jaap Kuiper, 2008).

51. Bobronev and Riazantsev, *Palachi i zhertvy,* 360.

52. Arsenii Roginskii, "The Embrace of Stalinism: Why Is Russia Romanticizing the Memory of Stalinism?" opening lecture at the International Conference on Approaches to Stalinism, Moscow, December 5, 2008.

53. Roy Medvedev, interview at his dacha, Moscow, June 19, 2005.

54. One such case was Alexander Chachulin, response to questionnaire by Stephen Cohen. Writing from Munich in June of 1985, he disclosed that remembering the terrible

things he had been through in the process of answering questions on his past repression was painful. He did not initially complete the questionnaire.

55. M. Frenkin, response to questionnaire by Stephen Cohen, October 29, 1983, Jerusalem.

56. Elena Pavlovna Karagaeva, interview, RGASPI, Moscow, March 17, 2008.

57. Ibid.

58. During research in the 1990s, I had the privilege of being one of the first readers of these documents (presumably since they had initially been collected in the 1960s).

59. See Juliane Fürst, "Prisoners of the Soviet Self? Political Youth Opposition in Late Stalinism," *Europe-Asia Studies* 54, 3 (2002): 368.

60. Ibid., 369.

61. Hyung-Min Joo, "Voices of Freedom: *Samizdat,*" *Europe-Asia Studies* 56, 4 (June 2004): 580.

62. *Istoriia Astrakhanskogo kraia* [The history of the Astrakhan krai] (Astrakhan': Izdatel'stvo Astrakhanskogo gosudarstvennogo pedagogicheskogo universiteta, 2000), as cited in *30 oktiabria* 77: 5.

63. Stephen F. Cohen and Katrina vanden Heuvel, *Voices of Glasnost: Interviews with Gorbachev's Reformers* (New York: W. W. Norton, 1989), 286.

64. Ibid., 291.

65. Ibid., 299.

66. Ibid., 294.

67. Zasedanie Politbiuro TsK KPSS [Meeting of the politburo of the CC CPSU], November 24, 1988, RGANI, f. 89, op. 42, d. 23, ll. 1–5.

68. Ibid., l. 2.

69. Ibid., l. 4.

70. See also Adler, *Gulag Survivor,* 5–7; and Adler, *Victims of Soviet Terror: The Story of the Memorial Movement* (Westport, CT: Praeger Publishers, 1993).

71. See Stephen Cohen's discussion on the causal factors in *Soviet Fates and Lost Alternatives: From Stalinism to the New Cold War* (New York: Columbia University Press, 2009), chapter 5.

72. See note 6, chapter 1.

73. Iakovlev et al., *Reabilitatsiia* 3:520.

74. Anonymous, author's questionnaire, December 12, 1995.

75. Ol'ga Konstantinovna Shireeva, author's questionnaire, December 12, 1995; Lev Emanuilovich Razgon, author's questionnaire, December 8, 1994.

76. Petr Lukianovich Kuziachkin, author's questionnaire, December 12, 1995.

77. L. S. Iardovskaia, author's questionnaire, December 12, 1995.

78. Ibid.

79. N. I. Zadorozhnaia, author's questionnaire, December 12, 1995.

80. Ibid.

81. Memorial, f. 1, op. 1, d. 610, l. 1407.

82. P. Iudenkov, "Nash Dolg [Our duty]," *Moskovskaia Pravda,* May 31, 1988.

83. Khrushchev was apprehensive about a flood (from the revelations) that would "sweep away the regime." Nikita Khrushchev, *Vospominaniia* [Memoirs] (New York: Chalidze Publications, 1979), 274–276.

84. E. Boldyreva, "Gde pustynia slivaetsia s nebom [Where the desert merges with the sky]," *Sovetskaia kultura,* September 14, 1989.

85. Ibid.

86. Roginskii, plenary speech, Itogi Stalinizma conference, Moscow, December 5, 2008.

5. The Legacies of the Repression

1. For more on the experiences of this group, see the richly documented volume by Cathy A. Frierson and Semyon S. Vilensky, *Children of the Gulag* (New Haven, CT: Yale University Press, 2010).

2. Iurii Feofanov, "XXX S'ezd KPSS v zale konstitutionnogo suda [Thirtieth Congress of the CPSU in the Constitutional Courtroom]," *Izvestiia,* July 8, 1992.

3. Ibid.

4. Ibid.

5. For more on children of special settlers, see Oxana Klimkova, "Special Settlements in Soviet Russia," *Kritika* 8, 1 (Winter 2007): 128–138. See also Figes, *The Whisperers,* 349, 352.

6. Roy Medvedev, interview at his Moscow dacha, June 19, 2005.

7. Nadezhda Ioffe, transcript of interview with Professor Albert Leong, November 17, 1997, 24.

8. Ibid.

9. See also Nadezhda A. Joffe, *Back in Time: My Life, My Fate, My Epoch,* trans. Frederick S. Choate (Oak Park, MI: Labor Publications, 1995).

10. His Party membership may have been returned at the same time as he was rehabilitated.

11. Felicity Barringer, "Soviet Survivor Relives 'Doctors' Plot'," *New York Times,* May 13, 1988. Natalia's memoirs were also published in journal form; see Natal'ia Rapoport, "Pamiat'—eto tozhe meditsina [Memory is also medicine]," in *Sputnik* 10–11 (May 16), 10 (May 23), 1988.

12. Barringer, "Soviet Survivor."

13. Orlando Figes, "The Family Histories," www.orlandofiges.com.

14. Evgeniia Vladimirovna Smirnova, interview, Moscow, March 18, 2008.

15. Ibid.

16. Ibid.

17. Evgeniia Smirnova, transcript of interview with Alena Kozlova, October 2004, 58–59.

18. Smirnova, interview, Moscow, March 18, 2008.

19. V. Tikhanova, ed. *Rasstrel'nye spiski,* Vypusk 1, Donskoe kladbishche, 1934–1940 [Execution lists, Donskoi cemetery, 1934–1940, vol. 1] (Moscow: NIPTs Memorial,

1993). This work encompasses the short biographies of 670 of the Moscow victims of execution on political charges whose ashes are buried at the Donskoi crematory. The list contains only the victims whose fates had been ascertained as of January 1, 1993. *Rasstrel'nye spiski* Vypusk 2, Vagan'kovskoe kladbishche 1926–1936 [Execution lists, Vagankov cemetery, 1926–1936, vol. 2] (Moscow: Memorial, 1995). This work contains short biographical information (as of June 1995) on executed victims of political repression whose ashes were strewn in the Vagankov Cemetery.

20. Smirnova, interview, March 18, 2008.

21. In a poignant tale of an American's search for the fate of his father, Isaiah Oggins, a leftist who was recruited as a spy for the Soviet Union and eventually executed in a Soviet prison, the son wonders if his father had changed his mind about Communism by the time of his incarceration. He concluded, "The worst thing for my father may have been realizing that he had been wrong all along. On the other hand, he may never have thought that. He may have believed in an ideal to the end, and thought that the train had been hijacked by lunatics" (C. J. Chivers, "A Soviet Horror Story, Buried for 60 Years," *International Herald Tribune,* November 5, 2008). From what we understand about the comfort of belief, the latter would be a more hopeful scenario.

22. Figes, "The Family Histories," www.orlandofiges.com.

23. Mariia Il'inichna Kuznetsova, interview, Moscow, March 15, 2008.

24. Ibid.

25. Mariia Il'inichna Kuznetsova, transcript of interview with Irina Ostrovskaia, October 2004, 39.

26. Ibid. Mariia's husband served as an economic advisor to the Ministry of Trade. They were stationed in Nepal and Libya, where Mariia had inevitable contact with foreigners. She referred to this manual up until 1985.

27. M. I. Kuznetsova, interview, March 15, 2008.

28. Ibid.

29. Frankl, *Man's Search for Meaning,* 99, 115. See also Gide in Crossman, *The God That Failed,* 166.

30. M. I. Kuznetsova, interview, March 15, 2008.

31. Ibid.

32. Ibid.

33. Ibid.

34. Such discussion was, of course, unlikely because of the secrecy surrounding these policies.

35. M. I. Kuznetsova, interview, March 15, 2008.

36. This so-called "minus" was a standard, reinforced passport restriction for returnees in the Stalinist era that restricted their freedom of movement, and forbade them to be closer than 101 kilometers from Moscow, Leningrad, Kiev, and a number of major cities.

37. Gertruda Evgen'evna Chuprun, interview, Moscow, March 20, 2008.

38. Ibid.

39. Ibid.

40. Philip J. Flores, "Addiction as an Attachment Disorder: Implications for Group Therapy," *International Journal of Group Psychotherapy* 51, 1 (2001): 63–81; Thomas R. Insel, "Is Social Attachment an Addictive Disorder?" *Physiology and Behavior* 79, 3 (2003): 351–357. Gerta neglected to mention—and I neglected to ask—if Dina had in fact quit smoking after Party reinstatement.

41. For an interesting comment on the complexities of the Soviet self that possesses "contradictory sensibilities" and exhibits "mixed emotions," see Chatterjee and Petrone, "Models of Selfhood," 984–985.

42. Chuprun, interview, March 20, 2008.

43. Levada Tsentr, "Rossiane o roli Stalina v istorii nashei strany [Russians on the role of Stalin in the history of our country]," December 21, 2005.

44. Levada Tsentr, "Vydaiushchiesia liudi vsekh vremen i narodov [Eminent figures of all times and peoples]," June 10, 2008.

45. Levada Tsentr, "Rossiane o Staline [Russians on Stalin]," March 5, 2010.

46. Anatolii Sivakov, "Stalin—luchshyi drug detei [Stalin—children's best friend]," *30 oktriabria,* 61, 2006.

47. Ibid.

48. *International Herald Tribune,* July 27, 1990.

49. Mike Eckel, "In Remarks, Putin Laments Soviet Fall," *The Boston Globe,* April 26, 2005.

50. Douglas Birch, "Vietnam Worse than Stalin Purges," *Associated Press,* June 21, 2007.

51. Leon Aron, "The Problematic Pages," *New Republic,* September 24, 2008.

52. A. V. Filippov, A. I. Utkin, and S. V. Sergeev, eds. *Noveishaia istoriia Rossii, 1945– 2006 gg.: Kniga dlia uchitelia* [New history of Russia, 1945–2006: Handbook for teachers] (Moscow: Prosveshchenie, 2007).

53. Cited in Orlando Figes, "Putin vs. the Truth," *The New York Review of Books* 56, 7 (April 30, 2009); see also Andrew E. Kramer, "Yes, a Lot of People Died, but . . . ," *New York Times,* August 12, 2007. See also the discussions by David Brandenberger, "A New Short Course? A. V. Filippov and the Russian State's Search for a 'Usable Past,'" in *Kritika: Explorations in Russian and Euroasian History* 10, 4 (Fall 2009): 825–833; Elena Zubkova, "The Filippov Syndrome," in *Kritika: Explorations in Russian and Euroasian History* 10, 4 (Fall 2009): 861–868.

54. See Aron, "The Problematic Pages."

55. "Uchitel'iam istorii veleno prepodnosit' stalinskii terror kak ratsional'nyi instrument razvitiia strany [Teachers are told to present the Stalinist terror as a rational instrument in the development of the country]," www.newsru.com.

56. See Memorial's critical commentary on the approval by an expert commission of a similarly oriented history of Russia by Aleksandr Barsenkov and Aleksandr Vdovin, "V uchebnoi literature proiskhodit reabilitatsiia stalinshchiny [In the educational literature a rehabilitation of Stalinism is taking place]," *30 oktiabria* 100, 2010.

57. See Cohen, *Soviet Fates,* chapter 5.

Epilogue

1. Dan Bilefsky, "After Years of Suppression, Serbs Rekindle Their Dark Wit," *International Herald Tribune,* December 3, 2007.

2. Ellen Barry, "Communism's Ghosts Haunt Moscow Streets," *International Herald Tribune,* October 14, 2008. At the Davos forum in January 2009, Russian Finance Minister Aleksei Kudrin predicted "the worst year for the economy in modern times. 2009 will be the most difficult for the Russian and world economies. I cannot remember a worse year since the end of World War II," *International Herald Tribune,* January 27, 2009; Pavel Aplekar, "A Partial Picture Distorts the Criminal Past," *Moscow Times,* June 25, 2007; "Stalin lidiruet v oprose," *30 oktiabria* 88, 2008; "Rossiia i istoricheskaia pamiat' [Russia and historical memory]" *30 oktiabria* 81, 2007; Iaroslav Leont'ev, "Marks perevernul'sia by v grobu [Marx would turn in his grave]," *30 oktiabria* 57, 2005; Elina Bestaeva, "Ch'ia eta ulitsa [Whose street is this?]," *30 oktiabria* 57, 2005; "Nostal'giia po tiranu [Nostalgia for the tyrant]," *30 oktiabria* 50, 2005; Douglas Birch, "Khrushchev kin allege family honor slurred," *Johnson's Russia List,* 141, August 4, 2008; Yevgeny Kiselyov, "Why Russians Put Stalin at the Top of the List," *Moscow Times,* October 1, 2008; Dan Bilefsky, "Stalin Still Haunts the Land of His Birth," *International Herald Tribune,* September 30, 2008; Sophia Kishkovsky, "What's in a Street Name? Moscow Is Finding Out," *International Herald Tribune,* September 19, 2008; "55 Years after Death Stalin in Style Again," *Itar-Tass,* March 5, 2008; "Russia Remembers Victims of Stalinism, But Tyrant Still Popular," *Itar-Tass,* October 30, 2008; Steven Lee Myers, "Estonia Sparks Outrage in Russia," *International Herald Tribune,* January 25, 2007.

3. Bilefsky, "Serbs at a Crossroads As Elections Approach: Vote Is a Choice Between East and West," *International Herald Tribune,* May 7, 2008. See also Jelena Obradovic-Wochnik, "Knowledge, Acknowledgement and Denial in Serbia's Responses to the Srebrenica Massacre," *Journal of Contemporary European Studies* 17, 1 (April 2009): 61–74.

4. Mark Freeman, "Transitional Justice: The Current State of the Field," paper, 60 Years Genocide Convention, The Hague, December 8, 2008.

5. Andreas Gross, "Draft Resolution and Report on the Use of Experience of 'Truth Commissions,'" report to the Council of Europe, December 4, 2007, 8.

6. Erik Ketelaar, "Truth, Memories, and Histories in the Archives of the ICTY," paper, 60 Years Genocide Convention, The Hague, December 8, 2008.

7. Roland Kostic, *Ambivalent Peace: External Peacebuilding, Threatened Identity and Reconciliation in Bosnia and Herzegovina,* Report No. 78 (Uppsala: Department of Peace and Conflict Research, 2007), 33.

8. Sonja Biserko, contribution to panel discussion Letting Go of the Past, Losing a Hold on the Future, The Hague, February 11, 2008.

9. Kostic, *Ambivalent Peace,* 256, 259.

10. For further discussion of reforms in education and changes in history textbooks, see Elizabeth A. Cole, "Transitional Justice and the Reform of History Education," *The International Journal of Transitional Justice* 1 (2007): 115–137.

11. Kostic, *Ambivalent Peace,* 157.

12. Natasa Kandic, director of the Humanitarian Law Center in Belgrade, cited in Dan Bilefsky, "Karadzic Sent to The Hague for Trial Despite Violent Protest by Loyalists," *International Herald Tribune,* July 30, 2008.

13. Bilefsky, "Karadzic Sent to The Hague."

14. Paul B. Miller, "Contested Memories: The Bosnian Genocide in Serb and Muslim Minds," *Journal of Genocide Research* 8, 3 (September 2006): 317, 320–321.

15. Aryeh Neier, "Fifteen Years of Progress," *International Herald Tribune,* May 13, 2008.

16. Ibid.

17. See Memorial's open letter to Moscow Mayor S. S. Sobianin, "On the Meaning and Importance of Memory for the State," December 7, 2010. See also Arsenii Roginskii, "The Embrace of Stalinism," speech at the opening plenary session of Approaches to Stalinism, Moscow, December 5, 2008; see also Paul Gregory, who aptly paraphrased Roginskii: "Instead of 'crimes without victims' Stalin somehow produced 'victims without criminals,'" in "The Liberals Fight Back: The Moscow Conference on Stalinism." My thanks to Professor Gregory for sharing this unpublished chronicle of his impressions of the Moscow gathering.

18. See Jonathan Brent, "Stalin's Russia and Russia's Stalin: A Report on the International Conference on the History of Stalinism"; my thanks also to Jonathan Brent for this unpublished paper, which included excerpts from his December 2008 interview with Iavlinskii. See also Brent's discussions with Aleksandr Iakovlev on the effects of unconstrained state power and Iakovlev's hopes and fears; Jonathan Brent, *Inside the Stalin Archives: Discovering the New Russia* (New York: Atlas, 2008), 252–255, 318.

19. "Opposition Leader Slams 'Features of Stalinism' in Russian Life," *Interfax,* March 5, 2008.

20. Writing in 1991, one former prisoner concluded: "In the historical perspective of the development of Russia, the history of the GULAG will not be repeated. But if time and again the liberals and thinkers, humanists, and politicians of the world do not draw the lessons from the GULAG and the historic defeat of its contemporaries, it is hard to believe in the triumph of higher reason." A. Sandler and M. Etlis, *Sovremenniki GULAGa: Kniga vospominanii i razmyshlenii* [Contemporaries of the GULAG: book of memoirs and reflections] (Magadan: Magadanskoe knizhnoe izdatel'stvo, 1991), 558. Perhaps unexpectedly even to the author, the years in which these lines were written ended up being the peak of anti-Stalinist revelations and public discourse on the Gulag.

21. See Viacheslav Feraposhkin, "Obysk v Sankt-Peterburgskom 'Memoriale' [Search at the St. Petersburg Memorial]" *30 Oktiabria* 90, December 2008; Orlando Figes, "The Raid on Memorial," letter to *New York Review of Books,* January 15, 2009.

22. "National Images of the Past: The Twentieth Century and the 'War of Memories,' an Appeal from the International Memorial Society," March 2008; see also Irina Flige, "Predmetnaia i material'naia pamiat' o Bol'shom Terror [Physical and material memory of the Great Terror]," draft paper, 2007.

23. Conversation with Irina Flige and Arsenii Roginskii, Moscow, December 7, 2008.

24. For a comment on latter-day dissidence, see Serge Schmemann, "The Case Against and for Khodorkovsky," *International Herald Tribune,* October 20, 2008.

25. Clifford J. Levy, "Purging History of Stalin's Terror," *International Herald Tribune,* November 27, 2008. I personally experienced this trend while working in the Party archive. Documents to which I had had access in 1996 were not available, nor were Party Control Commission statistics from the Brezhnev era on. The archive staff themselves did not seem to know the reason. Other researchers working in other places reported similar and even graver problems; see Badma Biurchiev, "Aleksandr Dudarev: My s Mikhailom Suprunom stali zhertvami politicheskikh represii [Aleksandr Dudarev: Mikhail Suprun and I became victims of political repression]," *30 oktriabria,* 100, 2010.

26. See Nikita Petrov's open appeal, "Landmark Decision by the Supreme Court: Is Access to Documents about Repressions being Closed Down in the Russian Federation?" February 2, 2011, http://hro.org/node/10136.

27. Similarly in Chechnya, a 2009 ally of Russia, the scars of war were being erased as Grozny had a makeover. The deputy mayor cited a Russian proverb that guided the process—"The one who recalls the past will lose an eye." In C. J. Chivers, "The New Chechnya Reconstructs its Past," *International Herald Tribune,* October 20, 2008.

28. Ian Rachinskii, "Nerazomknutyi krug [Vicious circle]," *30 oktiabria* 85, 2008, 4.

29. Ibid.

30. Ibid.

31. Paul Goble, "Medvedev Historical Falsification Commission 'Harmful' or 'Useless,' Memorial Expert Says," *Window on Eurasia,* May 20, 2009; see also Vladimir Rzyhkov, "History Under Lock and Key," *Moscow Times,* June 9, 2009; "Medvedev Seen Making History More 'Politicized' with Creation of Commission," *Vedomosti,* May 19, 2009; "Russian TV Looks at the Issues Facing Kremlin's New False-history Commission," *BBC Monitoring,* May 10, 2009.

32. Roginskii-Medvedev, "Eta programma ne tol'ko pro istoriiu [This program is not only about history]," www.org.org, February 7, 2011; Sergei Karaganov, "On the Perpetuation of the Memory of the Victims of the Totalitarian Regime and on National Reconciliation," *Rossiskaia gazeta,* April 8, 2011.

33. Semen Vilenskii, interview, Moscow, June 18, 2005.

34. Dan Bilefsky, "A Revisited Past Stirs Czechs' Discomfort: To Many, 5 Who Fled Were Terrorists," *International Herald Tribune,* June 2, 2008; see also Dan Bilefsky, "Who Betrayed Whom? Czechs Judge Kundera," *International Herald Tribune,* October 18–19, 2008.

35. Miranda Sissons, "Briefing Paper: Iraq's New 'Accountability and Justice' Law," International Center for Transitional Justice, January 22, 2008, 2.

36. Ibid., 5.

37. See Ella Rolfe, "Addressing the Baathist Legacy in Iraq," *ICTJ in the News,* February 26, 2010.

38. See Elazar Barkan's discussion "Truth and Reconciliation in History," *American Historical Review* (October 2009): 899–913; see also Jaime Malamud Goti, "Editorial Note: A Turbulent Past and the Problem with Memory," *The International Journal of Transitional Justice* 4 (2010): 153–165.

39. Barkan, "Truth and Reconciliation," 903.

40. Ketelaar, "Truth, Memories, and Histories," 13.

WORKS CITED

Archives

GARF (State Archive of the Russian Federation)

Memorial (microfilmed collection at the International Institute of Social History in Amsterdam and at Memorial headquarters in Moscow)

RGANI (Russian State Archive of Contemporary History, former Archive of the Central Committee of the CPSU)

RGASPI (Russian State Archive of Social and Political History, former Central Party Archive of the Institute of Marxism-Leninism)

Books

Adler, Nanci. *The Gulag Survivor: Beyond the Soviet System.* New Brunswick, NJ: Transaction Publishers, 2004.

———. *Trudnoe Vozvrashchenie: Sud'by Sovetskikh politzakliuchennykh v 1950–1990-e gody* [The difficult return: The fates of Soviet political prisoners from the 1950s–1990s]. Moscow: Zven'ia, 2005.

———. *Victims of Soviet Terror: The Story of the Memorial Movement.* Westport, CT: Praeger Publishers, 1993.

Aksiutin, Iurii. *Khrushchevskaia 'ottepel' i obshchestvennye nastroeniia v SSSR v 1953–1964gg.* [Khrushchev's 'thaw' and public attitudes in the USSR from 1953 to 1964]. Moscow: ROSSPEN, 2004.

Alexander, Richard D. *The Biology of Moral Systems.* Hawthorne, NY: DeGruyter, 1987.

Alexeeva, Ludmilla. *Soviet Dissent: Contemporary Movements for National, Religious, and Human Rights.* Trans. Carol Pearce and John Glad. Middletown, CT: Wesleyan University Press, 1985.

Alexopoulos, Golfo. *Stalin's Outcasts: Aliens, Citizens, and the Soviet State, 1926–1936.* Ithaca, NY: Cornell University Press, 2003.

Applebaum, Anne. *GULAG: A History.* New York: Doubleday, 2003.

Arendt, Hannah. *Crises of the Republic.* New York: Harcourt Brace Jovanovich, 1969.

Artizov, A. N., V. P. Naumov, et al. (compilers). *Nikita Khrushchev 1964: Stenogrammy plenuma TsK KPSS i drugie dokumenty* [Nikita Khrushchev 1964: Stenograms of the plenum of the CC of the CPSU and other documents]. Moscow: Materik, 2007.

Baitalsky, Mikhail. *Notebooks for the Grandchildren: Recollections of a Trotskyist Who Survived the Stalin Terror.* Atlantic Highlands, NJ: Humanities Press, 1995.

Berger, Joseph. *Shipwreck of a Generation: The Memoirs of Joseph Berger.* London: Harvill, 1971.

Bloch, Sidney, and Peter Reddaway. *Soviet Psychiatric Abuse: The Shadow over World Psychiatry.* London: Victor Gollancz, 1984.

Bobrenov, V. A., and V. B. Riazantsev. *Palachi i zhertvy* [Henchmen and victims]. Moscow: Voennoe izdatel'stvo, 1993.

Boobbyer, Philip. *Conscience, Dissent, and Reform in Soviet Russia.* London: Routledge, 2005.

Brent, Jonathan. *Inside the Stalin Archives: Discovering the New Russia.* New York: Atlas, 2008.

Bruner, Jerome. *Actual Minds, Possible Worlds.* Cambridge, MA: Harvard University Press, 1986.

Burleigh, Michael. *Earthly Powers: The Clash of Religion and Politics in Europe from the French Revolution to the Great War.* New York: Harper Collins, 2005.

Cherushev, N. S. *"Dorogoi nash tovarishch Stalin!" . . . i drugie tovarishchi: obrashcheniia rodstvennikov repressirovannykh komandirov krasnoi armii k rukovoditel'iam strany* [Our dear comrade Stalin! . . . and other comrades: appeals of relatives of repressed commanders of the Red Army to the leaders of the country]. Moscow: Zven'ia, 2001.

Cohen, Stanley. *States of Denial: Knowing About Atrocities and Suffering.* Cambridge, UK: Polity Press, 2001.

Cohen, Stephen F. *Soviet Fates and Lost Alternatives: From Stalinism to the New Cold War.* New York: Columbia University Press, 2009.

———. *The Victims Return: Survivors of the Gulag after Stalin.* Exeter, NH: Publishing Works, 2010.

Cohen, Stephen F., and Katrina vanden Heuvel. *Voices of Glasnost: Interviews with Gorbachev's Reformers.* New York: W. W. Norton, 1989.

Conquest, Robert. *The Great Terror: A Reassessment.* London: Pimlico, 1992.

Cornis-Pope, Marcel, and John Neubauer, eds. *History of the Literary Cultures of East-Central Europe; Junctures and Disjunctures in the 19th and 20th Centuries,* vol. 1. Amsterdam: John Benjamins, 2007.

Courtois, Stéphane, and Nicolas Werth. *The Black Book of Communism: Crimes, Terror, Repression*. Cambridge, MA: Harvard University Press, 1999.

Crossman, Richard, ed. *The God That Failed*. New York: Columbia University Press, 2001.

Daniel', A. I., and L. S. Eremina. *Uznitsy 'Alzhira'* [Prisoners of Alzhir]. Moscow: Zven'ia, 2003.

Daniel', Iulii, *Pis'ma iz zakliucheniia: Stikhi* [Letters from imprisonment, poems]. Moscow: Obshchestvo "Memorial," Zven'ia, 2000.

Dawkins, Richard. *The God Delusion*. New York: Bantam Books, 2006.

Deutscher, Isaac. *Stalin: A Political Biography*. London: Oxford University Press, 1967.

Diakov, Boris. *Povest' o perezhitom* [The story of what we (I) went through]. Moscow: Sovetskaia Rossiia, 1966.

Dobrol'skii, I. V., ed. *GULAG: Ego stroiteli, obitateli i geroi* [GULAG: Its builders, inhabitants, and heroes]. Moscow: Mezhdunarodnaia Obshchestvo Prav Cheloveka, 1999.

Dobson, Miriam. *Khrushchev's Cold Summer: Gulag Returnees, Crime, and the Fate of Reform after Stalin*. Ithaca, NY: Cornell University Press, 2009.

Druzhnikov, Iurii. *Informer 001: The Myth of Pavlik Morozov*. New Brunswick, NJ: Transaction Publishers, 1997.

Durkheim, Emile. *Selected Writings*. Cambridge: Cambridge University Press, 1972.

Eremina, L. S., and A. B. Roginskii, eds. *Rasstrel'nye spiski, Moskva, 1937–1941, "Kommunarka," Butovo: Kniga Pamiati zhertv politicheskikh represii* [Execution Lists, Moscow, 1937–1941, "Kommunarka," Butovo: Books of remembrance of victims of political repression]. Moscow: Zven'ia, 2000.

Etkind, Alexander. *Eros of the Impossible: The History of Psychoanalysis in Russia*. Boulder, CO: Westview, 1997.

Feldman, Marc D., and Jacqueline M. Feldman, with Roxanne Smith. *Stranger Than Fiction: When Our Minds Betray Us*. Washington, DC: American Psychiatric Press, 1998.

Festinger, Leon A. *A Theory of Cognitive Dissonance*. Stanford, CA: Stanford University Press, 1957.

Figes, Orlando. *The Whisperers: Private Life in Stalin's Russia*. London: Penguin Books, 2007.

Filippov, A. V., A. I. Utkin, and S. V. Sergeev, eds. *Noveishaia istoriia Rossii, 1945–2006 gg.: Kniga dlia uchitelia* [The new history of Russia, 1945–2006: Handbook for teachers]. Moscow: Prosveshchenie, 2007.

Fitzpatrick, Sheila, ed. *Stalinism: New Directions*. London: Routledge, 2000.

Frankl, Viktor. *Man's Search for Meaning: An Introduction to Logotherapy*. London: Hodder and Stoughton, 1959.

Freud, Anna. *The Ego and the Mechanisms of Defense*. London: Hogarth Press, 1937.

Frierson, Cathy A., and Semyon S. Vilensky. *Children of the Gulag*. New Haven, CT: Yale University Press, 2010.

Fülöp-Miller, René. *The Mind and Face of Bolshevism*. London: G. P. Putnam's Sons, 1926.

Galich, Aleksandr. *Pokolenie obrechennykh* [Generation of the doomed]. Frankfurt/Main: Posev, 1972.

Gerbner, G., Larry P. Gross, and William H. Melody, eds. *Communications Technology and Public Policy.* New York: John Wiley and Sons, 1973.

Geyer, Michael, and Sheila Fitzpatrick, eds. *Beyond Totalitarianism: Stalinism and Nazism Compared.* Cambridge: Cambridge University Press, 2009.

Gill, Graeme. *The Rules of the Communist Party of the Soviet Union.* New York: M. E. Sharpe, 1988.

Ginzburg, Eugenia. *Within the Whirlwind.* Trans. Ian Boland. San Diego, CA: Harcourt-Brace Jovanovich, 1982.

Ginzburg, Evgeniia. *Krutoi marshrut* 1. New York: Posev, 1985.

Gnedin, Evgenii. *Katastrofa: Vtoroe rozhdenie, memuarnye zapiski* [Catastrophe: Second birth, memoir notes]. Amsterdam: Alexander Herzen Foundation, 1977.

Goffman, Erving. *Asylums: Essays on the Social Situation of Mental Patients and Other Inmates.* New York: Anchor Books, 1961.

Goldman, Wendy Z. *Terror and Democracy in the Age of Stalin: The Social Dynamics of Repression.* New York: Cambridge University Press, 2007.

Golovkova, L. A., K. F. Liubimova, et al., eds. *Butovskii Poligon: Kniga pamiati zhertv politicheskikh represii* [Butovskii Poligon: Book of memory of the victims of political repression]. Moscow: ALSO, 2000.

———. *Butovskii Poligon: V rodnom kraiu. Dokumenty, svidetel'stva, sud'by . . .* [Butovskii Poligon: Right nearby. Documents, testimonies, fates]. Moscow: ALSO, 2004.

Grigorenko, Petro. *Memoirs: Pietro G. Grigorenko.* New York: W. W. Norton, 1984.

Grossman, Vasily. *Forever Flowing.* Trans. Thomas P. Whitney. New York: Harper & Row, 1972.

Gurvich, L. M., compiler. *Imet' silu pomnit'* [Have the strength to remember]. Moscow: Moskovskii Rabochyi, 1991.

Halfin, Igal. *Stalinist Confessions: Messianism and Terror at the Leningrad Communist University.* Pittsburgh: University of Pittsburgh Press, 2009.

———. *Terror in My Soul: Communist Autobiographies on Trial.* Cambridge, MA: Harvard University Press, 2003.

Harmon-Jones, Eddie, and Judson Mills. *Cognitive Dissonance: Progress on a Pivotal Theory in Social Psychology.* Washington, DC: American Psychological Association, 1997.

Hellbeck, Jochen. *Revolution on My Mind: Writing a Diary under Stalin.* Cambridge, MA: Harvard University Press, 2006.

Heller, Klaus, and Jan Plamper, eds. *Personality Cults in Stalinism.* Gottingen: V & R unipress GmbH, 2004.

Hollander, Paul. *The End of Commitment: Intellectuals, Revolutionaries, and Political Morality.* Chicago: Ivan R. Dee, 2006.

Hollander, Paul, ed. *From the Gulag to the Killing Fields: Personal Accounts of Political Violence and Repression in Communist States.* Wilmington, DE: ISI Books, 2006.

Hollander, Paul, ed. *Political Violence: Belief, Behavior, and Legitimation*. New York: Palgrave Macmillan, 2009.

Iakovlev, A. N., et al., eds. *Reabilitatsiia: Kak eto bylo*. T. 1, *Dokumenty prezidiuma TsK KPSS i drugie materialy, Mart 1953–fevral' 1956* [Rehabilitation: As it happened, T. 1. Documents of the presidium of the CC CPSU and other materials, March 1953–February 1956]. Moscow: Mezhdunarodnyi fond Demokratsiia, 2000.

———. *Reabilitatsiia: Kak eto bylo*. T. 2, *Fevral' 1956–nachalo 80-kh godov* [Rehabilitation: As it happened, vol. 2, February 1956–early 1980s]. Moscow: Materik, 2003.

———. *Reabilitatsiia: Kak eto bylo*. T. 3, *Seredina 80-kh godov–1991* [Rehabilitation: As it happened, vol. 3, mid-eighties–1991]. Moscow: Materik, 2004.

———. *Reabilitatsiia: Politicheskie Protsessy 30–50-kh godov* [Rehabilitation: Political trials 1930s–1950s]. Moscow: Izdatel'stvo politicheskoi literatury, 1991.

Ilic, Melanie. *Stalin's Terror Revisited*. Houndsmills: Palgrave Macmillan, 2006.

Inkeles, A., and R. Bauer. *The Soviet Citizen: Daily Life in a Totalitarian Society*. Cambridge, MA: Harvard University Press, 1961.

Ivanova, G. M. *Istoriia GULAGa, 1918–1958: Sotsial'no-ekonomicheskii i politico-pravovoi aspekty* [History of the GULAG, 1918–1958: Socioeconomic and political-legal aspects]. Moscow: Nauka, 2006.

Joffe, Nadezhda A. *Back in Time: My Life, My Fate, My Epoch*. Trans. Frederick S. Choate. Oak Park, IL: Labor Publications, 1995.

Jowitt, Ken. *New World Disorder: The Leninist Extinction*. Berkeley: University of California Press, 1992.

Kalyvas, Andreas. *Democracy and the Politics of the Extraordinary: Max Weber, Karl Schmitt, and Hannah Arendt*. Cambridge: Cambridge University Press, 2008.

Karsakova, G. N., compiler. *Uznitsy 'Alzhira'. Spisok zhenshchin-zakliuchennykh Akmolinskogo i drugikh otselenii Karlaga* [Prisoners of 'Alzhir'. List of women prisoners of the Akmolinsk camp and other Karlag settlements]. Moscow: Zven'ia, 2003.

Kharkhordin, Oleg. *The Collective and the Individual in Russia: A Study of Practices*. Berkeley: University of California Press, 1999.

Khlevniuk, Oleg V. *The History of the Gulag: From Collectivization to the Great Terror*. New Haven, CT: Yale University Press, 2004.

Khrushchev, Nikita. *Vospominaniia*. New York: Chalidze Publications, 1979.

Klinghoffer, Arthur Jay. *Red Apocalypse: The Religious Evolution of Soviet Communism*. Lanham, MD: University Press of America, 1996.

Koestler, Arthur. *Darkness at Noon*. London: Vintage Books, 2005.

Kokurin, A. I., and N. V. Petrov, compilers. *GULAG (Glavnoe Upravlenie lagerei), 1917–1960* [GULAG (Main Administration of Labor Camps), 1917–1960]. Moscow: Materik, 2000.

Kopelev, Lev. *Khranit' vechno* [To be preserved forever]. Ann Arbor: Ardis, 1975.

———. *The Education of a True Believer*. Trans. Gary Kern. New York: Harper & Row, 1980.

Korotkov, A. V., S. A. Melchin, and A. S. Stepanov, compilers. *Kremlevskii samosud: Sekret-nie dokumenty Politbiuro o pisatele A. Solzhenitsyne* [Kremlin lynching party: Secret po-litburo documents on the writer A. Solzhenitsyn]. Moscow: Rodina, 1994.

Kosenko, O. G. *Mir za koliuchei provolokoi: Lager' kak atribut totalitarnogo rezhima* [The wall behind barbed wire: Camp as an attribute of the totalitarian regime]. Voronezh: Voronezh'skii Gosudarstvennyi pedagogicheskii universitet, 2002.

Kostic, Roland. *Ambivalent Peace: External Peacebuilding, Threatened Identity and Recon-ciliation in Bosnia and Herzegovina,* Report No. 78. Uppsala: Department of Peace and Conflict Research, 2007.

Kotkin, Stephen. *Magnetic Mountain: Stalinism as a Civilization.* Berkeley: University of California Press, 1995.

Kozlov, V. A., and S. V. Mironenko, eds. *Kramola: Inakomyslie v SSSR pri Khrushcheve i Brezhneve 1952–1982* [Uprising: Dissidence in the USSR under Khrushchev and Brezh-nev 1952–1982]. Moscow: Materik, 2005.

———. *58-10: Nadzornye proizvodstva prokuratury SSSR po delam ob antisovetskoi agi-tatsii i propaganda* [58-10: Supervisory work of the Procuracy of the USSR on cases of anti-Soviet agitation and propaganda in the USSR] . Moscow: Mezhdunarodnyi fond Demokratsiia, 1999.

Kozlov, Vladimir. *Neizvestnyi SSSR: Protivostoianie naroda i vlasti 1953–1985 gg.* [Un-known USSR: Opposition of the people and the regime 1953–1985]. Moscow: Olma Press, 2006.

Kudriavtsev, V. N., and A. I. Trusov. *Politicheskaia iustitsiia v SSSR* [Political Justice in the USSR]. Moscow: Nauka, 2000.

Kuromiya, Hiroaki. *The Voices of the Dead: Stalin's Great Terror in the 1930s.* New Haven, CT: Yale University Press, 2007.

Kushner, Harvey W. *Encyclopedia of Terrorism.* Thousand Oaks, CA: Sage Publications, 2003.

Kut'ina, Dzhana, Andrei Broido, and Anton Kut'in. *Ob ushedshem veke: Rasskazyvaet Ol'ga Shatunovskaia* [On a century passed: Ol'ga Shatunovskaia speaks]. La Jolla: DAA Books, 2001.

Langer, Jo. *Convictions: Memories of a Life Shared with a Good Communist.* London: Andre Deutsch Limited, 1979.

Larina, Anna. *This I Cannot Forget: The Memoirs of Nikolai Bukharin's Widow.* London: Hutchinson, 1993.

Lar'kov, S. A. (compiler). *Memuary o politicheskikh repressiiakh v SSSR, khraniashchiesia v archive obshchestva "Memorial," annotirovannyi katalog* [Memoirs on political repres-sion in the USSR preserved in the archive of the society "Memorial," annotated cata-log]. Moscow: Zven'ia, 2007.

Levi, Primo. *If This Is a Man.* London: Sphere Books, 1987.

Lifton, Robert Jay. *Thought Reform and the Psychology of Totalism: A Study of "Brainwash-ing" in China.* New York: W. W. Norton, 1963.

Losskii, Nikolai. *Kharakter russkogo naroda* (in *Usloviia absoliutnogo dobra*) [Character of the Russian people, in Conditions of absolute good]. Moscow: Politicheskaia literatura, 1991.

Lourie, Richard. *Sakharov: A Biography*. Waltham, MA: Brandeis University Press, 2002.

Lunacharskii, Anatolii. *Religiia i sotsializm* [Religion and socialism], 2 vols. St. Petersburg: Shipovnik, 1908–1910.

Marx, Karl. *Marx's Critique of Hegel's Philosophy of Right (1843)*. Cambridge: Cambridge University Press, 1970.

McLoughlin, Barry, and Kevin McDermott. *Stalin's Terror: High Politics and Mass Repression in the Soviet Union*. Houndsmills: Palgrave Macmillan, 2004.

Medvedev, Roy. *Let History Judge: The Origins and Consequences of Stalinism*. Trans. George Shriver. New York: Columbia University Press, 1989.

Mercier, Louis Sebastien Mercier. *Het jaar twee duizend vier honderd en veertig: een droom, eerste deel* [Dutch translation of *L'An 2440;* The year 2440: a dream, part 1]. Haarlem: F. Bohn en A. Loosjes, 1787.

Merridale, Catherine. *Ivan's War: Life and Death in the Red Army, 1939–1945*. New York: Metropolitan Books, 2006.

———. *Night of Stone: Death and Memory in Russia*. London: Granta Books, 2000.

Mil'chakov, Aleksandr. *Molodost' svetlaia i tragicheskaia* [Bright and tragic youth]. Moscow: Moskovskii Rabochyi, 1988.

Milosz, Czeslaw. *The Captive Mind*. New York: Limited Editions Club, 1983.

Moon, David. *The Abolition of Serfdom in Russia, 1762–1907*. London: Pearson Education Limited, 2001.

Okhotin, N. G., and A. B. Roginskii. Sistema ispravitel'no-trudovykh lagerei v SSSR, 1923–1960 [System of forced labor camps in the USSR 1923–1960]. Moscow: Zven'ia, 1998.

Olitskaia, Ekaterina. *Moi vospominaniia* [My memoirs]. Frankfurt: Posev, 1971.

Orlova, I., N. Petrovskaia, et al. *Rasstrel'nye spiski, Vypusk 2, Vagan'kovskoe kladbishche, 1926–1936.* [Execution lists, volume 2, Vagankov cemetery, 1926–1936]. Moscow: Memorial, 1995.

Orlova, Raisa, and Lev Kopelev. *My zhili v Moskve* [We lived in Moscow]. Ann Arbor, MI: Ardis, 1988.

Rekemchik, Aleksandr. *Skudnyi materik* [Poor continent]. Moscow: Sovetskii pisatel', 1974.

Rogovin, V. *Partiia rasstreliannykh* [Party of the executed]. Moscow: V. Z. Rogovin, 1997.

Sandler, A., and M. Etlis. *Sovremenniki GULAGa: Kniga vospominanii i razmyshlenii* [Contemporaries of the GULAG: Book of memoirs and reflections]. Magadan: Magadanskoe knizhnoe izdatel'stvo, 1991.

Sarbin, Theodore R., and Karl E. Scheibe, eds. *Studies in Social Identity*. New York: Praeger, 1983.

Sats, Natalia. *Novelly moei zhizni* [Sketches from my life]. Moscow: Gosizdat, 1984.

Serebriakova, Galina. *Smerch* [Whirlwind]. Moscow: Pashkov Dom, 2005.

Shalamov, Varlam. *Sobranie sochinenii v chetyrekh tomakh,* t. 1 [Collected works in four volumes, vol. 1]. Moscow: Khudozhestvennaia literatura, Vagrius, 1998.

Shapovalov, Veronica, ed. *Remembering the Darkness: Women in Soviet Prisons.* Lanham, MD: Rowman & Littlefield, 2001.

Shikheeva-Gaister, Inna. *Semeinaia khronika: Vremen kul'ta lichnosti 1925–1953* [Family chronicle: The era of the cult of personality 1925–1953]. Moscow: N'iudiamed-AO, 1998.

Slezkine, Yuri. *The Jewish Century.* Princeton, NJ: Princeton University Press, 2004.

Solomon, Peter H., Jr. *Soviet Criminal Justice under Stalin.* Cambridge: Cambridge University Press, 1996.

Solzhenitsyn, Aleksandr. *The Gulag Archipelago.* Trans. Thomas P. Whitney and Harry Willetts. London: The Harvill Press, 1999.

———. *The Gulag Archipelago 1918–1956: An Experiment in Literary Investigation.* Trans. Harry Willetts. Vol. 3. New York: HarperPerennial, 1992.

Solzhenitsyn, Alexander. *One Day in the Life of Ivan Denisovich.* Trans. Max Hayward and Ronald Hingley. New York: Bantam Dell, 1963.

Taubman, William. *Khrushchev: The Man and His Era.* New York: W. W. Norton, 2003.

Tikhanova, V., et al., eds. *Rasstrel'nye spiski, Vypusk 1, Donskoe kladbishche, 1934–1940* [Execution lists, vol. 1, Donskoi cemetery, 1934–1940]. Moscow: Tekst, 1993.

Toker, Leona. *Return from the Archipelago: Narratives of Gulag Survivors.* Bloomington: Indiana University Press, 2000.

Tolczyk, Dariusz. *See No Evil: Literary Cover-ups and Discoveries of the Soviet Camp Experience.* New Haven, CT: Yale University Press, 1999.

Trivers, Robert L. *Social Evolution.* Menlo Park, CA: Benjamin/Cummins, 1985.

Tucker, Robert C., ed. *The Lenin Anthology.* New York: W. W. Norton, 1975.

Vaiskopf, Mikhail. *Pisatel' Stalin* [Stalin the writer] . Moscow: Novoe literaturnoe obozrenie, 2002.

Van Ree, Erik. *Bloed broeders: Stalin, Hitler en hun pact* [Blood brothers: Stalin, Hitler and their pact]. Amsterdam: Jan Mets, 1989.

———. *The Political Thought of Joseph Stalin.* London: RoutledgeCurzon, 2002.

Vilenskii, S. S., ed. *Dodnes' Tiagoteet.* T. 1, *Zapiski vashei sovremenitsy* [Till my tale is told, vol. 1, notes of your contemporaries]. Moscow: Vozvrashchenie, 2004.

———. *Dodnes' Tiagoteet.* T. 2, *Kolyma* [Till my tale is told, vol. 2, Kolyma]. Moscow: Vozvrashchenie, 2004.

———. *Soprotivlenie v Gulage* [Resistance in the Gulag]. Moscow: Vozvrashchenie, 1992.

Vilenskii, S. S., and A. I. Kokurin, compilers. *Deti GULAGa 1918–1956* [Children of the GULAG 1918–1956]. Moscow: Mezhdunarodnyi Fond "Demokratiia," 2002.

Vilensky, Simeon, ed. *Till My Tale is Told: Women's Memoirs of the Gulag.* Trans. John Crowfoot. Bloomington: Indiana University Press, 1999.

Weber, Max. *Wirtschaft und Gesellschaft, Grundriss der Verstehende Soziologie,* Fünfde, Revidierte Auflage [Economy and society, sketch of comprehensive sociology, fifth, revised edition]. Tübingen: J.C.B. Mohr, 1985.

Withuis, Jolande. *De jurk van de kosmonaute: Over politiek, cultuur, en psyche* [The cosmonaut's dress: On politics, culture, and the psyche]. Amsterdam: Boom, 1995.

———. *Opoffering en Heroik: De mentale wereld van een communistische vrouwenorganisatie in naoorlogs Nederland, 1946–1976* [Sacrifice and heroism: The mental world of a Communist women's organization in post-war Holland, 1946–1976]. Amsterdam: Boom Meppel, 1990.

Yakir, Petr Ionovich, *A Childhood in Prison.* London: Macmillan, 1972.

INDEX

Page numbers in italics indicate photographs.

authoritarianism: and faith-based belief, 11, 114; and justifications for rights violations, 112; and modernization efforts, 135; and reform efforts, 135; and thought reform, 93; and use of repression, 2

Ba'ath Party, 174
Baev, Aleksandr Aleksandrovich, 94
Bagirov, M. A., 131
Baitalskii, Mikhail, 33–34, 102
Baku Party Committee, 130–31
Barnes, Steven, 65–66, 67
Bauman (Technical) Institute, 159
belief-disconfirmation paradigm, 16, 182n67
Belomorkanal (White Sea Canal), *116*
Belovezh Accords, 99
benefit-finding, 74
Berger, Joseph, 53, 54–55
Beria, Lavrentiy: arrest of, 66–67; and blame for repression, 86–87, 136, 161; execution, 81; fall of, 35, 50; Gazarian on, 89; Mekhtiev on, 79–80; and Party reform efforts, 129; and the problem of evil, 44; and reinstatement requests, 15; and Shatunovskaia, 131; and Snegov, 128; trial of, 128
Big Zone, 41, 67
Bobrenev, V. A., 137
Bogoraz-Daniel family, 99
Bolsheviks and Bolshevism: and accountability for repression, 138; Bolshevism compared to religion, 24–33; contrasted with Stalinism, 94–102; criticisms of, 98; and faith-based belief, 10, 13, 25–26, 43–44; and identity crises, 171; and internal conflicts, 38–41, 43–44; and Kosterin, 105; and Lenin, 85; and Memorial, 172; and Old Bolsheviks, 78–79, 99–100, 139–41, 144; and Party reform efforts, 130; and

patriotism, 109; and realities of the camps, 41–43; and reinstatement requests, 15; and revolutionary legality, 33–38; and selfhood in the collective, 32; Serebriakov, 95
Bonner family, 99
Borian, Evgeniia, 104
Bosnia, 170
Bosnia-Herzegovina, 171
brainwashing, 16, 93–94
Brat, Anatolii, 55, 58–60
Brezhnev, Leonid: and corruption, 134; and the cult of personality, 78; and dissidents, 157; Ioelson-Grodzianskaia on, 162; and Jewish emigration, 138; Medvedev on, 19; and Party loyalists, 104; and re-Stalinization, 140, 157; and Shatunovskaia, 132; and a socially redeeming function of Gulag labor, 28, 29
The Bridge on the River Kwai (1957), 54
Bright and Tragic Youth (Milchakov), 87
"Bringing a Criminal to Death" (Mercier), 26
Brodsky, Joseph, 93
Buchenwald, 7
Bukharin, Nikolai: Berger on, 55; Brat on, 58; execution of, 32; fictional representation of, 48; and Party rehabilitation, 101, 139; and Rykov, 100, 101; and Shatunovskaia, 131–32; widow of, 98
Bureau of the Provincial Party Committee, 80
Burleigh, Michael, 30
Busarev, Nikolai Makarovich, 38, 51–52
Buzanov, Dmitrii Ivanovich, 145
Buzanov, Vasilii Ivanovich, 145
Buzanova, Dina Dmitrievna, 145

capitalism, 13
censorship: and access to archives, 211n25; and accountability for repression, 147; and credibility of subjects, 6; and faith-

based belief in the Party, 9; Gorbachev's lifting of, 158; and historical revisionism, 173; self-censorship, 144, 159, 162

Central Committee (Communist Party): assessment of Stalin era, 79; and the cult of personality, 136; and defense of the Party, 91; and Karpinskii, 141; and Kuznetsov, 36; and Lazarev, 88–89; and Lazarevna, 24; and Party reinstatements, 80; and Pisarev, 106; and rehabilitation requests, 35; and Shatunovskaia, 131, 133; and the Twentieth Party Congress, 64

Central Committee (of Komsomol), 84, 114–15, 133

Chachulin, Alexander, 204n54

Charents, E., 45

charismatic authority, 8, 12–13, 17, 49, 50

Charter of the CPSU, 81

Chebanov, Grigorii Ivanovich, 80–81

Chekists, 57, 89–92

Cherniak, 77

children of the repressed: burdens of, 148; Chuprun, 159–63; Ioffe, 150–51; Kuznetsova, 154–59; and Party loyalty, 82–83, 149–50, 154, 163–64; Rappaport, 151; Smirnova, 152–54; and youthful idealism, 83–84; Zadorozhnaia, 144

Children's Detention Center, 160

China, 78, 93–94

Christianity, 38

Chuprun, Gerta (Gertruda) Evgenevna, *124,* 159–63, 164

civil society, 3

Civil War, 68, 80, 95, 105, 152

class conflict, 5, 53, 64, 110

closed systems: and adaptive behaviors, 70, 94; and conformity, 46; and historical revisionism, 167; and indoctrination, 27; and self-deception, 60; and shaping of perceptions, 30

cognitive dissonance: and children of the repressed, 151; and coerced confessions, 50; and compartmentalization strategy, 134; and conversion, 184n90; and effort-justification paradigm, 182n67; and explanations for Party loyalty, 8; and historical revisionism, 167; neuroscience on, 182n68; and Party loyalty, 29; and personal narratives, 70; and religious view of Bolshevism, 29; theory of, 16–19; and the Twentieth Party Congress, 145

cognitive neuroscience, 8

cognitive psychology, 51

Cohen, Stephen, 128, 141, 204n54

collapse of the Soviet Union, 147–49, 159, 168–69, 171

collective memory, 33

collective punishment, 174

collectivization, 92, 144, 150, 178n10

Comintern, 53, 139

Commission to Counter Attempts to Falsify History to the Detriment of Russian Federation Interests, 173

Communist ideology: and children of the repressed, 154, 156–58, 161–62; compared to theology, 175; CPSU as "church-like" Party, 29–30; as faith-based belief system, 3, 9–11, 12–16, 17–18, 36, 43–44; and "historical necessity" view of repression, 51; ideology of, 9–12; and moral codes, 9–10; and Party loyalty, 47; and Party reinstatements, 143; and personal transformation, 31; and political use of mass violence, 54; and power of belief, 41; and practical reasons for Party membership, 102–104; and secularism, 8, 12, 25–26, 26–29, 30, 44; and Serebriakova, xii; and social exclusion, 45–46; subjects' commitment to, 8; Vozzhaev on, 65; youthful idealism, 83–84, 84–87

doomsday cults, 17
Dostoevsky, Fyodor, 56, 69
Dubcek, Alexander, 113
Duma, 164, 166
Durkheim, Emile, 31
Dzerzhinskii, Feliks, 57, 89, 98

education, 166–67
effort-justification paradigm, 182n67
ego mechanism of defense, 16
Engels, Friedrich, *117*
Etkind, Alexander, 13, 25
evidence-based belief systems, 9, 17–18,
    107, 114
evil, 37–38, 44
exclusion from the Party, 79–83. *See also*
    reinstatement to the Party
excommunication, 48

fabrication of evidence, 52
faith-based belief systems: and account-
    ability for state-sponsored crimes, 11;
    and Bolshevism, 10, 13, 25–26, 43–44;
    and Communist ideology, 3, 9–11, 12–
    16, 17–18, 36, 43–44; crises of faith,
    110; and enduring hardships, 107;
    and families of the repressed, 114; and
    Gavrilov, 107; and the Great Patriotic
    War, 110; and historical revisionism,
    167; and patriotism, 1; and subjectivity,
    162–63; and true believers, 39–41
false confessions, 32, 48–49, 49–50
famine, 3, 158, 178n10
Fascism, 62
Festinger, Leon, 16, 17
Filin, Vladimir, 140
Fitzpatrick, Sheila, 41
Flige, Irina, 172
Forever Flowing (Grossman), 42–43
Frankl, Viktor, 11, 29, 129
French Revolution, 30
Frenkin, M., 138–39

Freud, Anna, 16
Frunze Military Academy, 108
FSB (Federal Security Service), 159
Fülöp-Miller, René, 30
functionalism, 19–20, 28, 29
Furman, Leonid, 60
Fürst, Juliane, 140

Gagarin, Iurii, 114
Gagen, Evgenii Eduardovich, 60
Gagen-Torn, Nina, 3
Galich, Alexander, 39
Gal'per, Mariia, 59, *118*
Ganetskaia, Khanna Iakovlevna, 47–48
Gastev, Iurii, 133–34
Gavrilov, Lev, xii, 14, 107–108
Gazarian, Suren, 89–90
General Secretary, 52
Generation of the Doomed (Galich), 39
German Fascism, 62
Germany Democratic Republic, 139, 160
Gide, André, 12
Ginzburg, Evgeniia, 40, 85
glasnost, 127, 141, 143, 162
Gnedin, Evgenii, 62–63
The God That Failed (Crossman), 9
Goethe, Johann Wolfgang von, 69
Goldberg, Mariia Moiseevna, 40, 82–83
Gorb, Vasilii Ivanovich, 83–84
Gorbachev, Mikhail: and accountability
    for repression, 61; and Baev, 94; and
    children of the repressed, 151, 155; and
    corruption, 134; criticisms of, 157–58,
    163; and disclosures of repression, 157;
    and faith in the Communist Party, 43;
    and "historical necessity" view of re-
    pression, 54; and historical revisionism,
    166; and Iakovlev, 10; and legacy of So-
    viet system, 22; and loyalty to the Party,
    66, 127; and Memorial, 142, 144–45;
    and Milchakov, 87; and Party reinstate-
    ments, 3, 5, 82, 115, 143; and reform

efforts, 128, 142, 146, 147; and rehabilitations, 98, 144; and Serebriakova, 97, 98; and Shatunovskaia, 132; and Twenty-seventh Party Congress, 101

Gorbachev Foundation, 99

Gorkii State University, 49

Gorlizki, Yoram, 178n10

Great Depression, 13

Great Patriotic War, 106–10; and children of the repressed, 149; and cognitive dissonance theory, 17; Khrushchev on, 77; military service of Gulag prisoners, 183n88; and public opinion on Stalin, 164–65; and repression of Gulag history, 22

Great Purge of 1937, 166

Gregory, Paul, 210n17

Grigorenko, Petr, 105

Grigorevich, Ivan (character), 42–43

Grossman, Vasily, 42–43

group-needs system, 27

Gudzinskii, P. I., 77

Gulag Archipelago (Solzhenitsyn), 8, 18–19

The Hague, 171

Hale, Nathan, 94

Halfin, Igal, 13, 33, 55–57, 191n43

Harvard refugee project, 109

Harvard University, 75

"The Heirs to Stalin" (Yevtushenko), 98, 164

Hellbeck, Jochen, 15, 30–33

Henchmen and Victims (Kernes), 137

heroism, 12, 13, 32

Heuvel, Katrina vanden, 141

Historical Archive Institute, 138

"historical necessity" view of repression, 50–54

historical revisionism, 166–67, 169

"The History of Russia 1900–1945" (teachers' manual), 166–67

Hitler, Adolf, 109, 111, 174

Holocaust, 5, 111

housing issues, 89

human rights, 153, 174

humanism, xii, 27, 33

Iakovlev, Aleksandr Nikolaevich, 10–11, 22, 132–33, 163

Iardovskaia, L. S., 143

Iavlinskii, Grigorii, 171

idealism, 83–84

identification with the aggressor, 16

identity issues, 74–75, 89–92, 94–102

Igarka-Salekhard railway, *126*

Ilin, Feliks, 155

Ilin, Ilia Lvovich, *122, 155–59*

Ilin, Vladimir, *122,* 155

Ilina, Mariia Markovna, *122,* 155

indoctrination, 16, 27, 54–58

industrialization, 150, 167

informers, 57

ingrained patriotism, 54–55

initiation rites, 8, 182n67

Institute of History (Russian Academy of Sciences), 99

Institute of Marxism-Leninism, 37, *117,* 139

Institute of Molecular Biology, 94

Institute of the Refrigeration Industry, 159

intelligentsia, 73

International Conference on Approaches to Stalinism, xii–xiii

International Criminal Tribunal for the Former Yugoslavia (ICTY), 170–71

interpretive frames, 9

interrogation protocols, 55–56, 58–59

Ioelson-Grodzianskaia, Dina (Evdokiia) Sidorovna, *125,* 160–63

Ioelson-Grodzianskii, Aleksandr, 160

Ioelson-Grodzianskii, Evgenii Borisovich, 159

Ioffe, Adolf, 13, 150–51

Ioffe, Nadzhda, 150–51, 164

Ioffe, Natasha, 150–51, 164
Iraq, 174
Iron Curtain, 173–74
Ivan Denisovich (character), 41, 54
Izvestiia, 95, 141, 149

Jaspers, Karl, 43
Jews, 111, 138
Joseph K. (Kafka character), 45, 63
judicial exonerations, 57
judicial rehabilitation, 48, 80, 101, 103,
    192n68

Kafka, Franz, 45, 56, 63
Kaganovich, Lazar, 87
Kalinin, M. I., 108
Kandel, Eric, 21
Karadzic, Radovan, 171
Karagaeva, Elena Pavlovna, 139–40
Karlag, Mariia Gal'per, *118*
Karpinskii, Len, 140
Karpov, Vladimir Vasilievich, 108
kartsers, 80, 91, 96, *126*
*Katastrofa; Vtoroe rozhdenie, Memuarnye
    zapiski* (Gnedin), 62
Katkov, N., 133
Kazarian, Garnik, 15
Kengir, Kazakhstan, 65, 67–69
Kernes, Iosef, 136–37
KGB: archives, 137; Gazarian on, 90; and
    Karpinskii, 141; and Kosterin's funeral,
    105; Kuznetsova on, 159; and Pisarev,
    105; and Shatunovskaia, 132
Kharkhordin, Oleg, 32
Khlevniuk, Oleg, 178n10
Khronika Tekushchykh Sobytii, 153
Khrushchev, Nikita: and Aleksakhin, 135;
    and blame for repression, 41, 46–47,
    54, 62, 70; and children of the re-
    pressed, 153; on cult of personality, 17,
    76–79, 136; and dissociation from Sta-
    lin, 104; and faith in the Communist

Party, 43; fall of, 28; and functional-
    ism, 19; and Gazarian, 90; and Karpin-
    skii, 141; and liberation of prisoners,
    162; and Memorial, 145; and Milcha-
    kov, 86; and Party reinstatements, 5,
    143; and political rehabilitations, 64,
    77, 101, 115, 134; and public Gulag
    discussions, 28; and reform efforts, 82,
    129–30, 134, 138, 146; and release
    of prisoners, xii, xiii; and revision of
    Stalinism, 110; and Serebriakova, 97;
    and Shatunovskaia, 131, 132, 133; on
    size of Communist Party, 77; and Sne-
    gov, 128–29; and Tanin, 73, 74; and
    the Thaw, 5, 33, 110, 131, 134; and the
    Twentieth Party Congress, 14, 63–65.
    See also Secret Speech
Kiev Party, 57
Kiev Provincial Party Committee, 155
Kirov, Sergey, 132–33, 138
Koestler, Arthur, 47, 48–49
Kolchak, Aleksandr, 52
Kolyma: and death ships, 3, 103; and out-
    put quotas, 42, 152; and Party loyalists,
    66, 84, 105, 107, 115; and prisoner nar-
    ratives, 12, 14, 59–60; public revela-
    tion of conditions, 129, 136; and pun-
    ishment cells, 80; Shatunovskaia on,
    131–32
Kommunist, 101
Komsomol: and Baitalskii, 102; and Bol-
    shevism, 85; and camp staff, 91; and
    children of the repressed, 151, 152, 155,
    156–57, 160; and Goldberg, 83; and
    Karpinskii, 140; and Milchakov, 84,
    87; and Pikina, 115, 133; and Ravdel,
    103
Kopelev, Lev, 43, 92–93, 105, 140
Korallov, Marlen Mikhailovich, 68–69,
    120
Kosterin, Aleksei, 104–105
Kotkin, Stephen, 13, 15, 19, 29, 76

Marx, Karl, 10–11, 69, *117,* 162
Marxism, 32, 63–65, 77, 97, 105
Medvedev, Roy: on children of the repressed, 150; devotion to Leninism, 140; and the dissident movement, 19, 150, 164; on former prisoners, 2; and "historical necessity" view of repression, 50–51; and Karpinskii, 141; on Party loyalty, 66; and prisoners' stories, 19–20; and reform efforts, 142; and Snegov, 129–30; and the Twentieth Party Congress, 138
Medvedev, Vadim, 142
Mekhtiev, Bakhish, 79
Memorial: and Brat, 55, 58–59; and children of the repressed, 153–54; and Gorbachev, 142, 144–45; and Korallov, 69; and loyalty to the Soviet Constitution, 66; and monument to victims of Stalinism, 97; and Party reinstatements, 5; questionnaires, *118;* and rehabilitations, 144–45; and Roginskii, 135, 137, 173; and Shamaev, 82; and Sivakov, 165; and state repression, 168, 171–73; and statistics on Gulag population, 4
memory, 6–8
Mercier, Louis Sebastien, 26
Merridale, Catherine, 11, 25, 108–109, 110
The Metamorphosis (Kafka), 63
"method acting" view of Party loyalty, 19–20
Meyerhold, Vsevolod, 56–57
MGB, 35, 86–87, 189n10
Mikoyan, Anastas, 86–87, 128–29
Mikoyan, Sergo, 128, 130
Milchakov, Aleksandr Ivanovich, 84–87
military service, 67, 105, 154, 156, 183n88. *See also* Red Army
Milosevic, Slobodan, 171
The Mind and Face of Bolshevism (Fülöp-Miller), 30
Ministry of Education, 166

Mink, Louis, 7
"Misfortune and Bolshevik Conscience" (Adeev), 14
Mladic, Ratko, 171
The Modern History of Russia, 1945–2006 (textbook), 166
modernization, 135, 163
monopoly of power, 17–18
"The Moral Makeup of the Soviet Man" (lecture), 50
Morozov, Pavlik, 33–34, 112–13
Moscow City Court, 63
Moscow Party Committee, 131, 135
Mother Teresa, 163
MVD (Ministry of the Interior), 86–87, 89, 130

narrative "artifacts," 7
national identity, 137–38, 168, 169, 170, 172–73
Nazism, 37, 174, 183n88
"necessary evil" view of the repression, 50–54
neo-Stalinism, 140
neuroscience, 8, 21, 182n68
New Economic Policy, 98
Nietzsche, Friedrich, 11
Night of Stone: Death and Memory in Russia (Merridale), 11–12
Nikishov, I. F., 136
Nikolaev, Leonid, 133
Nineteenth Party Conference, 145
NKVD: and blame for repression, 44, 65, 71; and compliance of prisoners, 54; declassified materials, 52; fabrication of evidence, 52; Gazarian on, 90; and interrogations, 49, 55–56; jokes about, 47; and Kernes's arrest, 136; Lazarevna on, 24; and Party identity, 89–92; and punishment of prisoners, 56–57; and reform efforts, 128; and revolutionary legality, 33; and *sharashki,* 51

reinstatement to the Party: and Aleksakhin, 135; bureaucratic process of, 81; and children of the repressed, 151, 156; and Gagen, 61; and Ganetskaia, 48; and Gudzinskii, 77; importance of, 34; and judicial rehabilitation, 192n68; meaning of, 79–83; and Milchakov, 85; and Party loyalists, 100–101; and perestroika, 143–44; and post-Yagoda purge, 31; Slavianina, 79; and Teper, 103; and the Twentieth Party Congress, 14, 57, 61, 103–104, 143. *See also* Party Control Commission; rehabilitation

religion: and Bolshevism, 25–26; "churchlike" qualities of the Communist Party, 29–30; and faith in the Communist Party, 43–44, 111, 157–58; and faith-based belief, 9; Marx on, 10, 162; and Party membership, 174–75; religious prisoners, 38

revisionism, historical, 166–67, 169–71

revolutionary legality, 33–38

Revtribunal, 60

Riazantsev, V. B., 137

Roginskii, Arsenii, 4, 135, 137, 146, 173, 210n17

Rosenberg, Ethel, 195n6

Rosenberg, Julius, 195n6

RSFSR Ministry of Justice, 63

Rubashov (character), 48–49

Russia, 168, 169, 174

Russian Academy of Sciences, 99

Russian Orthodoxy, 12, 32

Russian Revolution, 30, 55, 105

Ryazan Memorial, 165

Rykov, Aleksei, 3, 99–100, 101, 131–32

Rykova, Nataliia, 3, 13, 99–102, *120*

Rykova, Nina Semenova, 100–101

sacred goals, 49

Sagoian, Petr, 57

Sakharov, Andrei, 98, 140

samizdat, 28, 153

sample selection, 5

Samsa, Gregor (Kafka character), 45

Samuelson, Lennart, 51

Sandratskaia, Mariia Karlovna, 83–84

Santayana, George, 22

Sats, Nataliia, 189n20

Schiller, Friedrich, 69

school curricula, 166–67, 170

scientific method, 9, 43

scope of study, 4–6

Scorpions (paramilitary unit), 170

Secret Speech: and the Central Committee, 136; and children of the repressed, 141; and liberation of Gulag prisoners, 18–19; and Mankovskii, 49; and Milchakov, 87; and Party approval, 76–77; and Party loyalists, 147; and Party reform efforts, 129; and rehabilitation requests, 4, 25, 77; and Shatunovskaia, 131

secularism: and Communist ideology, 8, 12, 25–26, 26–29, 30, 44; and repressive regimes, 1; secular humanism, 27–28; and selfhood in the collective, 32–33

Semprun, Jorge, 7–8

Serbia, 169, 170–71, 175

Serbia-Montenegro, 171

Serebriakov, Leonid, xi, 95, 97, 98

Serebriakova, Galina, xii, 43, 94–97

Serebriakova, Zoria, xi–xiii, 43, 96, 97–99

Seventeenth Party Congress, 64, 77

Shalamov, Varlam, 12, 42

Shamaev, Orest Ivanovich, 81–82

sharashki, 51

Shatrov, Mikhail, 141

Shatunovskaia, Olga, 33, 43, 87, 114, 129–33, 135

Shelest, Georgii, 107

shestidesiatniki, 130

Shipwreck of a Generation (Berger), 53

NANCI ADLER is senior researcher at the NIOD Institute for War, Holocaust, and Genocide Studies (Royal Netherlands Academy of Arts and Sciences, University of Amsterdam). She is author of *The Gulag Survivor: Beyond the Soviet System, Victims of Soviet Terror: The Story of the Memorial Movement,* and numerous scholarly articles on the Gulag, political rehabilitations, and the consequences of Stalinism. Her current research focuses on transitional justice and the legacy of Communism.